America through Transgender Eyes

J. E. SUMERAU
University of Tampa

LAIN A. B. MATHERS
University of Illinois at Chicago

D1554380

ROWMAN & LITTLEFIELD
Lanham • Boulder • New York • London

Executive Editor: Rolf Janke
Editorial Assistant: Courtney Packard
Senior Marketing Manager: Amy Whitaker

Published by Rowman & Littlefield
A wholly owned subsidiary of The Rowman & Littlefield Publishing Group, Inc.
4501 Forbes Boulevard, Suite 200, Lanham, Maryland 20706
www.rowman.com

6 Tinworth Street, London SE11 5AL, United Kingdom

British Library Cataloguing in Publication Information Available

Library of Congress Cataloging-in-Publication Data

Names: Sumerau, J. E., author. | Mathers, Lain A. B., 1990– author.
Title: America through transgender eyes / J. E. Sumerau, University of Tampa , Lain A. B. Mathers, University of Illinois at Chicago.
Description: Lanham : Rowman & Littlefield, [2019] | Includes bibliographical references and index.
Identifiers: LCCN 2019000252 (print) | LCCN 2019000928 (ebook) | ISBN 9781538122082 (electronic) | ISBN 9781538122068 (cloth) | ISBN 9781538122075 (pbk.)
Subjects: LCSH: Transgender people—United States. | Transgender people—United States—Identity.
Classification: LCC HQ77.95.U6 (ebook) | LCC HQ77.95.U6 S86 2019 (print) | DDC 306.76/80973—dc23
LC record available at https://lccn.loc.gov/2019000252

Contents

Acknowledgments   v

1 Introduction   1

2 Coming Out (or Not) as Trans   27

3 Transgender Experience in LGBTQIA Communities   51

4 Transgender Experience in Cisgender Realities   73

5 Transgender Experience with Religion   91

6 Transgender Experience with Medical Science   113

7 Conclusion   133

Methodological Appendix   147

Bibliography   161

Index   199

Acknowledgments

No book is written completely alone, and in this section, we would like to individually and collectively thank people who played important roles in the formation of this volume.

To begin, we would both like to thank the trans people who shared their stories with us both in the creation of the survey and within the survey itself—we hope that we have done your stories justice. We also feel indebted to all the trans artists, scholars, and activists who came before us, without whom this work in its current form would have been inconceivable. We further thank and continue to appreciate all the other trans artists, scholars, and activists currently engaged in a wide variety of areas throughout society for their influence, inspiration, and companionship both in navigating the current time period and in attempts like this book to make visible and heard voices from our communities. Additionally, we are indebted to the many other trans people we have encountered throughout our lives and development as people and scholars. Finally, we are also grateful to the Association for the Sociology of Religion for their support of this research through the Joseph H. Fichter Research Grant.

As the first author of this work, I, J. Sumerau, would also like to thank some people in my life who have been instrumental in this and other works in my career to date. First, thank you to my life partners for the many ways you support and embrace me every day throughout the good, bad, and everywhere in between that is this life. While each of you mean more than words to me, I want to especially thank Xan Nowakowski—life partner, spouse, and often writing collaborator and heroic protector—for the fact that I'm still breathing and for every little way over the last decade that you have brought me even more to life and worked with me to build the lives, partnerships, and careers we share today.

Looking back at the past decade, I also smile more and brighter than I ever thought possible when I think about the chosen family that makes all my work possible in little ways that go beyond any given moment or event. In this regard, I thank my coauthor in this book, Lain Mathers, for an ongoing conversation, friendship, and collaboration that continues to make me a better friend, writer, and person throughout my life. I would also especially like to note the overwhelming support and contributions of the other people in my little chosen family. Thank you so much, Eve, Brandy S., Nik, M, Eric, Brandy F., Mandi, Kate, Misha, Shay, Brittany, and Mercedes for all the inspiration, support, and kindness over the years. There are pieces of each of you in everything I'm able to do that I will never feel like I'm able to thank you for enough.

As I think of the people who have helped me to this point, I also think about the importance of mentorship and how lucky I have been to have wonderful mentors along the way. From the formal training I received at Augusta University and Florida State University, I am forever indebted especially to Drs. Irene Padavic, Kim Davies, Koji Ueno, Doug Schrock, Allen Scarboro, Saundra Reinke, Christos Bourdouvalis, John Reynolds, Jill Quadagno, and Patricia Yancey Martin. I am also personally forever indebted to Dr. Petra Doan for showing me it was possible for someone like me to make it in the academy, even though I was too scared to tell her so when I was lucky enough to meet and work with her. Beyond where I was educated, I also owe a debt of gratitude to brilliant scholars who were kind enough to help me along the path, including Drs. Kristen Schilt, Dawne Moon, Katie Acosta, Patricia Leavy, Richard Pitt, Staci Newmahr, Angela Jones, Charlese Edgley, and Dirk vom Lehn.

Finally, for me, I worked on this project over the past few years constantly thinking about and aware of the young trans people who came to my office, e-mailed me after reading one of my articles or books, or found me at conferences. While being visible comes with many costs within and beyond my field of work, the costs are far outweighed by the many younger people who have sought me out, whom I have been able to help or mentor, and/or who felt less alone because of my visibility. I think about these young folks now as I do every day, and I think about the small role I can play in trying to make it better for them, just as I think about the massive role they have played in encouraging me to continue to use my voice in what ways I can. Thank you to each of you: You are each beautiful in your own ways, and you are all part of this and my other continued attempts to speak. Despite the flaws in any work and the limitations of my or any other standpoint or perspective, I hope this is yet another piece that eases the road ahead for you, and in whatever ways I can, I promise to keep trying right alongside each of you.

As the second author of this work, I, Lain Mathers, would like to express my gratitude to a few people who played important roles in this and my other work to date. First, thank you to my coauthor J, who has been the greatest writing partner, mentor, and friend I could ask for. You are consistently a source of inspiration and support in more ways than I can possibly list here, and I would not be the person I am without knowing you for the past eight and a half years. I cannot imagine tackling this project with anyone else and am so excited that we got to work together to bring this book to fruition. I would also like to acknowledge my undergraduate mentors at Florida State University, Drs. Koji Ueno, Irene Padavic, Petra Doan, and Douglas Schrock, who collectively encouraged me to pursue graduate study. I am so very grateful for your early support and guidance.

Working on a book alongside my dissertation has been a unique experience, and I am forever grateful to my dissertation advisor and graduate school mentor at University of Illinois at Chicago, Dr. Lorena Garcia, who encouraged my work on this project from day one. Everyone should be so lucky as to have a dissertation chair as brilliant, insightful, and motivating as she is. I cannot envision navigating graduate school with anyone else as my advisor, and this book would not have been possible without knowing that she was in my corner the entire time. Thank you to Dr. Kristen Schilt for countless fun and uplifting conversations over coffee and for always reminding me that the work I am doing is important, and to Drs. Claire Decoteau and Laurie Schaffner, who have also consistently encouraged my academic endeavors. I am also grateful for all the things I've learned from Drs. stef shuster, Angela

Jones, Dawne Moon, Eric Anthony Grollman, and Brandy Simula; thank you for the wealth of knowledge you've shared with me along the way. Additionally, I have so much appreciation for the many undergraduate students at University of Illinois at Chicago and Northeastern Illinois University, who continuously remind me why I do what I do.

I would also like to especially thank some of my friends who have helped me along the path to completing this work. Sarah Steele has given me an incredible shoulder to lean on during my time in Chicago, and Sangi Ravichandran is always a source of encouragement when I need a break from working to sit back, laugh, and relax. I don't know what I would do without the intellectual and emotional sustenance provided by Katharine McCabe, who has been an unabashedly loving and loud supporter of me and my work from day one at UIC. My time in graduate school would not have been as bright without the steadfast friendship of Alison Moss who is (in every sense) one of the most rad people in my life. I am also forever thankful to have the honor of knowing and learning from Xan Nowakowski, without whom I wouldn't be half the scholar I am today. Their ability to push back, intellectually, professionally, and personally, against existing forms of inequality has undoubtedly inspired this work in more ways than we can count. Thank you also to Nik Lampe, who keeps me on my toes as a writer and mentor and is always there for me just as much as I am for them. Thank you to Eve Haydt, Chandra Palmer, Z Zahr, S Simmons, Misha Shuster, Michelle Manno, Michael Muñiz, Danielle Giffort, Brandy Fox, Lydia Hou, and Nick Rochin for your friendship; I am so grateful to know you all.

Lauren and Al Mathers have been the most incredible parents I could ask for and have been willing to grow and learn with me in ways I never imagined possible. I wish for a world where every trans person has parents like you. Last, but most certainly not least, unending love and gratitude to my life partner, Shay Phillips, who has cheered me on throughout this whole project, even when it meant many late nights and days working alone in my office. You push me to be a better person and scholar, and I cherish the privilege of walking through this strange forest of life with you. I am also appreciative of our three cats, Erving, Galahad, and Luca, who made valiant efforts to contribute to this book via jumping onto the keyboard more times than I can recall and, in so doing, served the important role of comic relief on some of the longer work days.

1

Introduction

A child sits in Sunday school learning the story of Adam and Eve. The child listens as the teacher of the week's lesson explains that God created Adam and Eve as complementary halves and that all the rest of human existence comes from this initial establishment of the world in the form of women and men created in God's image.

A middle-aged person walks into a meeting at work with a colleague, and upon entering, the two are greeted by a boss saying, "Oh there he is" to one of them, and, "You see, I knew she would find him" to the rest of the room while pointing at the other one of them as they take their seats with the rest of the team.

A student in an introduction to biology course reads about and hears a professor speak of the natural processes whereby human males and females evolved from other living things over time. The biology professor explains that women and men exist as separate but connected forms, and that the whole of human evolution involves the ways females and males accomplish mating, child rearing, and their natural urges for aggression (males) and nurturing (females) over time. The professor explains that this sexual dimorphism, shown in the understanding of females and males as oppositional and complementary halves of the human whole, is a foundational tenet of modern biophysical science.

A teenager spends the afternoon in the mall with friends from school. After checking out clothes at one of the shops, the teenager needs to use the restroom. The teenager walks to the area of the mall where the restrooms are located and encounters signs for a "men's room" and a "women's room."

A student in an introduction to sociology course reads about and hears a professor speak on the use of surveys to generalize broad patterns in society. The professor explains that survey methodologists seek to create "representative" surveys that allow us to take a limited number of cases and extrapolate what we find to the broader society we inhabit. The professor teaches the students that these surveys are considered representative because they are often weighted to match population estimates of males and females, age ranges, and other demographic cohorts in society. The professor notes that this process—substantive generalizability—is how someone can use a Pew data set or the General Social Survey to say that X percentage of the US population feels this way about same-sex marriage or that way about abortion or another way about other social issues.

A college graduate spends the afternoon with a human resources representative at a new job. The human resources representative hands the new graduate a stack of papers for taxes, insurance, employee records, and other managerial necessities. The forms ask the new graduate for a name, address, phone number, and other personal details, and require the graduate to check boxes identifying as either male or female and as a member of other social demographic categories commonly used by governmental agencies.

A twentysomething professional stops in a bar for a drink after work one day. While sitting at the bar enjoying a well-earned alcoholic beverage, the twentysomething is approached from behind by another person who says, "Well aren't you a pretty lady?" and turns around to see the source of the statement looking at the skin revealed by the skirt the twentysomething is wearing on this particular night.

What do these examples have in common? What is missing from each one? Would you, the reader, consider these situations easy to navigate—meaning they would not require much consideration—or would they be difficult to navigate, requiring you to choose your options carefully? In what ways do activities like the ones noted above influence your life, well-being, and daily experience in the United States of America? Although many cisgender people might read these examples and wonder why aspects of their "normal" everyday activities warrant mentioning or consideration in the first place, many transgender[1] and gender-nonconforming people (like the authors of this book)[2] see examples of or data drawn from the ways, to paraphrase Dorothy Smith,[3] the everyday cisgender world of contemporary US[4] society[5] is problematic.

In each case, the difference in interpretation of these commonplace activities arises from the viewer's experience of life as a person within, between, and/or beyond the sex/gender binary (i.e., one must only ever be a male man or a female woman) that is created and sustained by contemporary patterns embedded within social interactions and social structures.[6] As feminists have long noted,[7] the sex/gender binary structures the entirety of contemporary US social relations and requires every person to be held accountable for properly conforming to institutionalized notions of "what it means to be a man" and "what it means to be a woman."[8] For the many people willing and able to conform to the sex/gender binary (i.e., cisgender people), its operation in US society appears natural, taken for granted, ahistorical, and absolute (i.e., "just the way it is" or "the way it has always been")—or, in simpler terms, "easy." This is the case despite empirical evidence showing neither sex nor gender have ever been limited to only two binary options in the natural world.[9] For the authors of this book and the many other people who do not or cannot conform to the sex/gender binary (i.e., transgender and gender-nonconforming people), however, the operation of this societal system—as well as its influence on notions of race, class, sexualities, religion, science, and other social systems—represents (at least the possibility) of a continuous assault upon our existence, well-being, opportunity, and potential—or, in simpler terms, "difficult."

This is not to suggest that people who fit comfortably within the gender/sex binary do not find other aspects of their lives difficult, as many people have one or another characteristic or trait that pushes them outside of the idealized norms of society at a specific time or in a specific context (e.g., being African American, poor, or gay, for example). Even so, the sex/gender binary functions as a master status that intersects with all of these other traits.[10]

Which of the following joint identities will experience the world in even more "difficult" ways on average:[11] Cisgender men who are poor or transmen who are poor? Cisgender African American women or transgender African American women? A gay cisgender person or a gay nonbinary transgender person? In each case, combining a non-cisgender sex/gender label with other nonnormative identities has been shown to generally result in even greater difficulties navigating a judgmental, normative, cisgender world.[12]

In our work examining the experiences of Mormons identifying in more than a dozen ways beyond cisgender norms, we named the processes— individual, collective, and institutional—that facilitate such assault *cisgendering reality*.[13] Put simply, processes of cisgendering reality may be seen in any social setting, structural arrangement, or interaction wherein people— intentionally or otherwise—breathe into life an imagined world wherein only cisgender people exist; only cisgender people may move freely without punishment, shock, and stigmatization coming from others; and only cisgender people are recognized within language, structures, or stories about "the way this world is or once was."[14] In specific terms, cisgendering reality involves erasing, othering, and punishing non-cisgender existence and experience throughout mainstream social institutions, interactional patterns, and structural arrangements in ways that allow people to accept a world without non-cisgender people.

None of the experiences we shared to open this book, for example, feel necessarily safe to us, and many of them have led to violence in J's life as a nonbinary transwoman or harassment in Lain's life as a genderqueer person.[15] This is because these experiences can only seem "normal" or "natural" from a cisgender perspective, as each one relies upon the assumption of only cisgender people, history, bathroom needs, representation, and/or language that erases the existence of transgender possibility from daily life. In fact, the processes of cisgendering reality have been so successful in shaping US society to date that we often must explain and define the term *cisgender* to fellow PhDs (i.e., the most educated members of society) and even, on some occasions, to fellow PhDs who make their living studying gender in society.[16]

In case readers have fallen victim to these processes as well, at this point we should explicitly explain some key terminology before going further.[17] Simply put, *cisgender* is an umbrella term that refers to people who conform to the sex and/or gender they are assigned at birth by political, medical, religious, and/or familial authorities (i.e., you are told you are male and must become a man, so you do this by doing or performing gender in relation to current norms of manhood).[18] *Transgender*, on the other end of the spectrum, is an umbrella term for people who do not conform to the sex and/or gender they were assigned at birth by political, medical, religious, and/or familial authorities (i.e., you are told you are male and must become a man, but you instead become a woman who is assigned male at birth, or become a female woman utilizing gender affirming medical care, or become agender, genderqueer, or another nonbinary identity doing or performing gender by mixing current notions of manhood and womanhood). Although cisgender and transgender represent two broad umbrella terms on a spectrum of gender options, many people also identify between these options (i.e., gender-nonconforming people, or people who reject easy categorization into existing norms of cisgender or transgender and manhood or womanhood), and many people move back and forth between these ends in certain situations or over the life course.[19]

It is important to note that those indoctrinated into and conforming to binary views of the world—intentionally or otherwise—may be tempted to incorrectly see even this framework as yet another binary. Our aim here, however, is to argue that recognizing the spectrum of identities and experiences that exist beyond cisgender realities allows us to critically and systematically analyze cisgender privilege in much the same way recognizing other spectra of identification allows us to interrogate other forms of inequality.[20] For example, scholars pointing to racial identities beyond white,[21] a spectrum of cisgender experiences beyond ideal men on one end and ideal women on the other end,[22] and a spectrum of sexual experiences beyond heterosexual (e.g., gay/lesbian, bi+, and/or asexual [ace])[23] paved the way for outlining white, masculine, and hetero- and monosexual privilege in society. There are many ways to conceptualize the gender spectrum, but exploring cisgender and transgender interactions along this spectrum from a transgender perspective provides a framework for shining light on cisgender privileges[24] hidden by current interactional and structural arrangements in US society.[25]

Our argument is that shifting the focus from cisgender assumptions and norms to insights gleaned from transgender experience offers an opportunity to revise and transform not only social scientific studies of gender, but also our understanding of religion, medical science, research methodologies, and LG-BTQIA[26] experiences in society. At the same time as cisgender realities close off the possibility of gender fluidity, transition, experimentation, and equality, they also provide the sex and gender foundation for sexual inequalities, religious traditions predicated upon sexual and gender inequalities, and medical science based upon static assumptions about the "natural" connection between "normal" forms of sex, gender, and sexualities. As a result, cisgender realities collectively limit the opportunities, health options, and freedom of sexual, sex, gender, and other minority groups.[27] Stated another way, cisgender realities require political, religious, and scientific/medical simplification of the natural world, but also provide the initial separation—or doing of difference[28]—upon which politicians, religious leaders, and scientific practitioners justify ongoing marginalization (and often ignorance) of sex, gender, and sexual diversity in contemporary US interactional and structural arrangements.

The central goal of this book is to continue our prior work developing a theoretical framework for identifying how processes of cisgendering reality facilitate the erection and dissemination of sex, gender, and sexual differences that—alongside scientific and religious education on these topics—are often the primary predictors of US attitudes concerning every major social institution and population subgroup.[29] Further, we outline the ways a transgender perspective on US society reveals both the social construction and oppressive contents of cisgender realities. Specifically, we discuss how these patterns leave those of us who can't be neatly placed into cisgender binaries as both outsiders marginalized in society and insiders caught within systemic patterns of prejudice, discrimination, and marginalization. Finally, we outline the ways mainstream traditions of knowledge production—such as religion and medical science—commonly rely upon and promote cisgender realities. In developing these ideas, we utilize autoethnographic data from our own experiences as transgender researchers (like the data that opened this chapter) alongside a large-scale qualitative study of transgender experience to encourage our fellow Americans (regardless of gender) to "transition" from seeing only cisgender realities toward including recognition of transgender experiences in US society.

THE MISSING ROLE OF CISNORMATIVITY IN CONTEMPORARY KNOWLEDGE PRODUCTION

Social scientific disciplines have long defined religion and science as the primary sources of knowledge in contemporary societies. They have also regularly pointed out that education or socialization into these systems is generally one of the strongest—and often the strongest—predictor of attitudes concerning most social phenomena.[30] However, there have been very few theoretical interrogations of the ways cisnormativity (i.e., an ideology that assumes and expects that all people are and should be cisgender) is implicated in the production of religious and scientific knowledges.[31] There have further been very few analyses of the ways cisnormativity serves as an organizing principle in the development or dissemination of US science and religion over the course of time.

In recent years, researchers have begun to note and criticize the reliance upon only cisgender theories, methodologies, population samples, and assumptions in the physical sciences. Exploring medical, biological, and public health data sets regularly utilized in physical science traditions, for example, Megan Ivankovich and associates note that almost none of these data sources contain any information on transgender (or intersex and sexual minority) people, experiences, outcomes, or biological realities.[32] Similarly, in 2011 the US Institute of Medicine[33] sounded an alarm with a comprehensive study of patterns in the publication, education, and circulation of physical science research. Their findings noted the absence of any consideration of gender fluidity or sex variation in the bulk of biological, evolutionary, medical, and public health scholarship, theory, and data. In fact, these conclusions have led some medical schools, public health programs, and biological professional groups to begin adding videos and discussions about transgender experience to their websites, discussions of these topics into their graduate curricula, and workshops to reeducate their members at various conferences.[34]

We see a similar pattern of recent critique when we turn to debates currently occurring in the social sciences. Considering that the bulk of published social science research relies on quantitative methods and analysis, and that many programs require only quantitative training, which rarely includes discussion of measures that will capture sex/gender variation, mainstream social science seldom includes transgender people or perspectives in their theoretical and methodological endeavors.[35]

Researchers exploring the General Social Survey—often considered the gold standard of social scientific data—and other broad survey projects, for example, have begun to note that these "representative" data sets "represent" only cisgender experiences and should thus no longer be used to generalize findings about sex, gender, or sexuality.[36] Put simply, these emerging examinations reveal that much physical and social science may be capturing (at best) only cisgender realities.[37]

This picture of cisnormative knowledge production mirrors what has been taught for centuries by dominant religious traditions in the United States. This observation has even led some theorists to ask if the sciences do not simply—though likely unintentionally—mirror religious hegemony in some cases.[38] The two largest religious traditions in the world at present (i.e., Christianity and Islam), for example, are based on creation stories and sacred texts that have no mention of sex/gender variation at all.[39] Further, as we noted in our analysis of Mormon transgender experience, the bulk of religious activity and teaching in such traditions typically rests upon the assumption and enforcement of only cisgender realities, options, and ideas.[40] While some individual religious traditions—like some individual scientists and scientific groups—have begun to revise these sacred teachings, others have—like other scientific groups—responded harshly to increasing social awareness of sex/gender variation.[41]

When looking at these patterns in the majority of knowledge production that shapes the social attitudes of the US population, people like us and others who do not conform to cisgender realities—and thus notice the ways these versions of empirical reality are promoted throughout society—may very easily ask: Where are the transgender people?[42] If religious traditions claim that a specific deity or supernatural force created and controls this universe, and further, tells them about such efforts, why did this supreme being never mention people like us to its followers? If scientists claim that they study the natural world (and often claim to do so objectively), why have they managed to notice, for the most part, only the cisgender aspects of the world to date? What might these traditions of knowledge production look like if they evolved beyond cisgender realities? How might such a change impact the wide variety of social attitudes influenced by these institutions? These are the theoretical questions at the heart of this book.

RELOCATING SEX/GENDER DIVERSITY

Since we cannot generally turn to the primary sources of contemporary knowledge production—mainstream religions or sciences—for knowledge about the United States beyond cisgender binaries, one may ask, where can we turn to locate such phenomena? The answer is that we may turn to alternative knowledge producers, in the same way that cisgender women's rights groups,[43] people of color,[44] sexual minorities,[45] and some nonreligious populations[46] have over the years. Luckily, despite our absence in most mainstream religions and sciences, sex/gender diversity has at least existed in (1) Native American and other traditions mostly destroyed by colonialism and the rise of capitalism, (2) some historical and literary work in the humanities, (3) qualitative research in some social scientific disciplines, and (4) medical history concerning the construction of sex/gender/sexualities over time. In fact, much of this work emerges and/or provides the foundations for rapidly growing interdisciplinary transgender studies fields.

Researchers exploring Native nations have often noted that many such nations had much more expansive understandings of sex and gender than did the colonizers who invaded their lands and overthrew their cultures.[47] As part of the conquest of North America by illegal immigrants from Europe, for example, Native nations were forced by their captors to adopt cisgender, patriarchal, monosexual, and heterosexual selves and stories built upon Christian and Western scientific notions of complementarity.[48] Further, collections of Native mythology and stories reveal many prominent roles—in both the supernatural and natural realms—played by people of varied sexes, genders, and sexualities who were removed from human evolution or creation by the enforcement of scientific and religious complementarity over the past two centuries.[49] While these histories, mythologies, and stories are by no means entirely positive in their interpretations of sex/gender/sexual variation, they reveal a world of experiences, narratives, and possibilities before contemporary cisgender realities overtook recognition of the sex, gender, and sexual diversity of humankind.[50]

Like the aforementioned examples, the humanities—as social theorist Patricia Hill Collins notes regarding African American history and experience[51]—often contain more recognition of natural diversity in the case of transgender people than do mainstream sciences or religions. Following Collins, while this may sound counterintuitive to readers taught that science was built on empiricism and objectivity as well as those who see their religious or scientific preference as a form of "truth," the history of science itself—as Michel Foucault notes[52]— is a social process that has often fallen victim to the biases of its practitioners when facing minority communities and/or new information beyond its existing theoretical basis.[53] While most scholars are aware of this reality in the case of religion, there is often a tendency, as Herbert Blumer and Harold Garfinkel noted fifty years ago,[54] to forget the importance of skepticism when interpreting scientific claims.[55] Similar to other minority populations whose existence conflicted with dominant religious teachings as US science rose in the 1800s,[56] transgender[57] people disappeared for the most part from the dominant scientific and religious narratives while remaining visible—at least at times—in arts, literatures, histories, and music that were not as limited in their version of reality.

It is actually not hard to find evidence of the existence and experiences of sex/gender variant communities who would now be classified within the transgender umbrella in the humanities. Even so, cisgender realities far outnumber these examples in the humanities as well.[58] However, one may turn to gender variant artistic groups and performance companies active throughout the United States before, during, and after World War I; literature and music referencing gender (as well as sexual) variation in the 1920s and throughout the rest of the century; and even films and literary anthologies at least mentioning sex/gender variance at least as early as the 1970s, among many other examples. Further, readers may turn to historical accounts of protests in the 1950s in California, at the heart of what would come to be known as the Stonewall protests in New York City at the end of the 1960s, and the establishment of sex/gender variant support groups, community organizations, and even religious groups in the 1980s and 1990s, though very little of this history will be found in the social or physical scientific narratives of the times.[59] As Susan Stryker notes in her examination of transgender history, sex/gender variation may have been erased from dominant knowledges and structures, but these elements of social life continued to exist, live, and fight for civil rights the whole time.[60]

We also find confirmation of Stryker's observations about the existence of at least some coverage of transgender people in qualitative social science dating back at least to the early 1960s.[61] While the bulk of this work mirrors quantitative traditions by focusing on and limiting its attention to cisgender realities,[62] sex/gender variant people—or case studies—have at least emerged from time to time in qualitative sociology, psychology, anthropology, political science, public health, medical history and clinical care, social work, and interdisciplinary work across the humanities and sciences. At the same time, however, many of the studies published between the 1960s and the early 2000s sought to understand such people (and almost entirely transmen and transwomen only) through a cisgender lens. Specifically, these studies focused on the ways transmen and transwomen (i.e., people who identify as women or men contrary to their birth assignment, and often seek to transition socially, biologically, or in both ways partially or in full) performed gender in ways that challenged or reinforced sex/gender binaries through their efforts to exist. Such studies, however, generally did not analyze the cisgender realities that placed people like us in such circumstances in the first place.[63] Despite such problems, this line of literature at least reminded the sciences of some of the existence and experiences of our population.[64]

Since the early 2000s, however, the social sciences have seen more and more qualitative studies exploring transgender experience and critiquing cisnormativity. Such studies have demonstrated many ways that incorporating transgender people (mostly transmen and transwomen, but some nonbinary people as well) into existing scientific theory and methods complicates existing beliefs—or cisgender theories—about, for example, medicine, families, workplace politics and organization, social movements, romantic relationships, housework and emotions, legal systems, sexual interactions, military service, bathroom segregation, religion, and media.[65] While we do not mean to suggest that quantitative sciences cannot become more active in such efforts (and in fact we, along with others, have suggested ways to accomplish this),[66] at present, from a transgender perspective, the more empirical—in contrast with cisgender-only—studies almost entirely occur in qualitative studies that are published far less frequently than their quantitative counterparts, and almost entirely limited to small, localized case studies.

Throughout this book, we argue that the sex, gender, and sexual variation mostly missing in dominant religious and quantitative scientific traditions may be relocated by turning our attention to the ways transgender people—those like us and those otherwise situated—experience US society. We further provide qualitative experiences (like our own at the start of this book) beyond the numbers of large-scale transgender surveys, and patterns of transgender experience that show up beyond any given, specific local settings in qualitative case studies. As we have argued elsewhere, further incorporating sex/gender/sexual diversity into mainstream sources of knowledge would only require adjusting the ways we create mainstream religion and science to more closely resemble the natural world, and that it could dramatically impact the broad array of social attitudes these institutions influence.[67] As such, throughout this book we offer illustrative examples of some ways the United States may evolve beyond cisgender realities to better make sense of the version of the United States we inhabit as transgender people.

THE STUDY

Building on the insights and patterns noted above, this book examines—or reveals— processes of cisgendering reality experienced by transgender people throughout contemporary US society. Specifically, we utilize the statements and demographic characteristics of our respondents—alongside examples from our own lives—to note the ways transgender people navigate contemporary US society. Like cisgender women, people of color, and gay/lesbian people before us, we flip existing models of social science to present a portrait of US society from the perspective of a marginalized community in hopes of facilitating greater understanding and integration of transgender perspectives more broadly.[68] In so doing, our study provides the other side of the story generally missing from very important recent social scientific books focused on how cisgender people—be they parents, romantic partners, researchers, or strangers—experience us by adding how we experience them to the conversation.[69]

Rather than simply summarizing such patterns, however, we further extend previous studies on transgender experience, sexualities, gender, religion, and health. For example, we outline the ways patterns uncovered in specific local settings by qualitative researchers play out across the United States and provide the qualitative experiences behind the numbers from large-scale surveys of transgender experience in the United States. We then outline how transgender experience complicates and extends work on sexualities, gender, religion, and health science by extending such studies beyond cisnormative notions of sex/gender/sexualities. As other emerging transgender studies scholarship has noted at least since the 1990s, focusing on the ways our population experiences such phenomena allows us to explore conflicts and adjustments occurring (and/or being opposed) within and between varied sex/gender/sexual/religious/scientific communities at the present stage of US history.[70]

To this end, we utilize autoethnographic data from our own lives alongside an original mixed-methods study, which contains more than four hundred responses from transgender people of varied race, class, sex, gender, sexuality, age, and (non)religious identities.[71] Our work offers the largest qualitative collection of transgender experiences and responses available in the social and physical sciences to date, as well as a demonstration of the incredible diversity and variation that falls under the transgender umbrella and is missing from most existing scientific studies of gender, sexualities, religion, and health. We utilize patterns in these data to capture a portrait of both transgender experience and the diversity of transgender populations while suggesting many ways such patterns can extend existing sex/gender/sexualities scholarship throughout the book.

We focus specifically on transgender experiences in the United States to facilitate future discussion and consideration of three interrelated aspects of US society and cisgender realities revealed by carefully considering transgender experiences. First, we seek to direct attention to diversity that is missing in existing science. Next, we seek to outline similarities and differences in the ways transgender people occupying varied social locations experience cisnormativity in their daily lives and across the life course. Finally, we offer a demonstration of the similarities in both religious and scientific responses to transgender populations to reveal how cisnormativity—like heterosexuality, whiteness, and patriarchy at other historical moments—often finds a powerful voice in such institutions. As such, we demonstrate some ways viewing contemporary US society through transgender eyes—like our own and those of our respondents—brings to light the cisnormative foundations of contemporary US structural and interactional norms.

ORGANIZATION OF THE BOOK

Transgender people in the United States experience life in a wide variety of social locations, within a wide variety of local and regional contexts, and in relation to varied religious and scientific norms and expectations. We thus utilize chapter 2 to contextualize ourselves and our respondents in relation to the largest survey of transgender people in the United States to date. Though unintentional, our sample lines up fairly well demographically with this broader data set, which allows us to provide the experiences behind many of the numeric outcomes from such large-scale survey projects. At the same time, our sample spans the nation, which allows us to show how specific patterns noted in local case studies play out across US society. In chapter 2, we outline this approach to the work here and utilize an example common in both qualitative and quantitative studies (*outness*) to demonstrate this approach by exploring transgender coming-out experiences across the nation.

Since most scholarship that includes transgender populations to date occurs within and often focuses on relationships with broader LGBTQIA communities, we next turn to transgender experience in such communities in chapter 3. In so doing, we outline the ways transgender people experience such communities as outsiders within.[72] Specifically, we outline how broader social norms concerning sex, gender, and sexualities find voice in LGBTQIA communities when research examines the experiences of transgender, bi+, intersex, and/or ace people in such contexts. At the same time, however, we demonstrate that LGBTQIA communities are generally the most accepting places for transgender people and further outline conflicts that emerge within transgender communities. In so doing, chapter 3 expands existing LGBTQIA studies primarily focused on LG (and increasingly, sometimes T) experience while also contextualizing the location of transgender people within the communities we are most often associated with in mainstream social, political, religious, and scientific discussions.

After contextualizing transgender experience within transgender populations and LGBTQIA communities in chapters 2 and 3, we turn our attention to the broader landscape of contemporary US society. In so doing, chapter 4 focuses on the ways transgender people experience the bulk of interactions as outsiders within contemporary US expectations and norms concerning sex/gender/sexualities. Echoing earlier work by scholars—like Dorothy Smith, Adrienne Rich, and Patricia Hill Collins[73]—focused on the "problematic" nature of "normal society" from cisgender, lesbian, and/or black women's perspectives, we outline how cisnormativity embedded within US society negatively impacts transgender people throughout the majority of our interactions and structural encounters.

Although chapters 3 and 4 demonstrate the operation of cisnormativity throughout US society, such operation relies upon the lessons people receive concerning the sex/gender/sexual contours of the world. Since religion and science generally function as the primary sources of such education, we next turn to analyses of transgender experience with these traditions. In chapter 5, for example, we examine historical and contemporary conflicts about sex/gender/sexualities between religious and LGBTQIA populations, and the ways emphasis upon sex/gender complementarity structures much of these past and present debates. In so doing, we outline how transgender experiences with religion at present echo earlier experiences from sexual minorities throughout the last seven decades. Further, we discuss how religious teaching about sex/gender—like religious teaching about sexualities—plays a foundational role in US cisnormativity.

Especially since nonreligious reactions to transgender populations—again echoing responses to lesbian/gay people in the past—are often similar to religious reactions at present, we next turn to transgender experiences with science in chapter 6. We follow the lead of prior scholarship from lesbian/gay people and people of color by focusing our attention on medical science. In so doing, we demonstrate how transgender experience with medical science often mirrors such experience with religious people. Although this may seem odd to many people who view science and religion in oppositional terms or as very distinct social practices, here we point out that much contemporary US medical science relies upon the same belief in sex/gender complementarity as many religions and discuss the ways this influences medical and other scientific reactions to sex/gender diversity in the United States.

Taken together, these chapters paint a portrait of transgender experience in contemporary US society that expands beyond any given local setting and provides qualitative insights beyond broad-scale numeric portraits. The vast majority of social beings we encounter—whether drawing on lessons from science, religion, or both—rely upon cisnormativity to structure their lives. In the final chapter, we discuss some of the implications from these findings for broader US social and scholarly understandings of sex/gender/sexual politics as well as the role sciences and religions play in how the United States appears to transgender people at the current stage of history. Like other scholars who sought to foreground the ways society appears from the perspective of a specific marginalized population,[74] we conclude this work with a discussion of the potential—for transgender people and others—of a US society that transitions from cisnormativity to a society with more sex/gender/sexual freedom for all.

NOTES

1. Although sex/gender variation has been labeled in many ways both (1) within communities in different places and at different times in history and (2) by scholars,

historians, religious and political leaders, and other social authorities, here we follow Stryker by utilizing *transgender* as the umbrella term for people who do not conform to the sex assigned to them at birth by social authorities. This is similar to black feminist scholars using *black* and *people of color* to highlight the perspectives of such communities even when discussing time periods and examples where other types of language were more commonly used within communities and in how authorities talked about those communities (see, Collins, *Black Feminist Thought*). In so doing, we use language that highlights our positions as transgender people in contemporary US society, but also direct readers interested in historical variation in terms of sex/gender variation and terminology to see, for example, Stryker, *Transgender History*; Feinberg, *Transgender Warriors*; Karkazis, *Fixing Sex*; and others cited here for more information on such topics.

2. The first author of this book is a nonbinary transwoman who continues to vacillate between biological transition options, as she has since the 1990s, and presents as more masculine or more feminine at different times while utilizing both *they* and *she* pronoun structures. The second author of this book is a nonbinary transgender person who most often identifies as genderqueer and utilizes gender-neutral pronouns. Each of the moments utilized at the opening of this chapter come from data points in our lives that have, at different times, led to nothing remarkable or led to danger, fear, or serious problems. We use these autoethnographic examples, as we do with others at the opening of each chapter, to introduce topics with data drawn from our experiences as transgender people in the United States at present.

3. Smith, *The Everyday World as Problematic*.

4. Throughout this book, we use US as a common shorter version of the United States. Although we use references and note instances where other nations become relevant to the discussion, we focus here on how transgender people experience contemporary US society.

5. See Boylan, *She's Not There*; Grace and Ozzi, *Tranny*; McBee, *Amateur*; McBride and Biden, *Tomorrow Will Be Different*; Mock, *Redefining Realness*; Nutt, *Becoming Nicole*; and other transgender biographies and memoirs for more examples of transgender experiences in daily life in cisgender-dominated contexts. See also Mathers, "Navigating Genderqueer Existence," and Sumerau, "Embodying Nonexistence," for examples from the authors' own lives.

6. See Butler, *Gender Trouble*.

7. See, for example, Martin, "Gender as a Social Institution"; Padavic and Reskin, *Women and Men at Work*; and West and Zimmerman, "Doing Gender."

8. On what it means to be a man, see Bridges, "A Very 'Gay' Straight?"; Connell and Messerschmidt, "Hegemonic Masculinity"; Schrock and Schwalbe, "Men, Masculinity, and Manhood Acts"; and Vaccaro, "Male Bodies in Manhood Acts." On what it means to be a woman, see Connell, *Gender and Power*; Ezzell, "'Barbie Dolls' on the Pitch"; Sumerau and Cragun, "The Hallmarks of Righteous Women"; and Young, "Throwing Like a Girl."

9. See Davis, *Contesting Intersex*; Fausto-Sterling, *Sexing the Body*; Karkazis, *Fixing Sex*; and Stryker, *Transgender History*.

10. See Ridgeway, *Framed by Gender*.

11. We say "on average" here because situational contexts can create spaces where any given set of identities may experience social life in better or worse ways in a given moment, but certain patterns emerge in most cases when comparing such characteristics and contexts; see also Collins, *Black Feminist Thought*.

12. This pattern is evident in survey research on how transgender people are perceived more negatively than most other social groups by cisgender others (see Cragun and Sumerau, "The Last Bastion"; and Cragun and Sumerau, "No One Expects a Transgender Jew"). For analyses of the dynamics of transgender existence and the ways such existence intersects with other components of identity beyond survey research see, for example, Koyama, "Whose Feminism Is It Anyway?"; Roen, "Theory and Embodiment"; shuster, "Punctuating Accountability"; and Vidal-Ortiz, "The Figure of the Transwoman of Color."

13. Sumerau, Cragun, and Mathers, "Cisgendering Reality."

14. See Mathers, "Bathrooms, Boundaries, and Emotional Burdens"; Mathers, "Expanding on the Experiences"; Mathers, Sumerau, and Cragun, "The Limits of Homonormativity"; Nowakowski, Sumerau, and Mathers, "None of the Above"; Sumerau, "Embodying Nonexistence"; Sumerau and Cragun, "The Last Bastion"; Sumerau and Cragun, *God Loves (Almost) Everyone*; Sumerau, Cragun, and Mathers, "Cisgendering Reality"; Sumerau and Grollman, "Obscuring Oppression"; Sumerau, Mathers, and Cragun, "Incorporating Transgender Experience"; and Yavorsky, "Cisgendered Organizations."

15. For examples, see Sumerau, "Embodying Nonexistence."

16. Though it may surprise some readers, J learned the term *cisgender* (as well as the term *monosexual*, noted later in the book) before she was finished with high school in the 1990s simply by knowing and interacting with sex-, gender-, and sexually

diverse people. In fact, as Pfeffer (*Queering Families*) and others have noted, the term even showed up in some academic scholarship as soon as the early 1990s.

17. It is noteworthy that intersex people (i.e., people born between and/or beyond current assumptions about male and female bodies) may adopt cisgender and/or transgender identities (as well as identities located between these ends of the spectrum) in practice, since, as Davis (*Contesting Intersex*) notes, they are often missing completely from existing cisgender understandings predicated on only male/female sex options, and may find both acceptance and rejection at varied times in transgender communities.

18. See Butler, *Gender Trouble*; Serano, *Whipping Girl*; Stryker, *Transgender History*; Stein, *Unbound*; Travers, *The Trans Generation*; and Westbrook and Schilt, "Doing Gender, Determining Gender."

19. See Darwin, "Doing Gender beyond the Binary"; Serano, *Whipping Girl*; and Stryker, *Transgender History*.

20. See also Stryker, *Transgender History*, for a similar argument in relation to binary versus spectrum understandings of cisgender-transgender dynamics; see also Stryker and Whittle, *Transgender Studies Reader*, vol. 1; and Stryker and Aizura, *Transgender Studies Reader*, vol. 2.

21. See Bonilla-Silva, *Racism without Racists*; Buggs, "Dating in the Time of #BlackLivesMatter"; Cohen, "Punks, Bulldaggers, and Welfare Queens"; Collins, *Black Sexual Politics*; Crenshaw, "Mapping the Margins"; and Garcia, *Respect Yourself, Protect Yourself*.

22. See Cheng, "Marginalized Masculinities"; Demantas and Meyers, "'Step Up and Be a Man'"; Espiritu, "'We Don't Sleep Around'"; McCabe and Sumerau, "Reproductive Vocabularies"; Schilt, "'A Little Too Ironic'"; Schippers, "Recovering the Feminine Other"; and Sumerau, "'That's What a Man.'"

23. See Acosta, *Amigas y Amantes*; Ahmed, *Queer Phenomenology*; Eisner, *Notes for a Bisexual Revolution*; Moss, "Alternative Families, Alternative Lives"; Schippers, *Beyond Monogamy*; Steele, Collier, and Sumerau, "Lesbian, Gay, and Bisexual Contact"; and Warner, *The Trouble with Normal*.

24. See Pfeffer, *Queering Families*; Schilt and Westbrook, "Doing Gender, Doing Heteronormativity"; Stein, *Unbound*; Sumerau and Cragun, *God Loves (Almost) Everyone*; and Westbrook and Schilt, "Doing Gender, Determining Gender."

25. Let us provide another example of the importance of recognizing the cisgender and transgender spectrum for those who may have difficulty leaving binary thinking at the door before reading this book. Scholars and others upset by the use of the term *cisgender*, for example, often sound similar to those upset by the use of the term *whiteness*. However, the same way it is absurd to say "all lives matter" when the black ones are under attack mostly by white people and beliefs tied to whiteness, it is absurd to say "other ways to look at gender" when transgender people are the population under attack mostly by cisgender people and beliefs tied to cisgender realities. Here we are not saying there are not other ways to look at these dynamics or cases where cisgender might not be the most useful terminology, but rather, we use it to point out the current problem and supremacy of cisgender people in society (see also Stryker, *Transgender History*).

26. LGBTQIA is an umbrella term that refers to lesbian, gay, bisexual, transgender, queer/questioning, intersex, and asexual.

27. See Butler, *Gender Trouble*; Butler, *Undoing Gender*; Eisner, *Notes for a Bisexual Revolution*; Fausto-Sterling, *Sexing the Body*; Stryker, *Transgender History*; Serano, *Whipping Girl*; Stryker and Aizura, *Transgender Studies Reader*, vol. 2; and Stryker and Whittle, *Transgender Studies Reader*, vol. 1.

28. Building on the framework advanced by West and Zimmerman in "Doing Gender," the process of doing difference refers to the ways that one's existence in a given racial, class, and/or gender category is an ongoing accomplishment in social interactions. We see the process of doing difference play out when one suggests, for example, that a black student "sounds white," or a poor person "wastes money" by purchasing a nice dinner for their family. In these interactions, the "difference" of race and class are noted in the ways social others comment on or condemn another's behavior based on whether or not said behavior "fits" with culturally salient ideas of what it means to be black, white, rich, poor, man, woman, etc. See West and Fenstermaker, "Doing Difference."

29. See Cragun and Sumerau, "The Last Bastion"; Cragun and Sumerau, "No One Expects a Transgender Jew"; Mathers, "Bathrooms, Boundaries, and Emotional Burdens"; Mathers, "Expanding on the Experiences"; Mathers, "Navigating Genderqueer Existence"; Mathers, Sumerau, and Cragun, "The Limits of Homonormativity"; Nowakowski and Sumerau, *Other People's Oysters*; Nowakowski, Sumerau, and Mathers, "None of the Above"; Sumerau, *Cigarettes & Wine*; Sumerau, "Embodying Nonexistence"; Sumerau, *Essence*; Sumerau,

Homecoming Queens; Sumerau, *That Year*; Sumerau and Cragun, *God Loves (Almost) Everyone*; Sumerau, Cragun, and Mathers, "Cisgendering Reality"; Sumerau and Grollman, "Obscuring Oppression"; Sumerau, Mathers, and Cragun, "Incorporating Transgender Experience"; Sumerau, Mathers, Nowakowski, and Cragun, "Helping Quantitative Sociology."

30. For example, attitudinal surveys consistently show that education and religion are two of the strongest (and often *the* strongest) predictors of political identification; responses to social policies and laws; opinions on the criminal justice system; healthcare debates; civil rights campaigns for and against race, sex, class, gender, sexual, age, and ability equality; and conceptualizations of what it means to be an American; see Adamczyk, *Cross-National*, and Worthen, "An Argument," for reviews.

31. See Butler, *Gender Trouble*; Collins, *Black Sexual Politics*; Eisner, *Notes for a Bisexual Revolution*; Kuhn, *Scientific Revolutions*; Serano, *Whipping Girl*; shuster, "Passing as Experts"; Stryker, *Transgender History*; Sumerau, Cragun, and Mathers, "Cisgendering Reality"; Warner, *The Trouble with Normal*; and Westbrook and Saperstein, "New Categories."

32. Ivankovich, Leichliter, and Douglas, "Measurement of Sexual Health."

33. Institute of Medicine, "The Health of Lesbian, Gay, Bisexual, and Transgender People."

34. See Fine, "Explaining, or Sustaining, the Status Quo?"; Jordan-Young and Rumiati, "Hardwired for Sexism?"; Kraus, "Critical Studies"; Nikoleyczik, "Towards Diffractive Transdisciplinarity"; Roy, "Neuroethics, Gender"; and Vidal, "The Sexed Brain," for selections from a special issue of *Neuroethics* on some of these topics. See also current (as of this writing in 2018) calls from the National Institutes of Health for more transgender-inclusive medical research throughout the United States to use future studies to expand beyond existing limitations of US medical scientific knowledge.

35. Compton, Meadow, and Schilt, *Other, Please Specify*; Doan, "To Count or Not to Count"; Lombardi, "Trans Issues in Sociology"; Magliozzi, Saperstein, and Westbrook, "Scaling Up"; Miller and Grollman, "The Social Costs"; Sumerau, Mathers, Nowakowski, and Cragun, "Helping Quantitative Sociology"; Westbrook and Saperstein, "New Categories." See also, as of this writing in 2018, discussions of expanding sex/gender questioning practices in the General Social Survey.

36. See n. 28, above. See also Fenstermaker, "The Turn"; Grant et al., *Injustice at Every Turn*; Hughes, "Not Out in the Field"; James et al., *Report of the 2015 U.S. Transgender Survey*; Meadow, *Trans Kids*; O'Brien, "Seeing Agnes"; Schilt, "The Importance."

37. See also Fausto-Sterling, *Sexing the Body*.

38. See Butler, *Gender Trouble*; Sumerau, Cragun, and Mathers, "Cisgendering Reality"; Warner, *The Trouble with Normal*.

39. But see Hartke, *Transforming*, for examples of trans people beginning to become integrated into these traditions in terms of scriptural interpretation and activities—this mirrors a pattern seen among LGB people in years prior, which we discuss in chapter 5. (See Sumerau, "That's What a Man"; Wilcox, *Coming Out in Christianity*; Wilcox, *Queer Women*; and Wolkomir, *Be Not Deceived*.)

40. Sumerau, Cragun, and Mathers, "Cisgendering Reality." For more on this pattern in Protestant traditions, see Barton, *Pray the Gay Away*; Mathers, Sumerau, and Cragun, "The Limits of Homonormativity"; Sumerau and Cragun, *God Loves (Almost) Everyone*; Sumerau, Mathers, and Cragun, "Incorporating Transgender Experience"; and Sumerau, Mathers, and Lampe, "Learning from the Experiences." For more on this pattern in Jewish traditions, see Avishai, "'Doing Religion'"; and Dzmura, *Balancing*. For more on this pattern in Islamic traditions, see Rinaldo, *Mobilizing Piety*.

41. Following Stryker (*Transgender History*), we use the term *awareness* here because while many cisgender commentators within and beyond science see our populations as new as a result of erasure processes, gender variation and gender-variant people have long histories and have been noted, even in scientific studies in medical fields, since before the turn of the twentieth century.

42. See again Collins, *Black Feminist Thought*, for a similar discussion related to blackness in mostly white scholarship historically.

43. Martin, "Gender as a Social Institution"; Rossi, "The Formation of SWS"; Smith, *The Everyday World as Problematic*.

44. Anzaldua, *Borderlands*; Combahee River Collective, "A Black Feminist Statement"; Collins, *Black Sexual Politics*; Jones, *African American Civil Rights*.

45. Armstrong, *Forging Gay Identities*; Garber, *Bisexuality*; Warner, *The Trouble with Normal*.

46. Cimino and Smith, "Secular Humanism"; LeDrew, "Discovering Atheism"; Sumerau and Cragun, "'I Think Some People.'"

47. See, for example, Deer, *The Beginning*; Elledge, *Gay, Lesbian, Bisexual, and Transgender Myths*; and Smith, *Conquest*, for reviews.

48. Complementarity, as we discuss in chapter 5, refers to a belief system positing that the world is composed of only two sexes that complement each other in reproductive heterosexuality; see Moon and Tobin, "Sunsets and Solidarity," for a recent discussion of this topic.

49. Driskill, Justice, Miranda, and Tatonetti, *Sovereign Erotics*; Jacobs, Thomas, and Lang, *Two-Spirit People*.

50. It is important to note that in this short summary, we follow the suggestions of Towle and Morgan ("Romancing the Transgender Native"), who note the importance of (1) recognizing sex/gender variation in Native nations and other historically marginalized sectors of the world and historical politics while also (2) not assuming that such examples are necessarily similar to any other examples of sex/gender variation in the past or at present and remaining aware that such examples were/ are complicated and culturally specific rather than necessarily positive or negative or specifically comparative to a given current social context or setting.

51. Collins, *Black Sexual Politics*.

52. Foucault, *History of Sexuality*.

53. Collins, *Black Sexual Politics*; Kleinman, *Feminist Fieldwork*; and Kuhn, *Scientific Revolutions*.

54. Blumer, *Symbolic Interaction*; Garfinkel, *Ethnomethodology*.

55. As Thomas and Thomas noted in the 1920s (*The Child in America*), that which we define as real becomes real in its consequences. In terms of scientific literatures, it is often the case that a given finding, theory, or method becomes taken for granted over time and sanctified as the one "real" way to conduct scientific research (see again Compton, Meadow, and Schilt, *Other, Please Specify*), even in the face of competing empirical information that suggests such approaches to science need to be reevaluated and adjusted to better fit shifts in society. Interactionists and ethnomethodologists have long worked to disrupt these scientific assumptions by questioning the norms that are reproduced in scientific contexts. See Dingwall, "Notes toward an Intellectual History," for a review.

56. Collins, *Black Sexual Politics*; Foucault, *History of Sexuality*; Katz, *The Invention of Heterosexuality*; Stryker, *Transgender History*; Stryker and Aizura, *Transgender Studies Reader*, vol. 2; Stryker and Whittle, *Transgender Studies Reader*, vol. 1.

57. It is important to note that the term *transgender* did not gain widespread use until the 1990s. Although some scholars prefer not using it to discuss time periods before the 1990s, we respectfully disagree with them for three reasons drawn from our experiences as transgender people studying transgender people. First, J has often talked—professionally and informally—with people as old as eighty-three years of age who prefer this term because most prior terminology emerged via the medical, political, and religious efforts of cisgender people and was often used against our communities. Second, it is difficult to decide what time-specific terminology to use as scientists because if we use terms in scientific literature we are not necessarily using the terms of our community at the same times, and if we use the terms of our communities at the time, we have to pick which terms and may use terminology that those who have only prior scholarship to understand our pasts will not know about or recognize. Third, we agree with people of color—and especially black and African American people—who argue that utilization of the time-specific language for their communities reinforces the power of historical authorities rather than emphasizing the perspectives of the people themselves. As a result, the same way many terms used historically for people of color are not utilized by researchers (of color or otherwise) now, we prefer to use our community terms instead of historical terms associated with our community (mostly by others).

58. See, for example, the lives of famous transgender people throughout history such as Christine Jorgensen, Tracy Africa Norman, Lili Elbe, April Ashley, Aleisha Brevard, Sylvia Rivera, Marsha P. Johnson, Michael Dillon, and Candy Darling, just to name a few. See also the memoirs mentioned in n. 2 of this chapter. See also books, both fiction and nonfiction, such as Bornstein, *Gender Outlaw*; Feinberg, *Stone Butch Blues*; Gill, *Already Doing It*; Irving, *In One Person*; Kennedy, *The First Man-Made Man*; Krieger, *Nina Here*; Nowakowski and Sumerau, *Other People's Oysters*; Rosenberg, *Jane Crow*; Samuels, *Fantasies of Identification*; Snorton, *Black on Both Sides*; and Sumerau, *Cigarettes & Wine*, *Homecoming Queens*, *Essence*, and *That Year*. See the influence of transgender people in other art forms: *Transgender Dysphoria Blues* and *Shape Shift with Me*, both albums by the band Against Me!; DeCurtis, *Lou Reed*; Gallardo, "The Transgender Muse"; Gibson, *Pole Dancing*, *The Madness Vase*, and *Pansy*; Tolbert and Peterson, *Troubling the Line*. For a review of transgender visibility and influence in art and culture, see Gossett, Stanley, and

Burton, *Trap Door*. Finally, see the list in the sources within Stryker, *Transgender History*, for even more examples.

59. But see, for example, Dozier, "Beards, Breasts, and Bodies"; Schrock, "Transsexuals' Narrative Construction"; Schrock, Reid, and Boyd, "Transsexuals' Embodiment"; and Sumerau, Schrock, and Reese, "Transsexuals' Gender Presentations," for examples wherein such events are noted in qualitative research projects over time.

60. See also Bauer, "Transgressive and Transformative"; Beemyn and Rankin, *The Lives*; Benjamin, *Transsexual Phenomenon*; Boylan, *She's Not There*; Brubaker, *Trans*; Connell, "Doing, Undoing, or Redoing"; Cromwell, *Transmen*; Currah, "Expecting Bodies"; Devor, *FTM*; Fausto-Sterling, *Sex/Gender*; Green, *Becoming a Visible Man*; Halberstam, *Female Masculinity*; Kessler, *Lessons*; Lev, *Transgender Emergence*; Manion, "Transbutch"; Martinez–San Miguel and Tobias, *Trans Studies*; Plemons, "Description of Sex Difference"; Psihopaidas, "Intimate Standards"; Reisner et al., "Legal Protections"; Rubin, *Self-Made Men*; Schilt, *Just One of the Guys?*; Schilt and Westbrook, "Doing Gender, Doing Heteronormativity"; shuster, "Uncertain Expertise"; and Spade, *Normal Life*. See also the journal *Transgender Studies Quarterly* for more studies, and Stryker, *Transgender History*, for a historical review.

61. Stryker, *Transgender History*.

62. Schilt and Lagos, "The Development"; Sumerau, Schrock, and Reese, "Transsexuals' Gender Presentations."

63. See Ekins and King, "Towards a Sociology"; Gagné, Tewksbury, and McGaughey, "Coming Out and Crossing Over"; Garfinkel, *Ethnomethodology*; Goffman, *Stigma*; Lewins, *Transsexualism in Society*; and Schrock, "Transsexuals' Narrative Construction," for examples of this line of scholarship.

64. See Fenstermaker, "The Turn"; O'Brien, "Seeing Agnes"; Schilt, "The Importance"; Schilt and Lagos, "The Development"; Stryker and Aizura, *Transgender Studies Reader*, vol. 2; and Stryker and Whittle, *Transgender Studies Reader*, vol. 1.

65. Connell, "Doing, Undoing, or Redoing"; Halberstam, *In a Queer Time*; Mathers, "Bathrooms, Boundaries, and Emotional Burdens"; Mizock and Lewis, "Trauma in Transgender Populations"; Pfeffer, "'Women's Work'?"; Pfeffer, "Normative Resistance"; Reese, "Gendered Identity Work"; Samons, "Can this Marriage"; Schilt, *Just One of the Guys?*; Schilt and Westbrook, "Doing Gender, Doing

Heteronormativity"; Stone, "More than Adding a T"; Sumerau and Cragun, *God Loves (Almost) Everyone*; Sumerau, Cragun, and Mathers, "Cisgendering Reality"; Westbrook and Schilt, "Doing Gender, Determining Gender."

66. Compton, Meadow, and Schilt, *Other, Please Specify*; Doan, "To Count or Not to Count"; Magliozzi, Saperstein, and Westbrook, "Scaling Up"; Nowakowski, Sumerau, and Mathers, "None of the Above"; Sumerau, Mathers, Nowakowski, and Cragun, "Helping Quantitative Sociology"; Westbrook and Saperstein, "New Categories."

67. Sumerau, Mathers, Nowakowski, and Cragun, "Helping Quantitative Sociology." See also n. 55 in this chapter.

68. Collins, *Black Sexual Politics*; Rich, "Compulsory Heterosexuality"; Smith, *The Everyday World as Problematic*; and Warner, *The Trouble with Normal*.

69. It is important to note that we appreciate the analyses the authors present in each of these books and hope to see more such work published in the future. However, the analytic focus of these works, as well as the attention and acclaim they've received within and beyond the social sciences, show that—thus far—the stories that get the greatest attention are more focused on cisgender experiences and realities in relation to transgender people than on studies undertaken by transgender people ourselves or the experiences of transgender people in relation to cisgender others.

70. Erickson-Schroth, *Trans Bodies*; Serano, *Whipping Girl*; Stryker, *Transgender History*; Stryker and Aizura, *Transgender Studies Reader*, vol. 2; and Stryker and Whittle, *Transgender Studies Reader*, vol. 1.

71. As discussed in the methodological appendix, 74 international respondents were also captured in the survey, which puts the total number at 395 U.S. transgender respondents. However, it is noteworthy that the experiences shared by the international respondents were very similar to the U.S. ones. See the methodological appendix at the end of the book for more details.

72. See chapter 3 for further discussion of Patricia Hill Collins's concept of outsider within.

73. See again n. 65 in this chapter.

74. See again n. 65 in this chapter; see also Serano, *Whipping Girl*; Stryker, *Transgender History*; Eisner, *Notes for a Bisexual Revolution*; and Halberstam, *In a Queer Time*.

Coming Out (or Not) as Trans

"What was it like when you first realized you were really a girl?" I (Lain) asked J on the phone after class one day at the end of my first year of graduate study. I remember feeling nervous and worrying that this was a bad—or maybe just impolite—question, but J just laughed and said, "You know, I was so young, I don't know if I really remember ever feeling like anything else, if I ever did." I heard my own lack of fit with the sex and gender assigned to me throughout my life in those words, and over the next hour or so (and for many weeks and months to come) I talked about my nonbinary transgender selfhood with another person for the first time in my life. As I've written about elsewhere, I was early into graduate school in the 2010s and people like me were becoming hot topics and even finding some welcome in some academic spaces as I began navigating my life as an openly nonbinary transgender person.[1] Although this has come with many costs alongside other beautiful moments, my coming-out experiences have been more positive than negative overall, allowing me to bond and work with other young trans and LGBQIA scholars emerging in my field and society more broadly.

My story is one version of coming out, but J's is a more complicated tale. When she entered graduate school at the age of twenty-seven in 2008, J specifically worked with seasoned feminist scholars who were supportive of her interests in more expansive notions of sex, gender, and sexualities, but J kept their[2] own gender identity secret and separate from professional settings. In

27

fact, she even remained quiet when granted the luxury of having a fellow transgender person become part of her graduate student research experience as a mentor right before she earned her PhD in 2012. Still in the process of recovering from trans-, bi-, and homophobic violence that left her face, back, and legs scarred in many places (some still visible today even after much health care intervention), and having been turned away by "scientists" called *doctors* in her early twenties,[3] J chose to remain hidden in plain sight at first, then slowly came out as nonbinary publicly and professionally after graduate school. She has only recently (for the first time since before entering the academy) begun sharing her experiences as a nonbinary transwoman beyond her supportive inner circle of family and friends in the last couple years.[4] Whereas I have had at least some support and been able to be more out professionally and in my personal relationships to date, J's trajectory more closely resembles the selective disclosure (i.e., picking and choosing who knows based on safety and other concerns) often found in older transgender populations, bi+ communities, and ace populations.[5]

The above examples speak to both variations in transgender experience related to coming out[6] and the ways various social factors influence processes of coming out (or not) within and between different populations within transgender communities.[7] At the same time, our experiences are just two of many types of stories transgender people have in relation to how (or if) they come out as transgender in their lives. In this chapter, we introduce readers to the variations in our sample of transgender people to set up the overall population captured throughout this book and explore experiences with coming out and reasons for not coming out offered by our participants. In so doing, we set the stage for later chapters that focus on how transgender people occupying varied social locations experience and discuss their encounters with others in contemporary US society.

CONTEXTUALIZING TRANSGENDER EXPERIENCE

At the time of this writing, J and Lain are both white,[8] bi+, agnostic, transgender people working in the academy as researchers and teachers. Although J was born into, given up for adoption in, adopted within, and raised in the lower working class, she is now considered upper class in terms of her economic standing and educational attainment. On the other hand, Lain was born into and raised in a middle-class family, but, like most graduate students, currently subsists economically around the US poverty line while possessing advanced degrees. As noted above, Lain and J have two different gender identities within the broader transgender umbrella, and are from two different generational cohorts, as Lain is in their late twenties and J is in their late thirties. Both researchers manage chronic health conditions in their daily lives, and both engage in research and teaching related to gender, sexualities, health, religion, inequalities, and violence in society. While Lain is monogamous in their romantic desires, J is an openly polyamorous person with multiple committed partnerships at present.

These disclosures speak to a topic theorists have noted over the past fifty years: Personal and broader social contexts play powerful roles in the experiences of social life as well as the construction of any text—research or otherwise—about social life.[9] We thus share these aspects of ourselves both because they impact the context of this writing, and because our own sociodemographic characteristics come to light in the coming-out experiences and other personal examples we utilize in this book. Put simply, this book offers a view of the United States through both our own transgender eyes and the sightlines of our respondents, filtered by our decisions about how to use and present their stories.

We thus begin the substantive chapters of our discussion of transgender experiences in contemporary US society by using this chapter to (1) contextualize the transgender people whose voices make up the bulk of this book as they relate to broader knowledge about transgender populations in US society at present, and (2) utilize an issue—coming out or outness—also captured in the largest survey study of transgender populations to date. We do this to present a comparative picture of this process before moving into qualitative analyses of topics that are not the focus of quantitative studies about our communities. We also do this to highlight the diversity of both transgender populations and the standpoints shared here.

As suggested by the references throughout this book, the expansion of transgender studies in the past couple decades has allowed the voices of our communities unprecedented exposure in academic and mainstream contexts. The 2015 U.S. Transgender Survey (USTS), for example, provides a powerful quantitative snapshot of the demographic variety and experience of transgender people in the United States.[10] Like its predecessors, the USTS offers a large-scale numeric portrait of the identities and issues faced by transgender people within multiple US institutions, as well as information regarding their interactions with friends, families, and strangers across the country. At the same time, myriad case studies and memoirs have been published in recent years. Such efforts focus attention on specific members or population groups under the transgender umbrella and offer in-depth qualitative portraits of transgender experience in specific contexts. Similarly, recent years have witnessed more work on transgender histories, theorizing in the sciences and humanities, and media representations across the nation, each of which influences continually emerging surveys and case studies.

While the importance of these works cannot be understated,[11] here we outline a path between the massive surveys and localized studies available at present. Specifically, we utilize this book to paint a vast, qualitative portrait of transgender experience across the United States beyond a given local context or specific demographic group. In so doing, we offer stories behind the numbers captured in existing large-scale surveys as well as broader patterns transgender people speak of, which focused case studies can tease apart in more in-depth and nuanced ways. To this end, we draw upon each of the aforementioned types of media representations and emerging transgender studies scholarship to provide context—local and national—for the experiences shared throughout this book.

We thus begin by painting the overall demographic portrait of the people whose experiences are shared in this study. Like the USTS, we designed our survey to allow freedom for respondents to identify in relation to current demographic categories. As a result, our survey captured responses from transgender people occupying a wide array of gender, sexual, race, religious, class, and age categories. At the same time, our respondents were mostly white (67 percent) and fairly well-educated compared to the broader US population (73.7 percent had at least some college). Furthermore, most people in our sample were on the lower and middle portions of the economic ranks of society (61.4 percent earned less than $40,000 per year) despite being more well-educated than most people in the United States. Though we did not set out to ensure this would be the case, our sample lines up fairly well with the USTS, where most respondents were white (62.2 percent), more educated on average than the broader US population (87 percent with at least some college), and more likely to be on the lower and

Table 2.1.   Gender Identities (*n* = 469)

Gender Identity	Number of Respondents
Transgender	87
Transman	78
Transwoman	71
Nonbinary	70
Genderqueer	53
Agender	33
Gender Fluid	28
Transsexual	21
Gender Neutral	15
Bi-gender	6
Intersex	5
Cross-dresser	2

middle sections of the economic ranks despite such educational attainment (74 percent earned less than $50,000 per year).

In terms of gender identity, our survey respondents identified in twelve different ways (see table 2.1). Although this is fewer than the USTS survey, which noted twenty-five different gender identities, our sample matches that in the sense that the four most common gender identities in the USTS are also the four most common gender identities in our sample: transgender, transwoman, transman, and nonbinary.[12] Although most of our respondents were white, we also see similar racial diversity to that of the USTS with respondents of Hispanic, black, Asian, Native American, and multiracial experience represented in our data (see table 2.2). Similarly, our sample includes transgender people who identify with myriad sexual identities, including gay/lesbian, straight/heterosexual, bisexual, pansexual, queer, and ace, with queer being the most common sexual identity in the sample, as it is in the USTS. Although we focus on the overall patterns in our data set, such diversity lends weight to increasing calls to ascertain racial and sexual variation within transgender populations and experiences in society.[13]

Alongside gender, race, and sexualities, researchers—within and beyond transgender studies—have long noted the influence of socioeconomic status on social life.[14] As table 2.3 demonstrates, transgender people occupy a curious social position in relation to usual measures of socioeconomic status such as income and educational attainment. Like the respondents in the USTS, for example, our respondents are much more likely than the average US citizen to live in poverty (38.4 percent) but are also more likely than the average US

Table 2.2.   Racial and Sexual Identities (n = 415[a]; n = 413)

Racial Identity	Number of Respondents	Sexual Identity	Number of Respondents
White	315	Queer	126
Black	27	Pansexual	70
Hispanic	27	Asexual[b]	57
Multiracial	16	Lesbian	50
Native American	12	Bisexual	41
Asian	10	Heterosexual	41
		Fluid	12

[a]Different total numbers (n) are due to (1) our survey not forcing anyone to respond to any question and (2) respondents choosing, as a result, not to disclose certain information.
[b]Asexual people who identify as romantic (n = 43) and aromantic (n = 14).

citizen to have a college or graduate degree (48.8 percent). Considering that much research and political commentary suggests that education—across other demographic factors—generally correlates with income and other economic indicators, this pattern in our data and the USTS suggests that the limitation of most surveys to cisgender populations may be obfuscating the impact of transphobia or other aspects of gender on hypothesized relationships between education and economic status.[15] However, our respondents appear to utilize education rather than income when defining themselves, since more than half of them identify as middle class despite almost half of them in living in poverty.[16]

The USTS, alongside the past thirty years of scholarship on lesbian and gay (and, recently, occasionally bi+) religious experience, also suggests complicated relationships between religion, sexualities, and gender that impact transgender people's lives.[17] As in the USTS, table 2.4 shows that our respondents are more likely to be nonreligious than religious, and the most common religious identifications are Christian and pagan. Also, as we outline in

Table 2.3.   Educational Attainment and Income (n = 412; n = 371)

Educational Attainment	Number of Respondents	Income Per Year	Number of Respondents
Did Not Graduate High School	10	Less than $20,000	180
High School or GED	56	$20,001–40,000	108
Some College	117	$40,001–60,000	35
Bachelor's Degree	138	$60,001–80,000	19
Master's Degree	61	$80,001–100,000	13
Juris or Medical Doctorate	15	Over $100,000	16
Academic Doctorate	15		

Table 2.4. Religious Identities, Political Orientation, and Age (n = 290; n = 384; n = 469)

Religious Identity	Number of Respondents	Political Orientation	Number of Respondents	Age	Number of Respondents
Nonreligious or None	145	Conservative	7	19–29	260
		Moderate	69	30–39	108
Christian	55	Liberal	358	40–49	44
Pagan	37			50+	57
Muslim	25				
Jewish	14				
Buddhist	12				
Sikh	1				
Hindu	1				

chapter 5, our respondents mirror those in the USTS by reporting experiences with religious organizations and leaders ranging from outright rejection to loving embrace. Especially considering the role religion plays in US society overall and the formation of US attitudes on political and social issues, and even more so in campaigns for and against sexual and gender rights, such patterns suggest a wealth of possibilities in emerging studies of transgender religious experience and the ways religious people and organizations respond to increased transgender visibility.

Table 2.4 shows similar political views among our respondents to those in the USTS. Our participants overwhelmingly identified on the moderate-to-left end of the political spectrum. Considering ongoing disparities in housing, healthcare access, criminal justice system encounters, identification documents, legal recognition, schools, and public accommodations, it is not surprising that transgender people are more likely to identify with politics geared toward changing rather than conserving existing social arrangements. Further, considering the role of religion in attitudes concerning each of the aforementioned issues, this pattern also reveals the importance of studies incorporating religion into understandings of transgender experience. Moreover, as table 2.4 shows, this is not just a case of young people drawn to liberalism, as our sample includes people in all age groups, much like the USTS. Further, our respondents, like those in the USTS, come from all over the United States rather than from any given specific or localized sociopolitical setting or context within the nation.[18]

The qualitative portrait outlined in this book thus provides a snapshot of transgender experience throughout contemporary US society. Our data mirror the diversity of large-scale quantitative assessments of our population while simultaneously presenting a rich opportunity for innovative qualitative analysis reaching beyond most localized case studies. As an illustration of this approach, we now turn our focus to an issue captured in the USTS and other statistical surveys to outline the stories that go along with existing quantitative observations. This exercise also demonstrates that patterns found in specific case studies in distinct settings represent a broader general pattern across the United States.

ELABORATING ON OUTNESS

Throughout this book we seek to share the ways transgender people—both those sharing and those in different social locations than us—narrate lived experience in the United States at present. Although case studies can provide detailed and deep exploration of the intersectional factors that influence transgender experience in specific contexts, here we focus on the overall patterns transgender people in our sample note beyond a given context.[19] Likewise, while large-scale surveys can show us overall demographics and outcomes as well as intersectional variations in such measures, here we add the stories of the people behind such numbers to understandings of the overall experiences of transgender people in the United States at present.[20]

As an illustration of this approach, we utilize questions about whether transgender people are out (i.e., if others know they are trans) that emerge in both localized case studies and broad-scale surveys. Within case studies concerning outness (i.e., the level at which one is known as transgender to others), for example, researchers find that transgender people of color face even more economic, structural, and violent experiences when out to others in their lives.[21] At the same time, studies show that some transmen gain more social standing in cases of transition whether or not they are out about their transgender identity, and transwomen often lose social standing in the same cases.[22] Studies also find that coming out as transgender is more likely to be received positively by LGBQ people overall, but even here, results are mixed and often complicated in relation to race, class, specific sexual identity, and other factors.[23] Studies also show that transwomen—and especially transwomen of color—are most likely to experience interpersonal and structural violence when identified as transgender by (especially cisgender) others.[24] Finally, studies demonstrate that economic class, religion, age, and regional location may dramatically impact whether or not transgender people come out, as well as how coming out may go in such circumstances. Each of these findings reveals nuances requiring even more attention from researchers across the sciences and operating in different specialty areas.

At the same time, however, survey research shows that despite issues transgender people may face when they come out, the majority of those who participate in surveys are out to some degree. In fact, the USTS notes that even though many transgender people do not need to be out in any absolute sense (i.e., more than half of respondents report that others cannot tell if they are transgender), 8 percent are out to everyone in their lives, while another 48 percent are out to most and 43 percent are out to some. Interestingly, the USTS notes that some transgender people of color (i.e., black and Native American) are a little bit more likely to be out than others, and that about 60 percent of USTS respondents reported receiving at least some support from families upon coming out. At the same time, however, half of USTS respondents experienced some form of rejection upon coming out, and more than a quarter (27 percent) lost romantic relationships as a result of coming out. Further, 10 percent of respondents experienced familial violence and 8 percent were kicked out by their families upon coming out as transgender.[25] Echoing case studies on this dynamic, these numbers reveal a complex situation for transgender people in terms of outness to others.

This same type of complexity shows up with our respondents. Although we asked our respondents only if they were out, without any qualifications, even the statistical portrait of their responses creates a complex picture. Specifically, 61.7 percent of our respondents said they were out, while only 10.1 percent said they were not out and another 28.1 percent chose not to answer the question. Such responses suggest that almost two-thirds of our respondents are out to at least someone in their lives, and that given the option,[26] just over one-fourth of the respondents chose not to disclose this information. In the rest of this section, we explore this complexity by outlining the experiences shared by respondents who said they were or were not out to others.

Invisibility

An important topic within and beyond transgender populations involves increased visibility of some transgender people in recent years. J, for example, remembers telling people she was a transwoman or a transsexual in the 1990s, and often learning that many people had no clue what such terms meant.[27] In more recent times, however, the appearance of some transgender people in media has shifted the contours of visibility wherein many cisgender Americans have at least heard of people like Laverne Cox and Caitlyn Jenner or transgender characters in various television shows or movies. At the same time, however, increased visibility—as has been the case for other populations over time—is not distributed equally. In our sample, there were transgender people—like J and others in the 1990s—who came out only to recognize their invisibility in the cisgender realities of others. However, all the people who reported such experiences were respondents who identified in varied nonbinary ways (i.e., not as transmen or transwomen or even using the umbrella term *transgender*).

For LGBTQIA people who may be older, the visibility issues noted by nonbinary respondents are eerily familiar. Echoing some transmen and transwomen in studies from the past, for example, a twenty-six-year-old middle-class, queer, genderqueer person who came out at the age of fourteen wrote:

> Frustrating, because everyone responds to gender queer identity as if it is not a thing: the mainstream thinks it's just bullshit and the radicals think it's just a way for white cis people to pretend like they are less privileged than they are. No one seems ready to acknowledge that a non-binary identity is possible, particularly if you aren't constantly genderfucking. And that's the same from the first time I came out through the present.

A thirty-year-old middle-class, queer, nonbinary person who came out at seventeen offers a similar example: "My mom . . . insisted it was impossible because I had liked feminine things as a child, and would not listen to what I had to say." Likewise, a thirty-year-old lower-class, fluid person who came out at twenty-three noted: "They couldn't understand what that really meant. . . . I had to do a lot of work explaining myself over and over again." Like J and respondents in earlier studies of transmen and transwomen, our nonbinary respondents often came out to cisgender people who were completely unware nonbinary identities existed.

Also echoing earlier studies on transwomen and transmen, these respondents noted the ways such societal invisibility influenced their own attempts to understand themselves.[28] A forty-two-year-old working-class, bisexual, genderqueer person who came out at twenty-five offers a typical case: "I didn't even have words yet for being genderqueer." A thirty-year-old lower-class, asexual romantic, gender-fluid person who came out at twenty-eight added: "It was uncomfortable because I wasn't sure how to express what my gender is actually like, and it was difficult to ask for people to use neutral pronouns when referring to me." Such examples—even for people who came out as non-binary as early as the late 1990s[29]—may suggest nonbinary people face similar visibility issues seen among transmen and transwomen in earlier decades. It is also potentially interesting that all the respondents who noted trouble understanding themselves were from the Midwest and South, and all the respondents who noted visibility issues were white nonbinary transgender people.[30]

A Mixed Bag

The common refrain from our respondents regardless of gender, racial, sexual, religious, and class identities involved mixtures of negative and positive experiences coming out to others. While this sometimes involved some respondents having only positive experiences and others having only negative experiences, most noted some combination of the two. Like patterns captured in the statistical portraits of the USTS and many localized qualitative studies, our respondents noted fears about how (especially cisgender) people would react, as well as the inability to ever know how any given audience might respond to their violation of cisgender assumptions. In fact, many—as shown in the next quote from a forty-two-year-old middle-class, white, lesbian transwoman who came out at fourteen—experienced coming out as both a gradual process and one that, while plagued by fear and mixed reactions from others, was deeply important for their own life: "I downplayed it using humor; only over time did I convey the severity and integral nature, and only to my closest friends who I knew would be accepting. Yet, each step I took in revealing myself was fraught with concerns that I would be viewed as being sick, a freak, or even worse."

In some cases, respondents shared deeply negative experiences when they became known as transgender to (mostly cisgender) others in their lives. A fifty-nine-year-old lower-class, Hispanic, asexual romantic transwoman who came out at nineteen added: "It was something I had to do. It was not fun, and not a joy to do. It had to be done no matter what happened, and I knew what could happen (most of which did happen)." Likewise, a thirty-five-year-old middle-class, white, queer transman who came out at twenty noted: "I was told I was a freak. I felt ashamed and didn't mention it again to anyone for at least another year. What's worse is that it confirmed my own fears that I really was a freak." Similarly, a twenty-six-year-old lower-class, white, pansexual, nonbinary person who came out at fourteen wrote: "I made an appointment with the school counselor to get hormones . . . then they called my mom and it was horrible." Although visibility has increased in recent years for some transgender people, these stories point out that very negative consequences may await transgender people who come out in the context of cisgender realities at present—consequences not unlike the ones transgender people faced forty years ago.

In fact, reports from our respondents who have come out even more recently than the examples above often contain similar hardships, as suggested in statistical and media analyses in recent years. A twenty-six-year-old lower-class, white, queer, nonbinary person who came out at twenty in 2010 noted: "A few people accused me of having an 'identity crisis' or mental illness. Others stopped talking to me. I hadn't realized my vagina played such a large role in my platonic relationships until I came out as trans." A forty-six-year-old middle-class, Native American, pansexual transwoman who came out at thirty-five in 2005 added:

> I came out while in jail[31] for driving on a suspended license. I came out to my wife in monitored phone calls. The corrections officers and staff persecuted me in imaginable and unimaginable ways. The warden penalized me . . . by holding me for an unexplained additional two weeks. . . . It did not improve much when I was released. I was ostracized and ultimately chased out of my marriage, my home, my town, and my child's life.

Even more recently, a nineteen-year-old lower-class, white, asexual romantic, transgender person who came out at seventeen in 2014 noted: "Most people didn't understand. I faced a lot of bigotry from my parents and siblings. I was told, 'It's just a phase'; it was so bad." As these examples and others like them reveal, many transgender people—of varied racial, sexual, gender, and other social identities—still come out to a harsh cisgender reality where persecution and pain await.

At the same time, we were heartened—as so many others are—to see more positive experiences in some of the stories our respondents shared. As noted by a twenty-seven-year-old middle-class, white, asexual romantic, transgender person who came out at twenty-four in 2013, some of us (like Lain) come out to supportive others that help ease the process: "I was terrified and miserable, still deeply in denial; the person I was coming out to was incredibly supportive, though." A twenty-four-year-old middle-class, Hispanic, bisexual, agender person who came out at twenty-one added: "I was already accepted as bisexual, so I did not feel very concerned about coming out with gender and it went well." Echoing many of the respondents with positive experiences, a twenty-two-year-old lower-class, white, queer, genderqueer person who came out at nineteen in 2013 offered:

> The very first person I talked to about it was a friend I had met about a year earlier. I didn't have as much to lose if she rejected me than if I tried to tell a family member or old friend. I talked to her about the idea of dimensions of gender, and how I didn't really fit into one gender, while I still considered myself to be exploring the idea rather than identifying as trans. She reacted very well, patiently listening and reassuring me that she didn't mind me talking about it, talking with me and helping me to explore my own thoughts, and actually came out to me as having similar feelings. Later we "came out" to each other as genderfluid (I later decided genderqueer fits better) and agender.

Another illustrative case of the positive experiences respondents noted comes from a forty-seven-year-old lower-class, white, lesbian transwoman who came out at thirty-four: "I felt amazing by being truthful for the first time in my life. I came out to my therapist and then my ex-wife. Both were very supportive."

As the quotes above suggest, negative reactions are not universal, which suggests that anyone could react in positive and supportive ways. This, of course, leads to pressing questions in US society today: What factors may facilitate more positive or negative reactions to transgender people in society, and how might shifts in existing cisgender realities—specifically shifts to facilitate the incorporation of transgender people more fully into society— impact the gendered and other sociodemographic contours of the United States? Although only time may answer such questions, greater support of transgender people—as some people have shown in our lives and the lives of some of our respondents—is something anyone *could* offer, for starters.

What about Significant Others?

An important book by sociologist Carla Pfeffer called *Queering Families* focuses on the experiences of cisgender women who have or have had romantic-sexual partnerships with transmen. In 2018, this book won the American Sociological Association Section on Sex and Gender Distinguished Book Award and was selected for inclusion in the American Library Association's Over the Rainbow List for top titles in LGBTQ nonfiction. In many ways, Pfeffer's work represents a groundbreaking study in the relationships of transgender people that many people within the broader transgender community (including the authors of this book) applaud. At the same time, it—as well as the prestige, awards, and honors received by it—leads to another question often missing from studies of romantic-sexual relationships: How do transgender people experience our partners, cisgender or otherwise?

Although it is beyond the purview of the current study to systematically explore this question,[32] some work on this topic shows that transgender people have to engage in significant emotional and other labor to manage relationships with cisgender people, and that such patterns may be even more pronounced for transgender people of color.[33] In this section, we join such work by examining the issue of significant others in the coming-out stories of our respondents, which came up in more than one-third of their responses. In so doing, we join Pfeffer and others calling for more incorporation of transgender experiences in future studies of sexual-romantic relationships.[34]

Echoing the cisgender women subjects of varied sexualities previous research has focused on in studies of romantic-sexual relationships involving transgender people, our respondents noted many ways that—as illustrated by a thirty-three-year-old middle-class, white, heterosexual, genderqueer person who came out at twenty-five—coming out as transgender complicated things with partners:

> My partner is okay with it, but has complained I talk too much about it. She's worried I'll eventually identify as a transwoman and she's not sure what she'd do since she's not attracted to women. This took many conversations over 1.5 years (after we were married). She felt like she didn't know about this before marriage, but we had talked about it some. Now it's sometimes a joke (sometimes a bit uncomfortable, like joking about a recent negative event, but sometimes it's just

fun) like "why can't you be more genderqueer about not farting in bed" or "go genderqueer on that shit" (in reference to a task like cooking for a party).

Respondents also noted situations where partners sought to maintain cisgender and monosexual realities predicated upon static, binary notions of sex, gender, and sexualities. For example, a twenty-nine-year-old middle-class, white, asexual, nonbinary person who came out at twenty-five wrote: "My significant other of the time told me that it was a deal breaker if I wanted to transition in any way." Similarly, a thirty-three-year-old middle-class, black, queer, nonbinary person who came out at twenty-eight noted: "It was awful. My partner at the time went on and on about how I was beautiful and 'all woman.'" A nineteen-year-old lower-class, white, pansexual, gender-neutral person who came out at eighteen summed up many such examples by adding: "My boyfriend at the time was the first person I came out to. He said he respected my feelings, but that he could only ever think of me as a girl because he's straight. He also flat out refused to respect my pronouns." In most cases, significant others responded to transgender partners with negotiation, rejection, or the suggestion of support that did not find follow-through in their actions.[35]

Not Out

Our analyses also included transgender people who were not out. In some cases, for example, our respondents did not wish to be out. A thirty-two-year-old lower-class, black, fluid transman put it succinctly: "It is no one's business." A thirty-eight-year-old middle-class, heterosexual transsexual who did not disclose a racial identity added: "Because I'm transitioning to finally be part of the group I was supposed to be part of. Why go to another group that only represents my medical condition, not my true identity?" A thirty-one-year-old middle-class, white, asexual, nonbinary person added: "I am usually comfortable presenting as I present, and so I will be referred to as 'female' most of the time. Unless I'm exhausted or under a lot of stress, it doesn't bother me because it's an adequate summary of my public existence, which is the only contact with me most people have." A forty-three-year-old middle-class, white, bisexual transwoman added: "I am transitioning, but I don't consider myself transgender. I am female, and I am my own person. I want people to know me, not a label."

Like these respondents, all the people who expressed similar sentiments in our sample were at least thirty years old, which may be tied to generational differences within transgender populations. In an examination of conflicts between older and younger transgender people, for example, medical sociologist stef shuster demonstrates differential norms and expectations for what it means to be transgender, how one should experience gender identity, and conflicts between nonbinary and binary understandings of sex and gender between transwomen and transmen and nonbinary people as well as between older and younger transgender people.[36] While shuster examined older transmen and transwomen and younger nonbinary transgender people, here we see generational differences within each of these groups concerning whether or not one should come out. Although there is no way to tease out possible age-related nuances in the present study, our observations here lend weight to shuster's call for intergenerational transgender studies.

Potentially drawing on understandings of the societal invisibility of nonbinary experience within cisgender realities, some nonbinary respondents who were not out cited concerns that cisgender others would not understand or recognize them if they did come out. As a twenty-two-year-old middle-class, Hispanic, lesbian, gender-fluid person put it: "I can't tell my parents about it because they have a hard enough time understanding my sexuality." A thirty-nine-year-old lower-class, white, gender-neutral person who did not disclose a sexual identity added: "It's hard to explain to others that I'm a person, not a woman or a man. There's no 'none' box to check off on forms, and worse, I have female genitalia and see a doctor every so often to get those parts checked out. And my partner is a cisgender male, so no one would ever believe me if I said I had no gender." A twenty-three-year-old lower-class, white, pansexual cross-dresser agreed: "My want to be none or both genders would just not be accepted." Further, a nineteen-year-old middle-class, multiracial, asexual romantic, nonbinary person noted: "People I know wouldn't understand it and would tell me I'm faking it or they don't think it's a real thing." In such cases, nonbinary respondents who were not out said they did not disclose information about their trans identities because they feared the reactions that nonbinary respondents who did come out received from others.[37]

In fact, fear was a common thread throughout the responses of transgender people who were not out in this study. A twenty-four-year-old middle-class, white, heterosexual transman wrote: "I am afraid to disappoint and destabilize people close to me." A twenty-year-old middle-class, black, queer, genderqueer person added: "I'm afraid of what others will think of me, and of losing financial support from my parents." A nineteen-year-old upper-class, white, asexual romantic transman summed up other examples of the effect of fear on decisions about coming out: "I am extremely afraid. My family are very conservative and last night, my mother called me a freak. I was considering coming out to her in later years, but I have decided not to due to the terrible way she made me feel. I assume I must hide my identity until, perhaps, college." Echoing decades of scholarship on the coming out experiences of sexual minorities, respondents (especially younger ones) who were not out generally cited fear as the main reason.

As suggested by the respondent just quoted, however, it is important to remember that this fear is not only understandable but likely an educated guess regarding how others will respond to such disclosure. Considering the severity and large number of issues transgender people face when they become known to cisgender others and in the context of structural settings outlined in the USTS and other research, it would be more surprising if respondents were *not* afraid to speak openly about being transgender. As a sixty-year-old middle-class, heterosexual transman who did not disclose a racial identity put it: "It's dangerous; I have a family to protect and I live in a smaller city." Stated another way, respondents noted that coming out could "get them," for example, "killed," "attacked," "fired," "disowned," and/or put them in situations where they could "lose" their "families," "home," and/or "marriage."[38]

Such fear is not simply an abstract understanding of what many transgender people face in US society. Rather, respondents often noted experiences where they had already experienced empirical demonstrations of cisgender violence, such as in the example from this twenty-two-year-old middle-class, white, pansexual transman: "I'm afraid of being hurt. My brother pointed a gun in my face because I said something he disagreed with, and he *hates* anyone who is not a cis white man, so he would kill me if he found out." Further, respondents were well aware of cisgender people's "inability to accept things that are different from what they already know or believe."[39] As a twenty-seven-year-old middle-class, multiracial, queer transwoman wrote in summation of recent research on US attitudes toward sexual and gender minority groups: "It's easier, for example, for a person to be openly gay than to be openly transgender. I would only come out to be able to transition, and since I am not free to transition, I won't be coming out." Put simply, many respondents who were not out cited fear concerning the potential—and even likely, in many cases—negative consequences of being known as transgender within the cisgender social order of contemporary US society.

LOOKING BACK AND MOVING FORWARD

As we illustrated in this chapter, our goal in this book is to shed light upon the space betwixt and between, on the one hand, large-scale statistical portraits of transgender populations, and on the other hand, localized in-depth case studies of specific sociodemographic groups within distinct sociocultural settings and contexts. We do this by bringing forth the stories of transgender people across the nation (both occupying similar social locations to us and otherwise) to reveal common issues and experiences that may be analyzed within and across specific settings and groups. In short, we outline the ways transgender people experience the events captured in statistical patterns from broader surveys in their own words. To this end, we utilized a common element of both large-scale and localized studies—outness—to add texture to the stories behind the numbers and demonstrate how patterns outlined in local settings show up more broadly across the nation and beyond any one demographic group.

Building on this example, the following chapters expand beyond the contours of existing large-scale surveys and specific case studies to outline common ways transgender people negotiate encounters with LGBTQIA communities, cisgender people in general, religion, and medical science. As we did here, throughout the chapters that follow we explore the ways transgender people navigate US cisgender realities predicated upon our marginalization, invisibility, and pain. We also shed light on the ways turning our analytic focus toward the oppressive actions of cisgender people, which maintain the social structures of a cisgender reality, may create opportunities for the betterment of transgender people's standing in society and open doors for expanding scientific studies beyond existing limitations and blind spots.

NOTES

1. See again Mathers, "Navigating Genderqueer Existence."

2. Throughout the text, "she/her" and "they" pronouns are used interchangeably when referring to J.

3. See again Sumerau, "Embodying Nonexistence"; see also Sumerau, *Cigarettes & Wine* and *Homecoming Queens*. For potential harassment and marginalization in social science even cisgender people may face when they show concern for or study transgender people, see also Schilt, "The 'Not Sociology' Problem"; for difficulties being known as transgender in social scientific fields, see also Hughes, "Not Out in the Field"; and Lombardi, "Trans Issues in Sociology."

4. In fact, especially if they have internalized cisnormativity to the point where they have sought to assign J's sex/gender identities without asking J about it, for example, this long-term history in J's life may be surprising to many of our colleagues. Specifically, when asked in professional settings, J has almost always responded that she is trans, without further elaborating, until very recently. At the same time, however, we have both noticed (as have others who remarked on it) the distinct differences in how even other academics respond to J when she is more obviously presenting as feminine in clothing and demeanor rather than as a butch woman who others may read as either a nonbinary person or a man, based on their own internalized notions of how one is supposed to do or perform gender.

5. See Dozier, "Beards, Breasts, and Bodies"; Gupta, "'And Now I'm Just Different'"; Mathers, "Sibling Relationships"; McLean, "Hiding in the Closet?"; Schilt, *Just One of the Guys?*; Schrock, "Transsexuals' Narrative Construction."

6. See Hoffman-Fox, *You and Your Gender Identity*. See also Boylan, *She's Not There*; Grace and Ozzi, *Tranny*; McBee, *Amateur*; McBride and Biden, *Tomorrow Will Be Different*; Mock, *Redefining Realness*; and Nutt, *Becoming Nicole*.

7. See Davis, Dewey, and Murphy, "Giving Sex"; Doan, "Coming Out"; Schilt, *Just One of the Guys?*; Stryker, *Transgender History*; Vidal-Ortiz, "The Figure of the Transwoman of Color."

8. As she has written about elsewhere, J is also sometimes read as or assumed to be Hispanic in social interactions due to facial and skin features that are more or less visible at different times and in different climates. Although there is Native American/Hispanic ancestry in J's biological case, J was adopted and raised by white people who both thought J's birth mother was Hispanic and raised J as white, which is also what J is legally assigned (since birth) in the United States. At the same time, however, J is mostly read as white by others and as a result of legal assignment, likely benefits from not only interpersonal but structural forms of white privilege alongside occasional very different experiences when read as nonwhite by (almost entirely) Hispanic and white others. For examples of how these dynamics sometimes play out in daily life, see Sumerau, "Embodying Nonexistence."

9. Interactionists have long pointed to the ways that social context is central to the ways people present themselves to others in the social world, as well as the ways the biographies individuals bring into their research and knowledge production efforts shape the construction and dissemination of knowledge. Feminist, queer, and scholars of color have extended these ideas to discuss the ways that one's standpoint is rooted in relations of power, and thus these relations impact the types of knowledge that are considered "correct" in a given society. For notes on the interactionist history of standpoint theories, see, for example, Goffman, *The Presentation of Self*, and Mead, *Mind, Self, and Society*. For expansion on this dynamic by queer, feminist, and/or scholars of color, see, Collins, *Black Sexual Politics*; Harding, *Feminist Standpoint Theory*; and Rich, "Compulsory Heterosexuality."

10. See Grant et al., *Injustice at Every Turn*; James et al., *Report of the 2015 U.S. Transgender Survey*.

11. J, for example, remembers when it felt like finding out anything about transgender people was equivalent to searching for the Holy Grail despite their knowledge of other people like them in the world.

12. In the USTS, the second most often chosen identity was trans, which is often used as shorthand for transgender, as we interpret it here, but we recognize that the term could be emerging as a separate or distinct identity as well, though we are unable to ascertain such potential at present.

13. See, James, Brown, and Wilson, *2015 U.S. Transgender Survey: Experiences of Black Respondents*; James et al., *Report of the 2015 U.S. Transgender Survey*; James, Jackson, and Jim, *2015 U.S. Transgender Survey: American Indian Alaska Native Respondents*; James and Magpantay, *2015 U.S. Transgender Survey: Asian, Native Hawaiian, Pacific Islander Respondents*; James and Salcedo, *2015 U.S. Transgender Survey: Latino/a Respondents*; Movement Advancement Project, "A Closer Look"; and Vidal-Ortiz, "The Figure of the Transwoman of Color." Furthermore, intersectional scholars have pointed to the ways that individuals experience life in vastly different, and sometimes similar, ways based on the multiple positions they occupy in relation to various structures of inequality (see Collins, *Black Sexual Politics*, for an overview). Researchers also find variations in experience of LGBTQIA people in relation to different racial identities, backgrounds, and contexts that shape the experience of both self and society throughout the life course (see Vidal-Ortiz, Robinson, and Khan, *Race and Sexuality*). For the purposes of this book, we focus on the broad ways that the transgender people in our sample experience the dynamics of cisgender realities. We do, however, speak to the

intersections of their existence in terms of race, class, sexuality, education, religion, and other axes of inequality throughout the book when patterns emerge, while also working to present an overall portrait of shared transgender experience reported across these social locations in the contemporary US context.

14. See Robinson, "Conditional Families," for discussion of this topic specifically focused on LGBTQIA populations.

15. See Bourdieu, *Cultural Reproduction*; Feliciano and Rumbaut, "Gendered Paths"; Keller and Tillman, "Post-Secondary Educational Attainment"; Kirkpatrick and Reynolds, "Educational Expectation Trajectories"; Reynolds and Baird, "Is There a Downside"; Reynolds, Stewart, MacDonald, and Sischo, "Have Adolescents Become"; and Reynolds and Burge, "Educational Expectations."

16. In our sample, 140 people (or 29.9 percent) identify as lower class, 252 (or 53.7 percent) identify as middle class, 9 (or 1.9 percent) identify as upper class, and 68 (or 14.5 percent) chose no response to our question about class identity.

17. See, for example, Mathers, "Expanding on the Experiences"; Sumerau, Cragun, and Mathers, "Cisgendering Reality"; Wilcox, *Queer Women*; and Wolkomir, *Be Not Deceived*.

18. One hundred fifteen respondents live in the western United States, 98 respondents live in the Midwest, 68 respondents live in the Southeast, and 64 live in the Northeast, while 50 chose not to disclose the state in which they reside. As noted earlier, our survey also acquired 74 international respondents whose responses are used in statistics from the survey, but who are not included in the qualitative analyses throughout the book, even though their experiences were very similar to those of US transgender respondents. We do not, however, note such geographic locations when introducing respondents due to concerns about confidentiality in cases where transgender populations in certain states may be more or less safe, more or less easy to identify, and/or more or less easily recognizable in relation to other demographic aspects. For more on the importance of studying LGBT populations across all US contexts, see Stone, "The Geography."

19. While we generally take a broader view of the shared experiences of the respondents in our sample, as we note in n. 10 in this chapter, we aim to tease apart the ways these experiences may differ based on respondents' other social locations whenever we are able and it is relevant to do so.

20. While existing surveys are useful for demonstrating demographic patterns among transgender populations, and case studies are useful for parsing local

dynamics among transgender communities, our data fall in between these two approaches by providing qualitative responses to open-ended questions from transgender people across the country. While there are significant strengths to this approach, there are also weaknesses. For example, we were not able to probe or ask follow-up questions to the individuals who completed our survey, which means our data are limited to what people typed in response to the open-ended questions on the survey. Additionally, respondents were able to share the survey among their networks, which may have impacted the race, class, and religious makeup of our sample (despite our efforts to share the survey among multiple diverse social networks and groups). Despite these limitations, a strength of this work involves a broad qualitative portrait of transgender experience, and opportunities for transgender people to speak/write freely without interaction with a specific researcher who may or may not influence what we are or are not willing to share. As such, our data are unique in the sense that they lend themselves to a meso-level analysis of transgender experience in the United States at present, which may guide continuing macro and micro studies in the field.

21. See Jauk, "Gender Violence Revisited"; and Schilt, "Just One of the Guys?"

22. See Schilt, *Just One of the Guys?*; Yavorsky, "Cisgendered Organizations."

23. See Spade, *Normal Life*; Stryker and Aizura, *Transgender Studies Reader*, vol. 2; Stryker and Whittle, *Transgender Studies Reader*, vol. 1.

24. See Schilt and Westbrook, "Doing Gender, Doing Heteronormativity."

25. See the citations in n. 10 of this chapter.

26. None of the questions on our survey required or forced completion, as is common on other surveys. The USTS survey question on outness (see question 4.5 in appendix B of the USTS), for example, has no option for "no response," so similar respondents in the USTS may have been dropped (though this question is not listed in the questions necessary for staying in the survey pool in appendix C) or may have been coded as missing.

27. See, for example, Schrock, "Transsexuals' Narrative Construction"; Schrock and Reid, "Transsexuals' Sexual Stories"; and Schrock, Reid, and Boyd, "Transsexuals' Embodiment," for discussions of visibility and transgender experience in the 1990s. See also Stein, *Unbound*, where she discusses experiencing current transmen as a new phenomenon prior to her study of transition among four transmasculine people. See also Bornstein, *Gender Outlaw*; Halberstam, *Female Masculinity*; and Stryker, *Transgender History*, for more examples of these dynamics.

28. See, for example, Cromwell, *Transmen*; Devor, *FTM*; Feinberg, *Stone Butch Blues*; and Feinberg, *Trans Liberation*.

29. This date may surprise some cisgender social scientists, as such fields have only recently begun to publish much research related to nonbinary gender identities. See, for example, Darwin, "Doing Gender beyond the Binary"; and shuster, "Punctuating Accountability," both of which were published in 2017. See also our own work (Sumerau, Cragun, and Mathers, "Cisgendering Reality"; Sumerau, Mathers, and Cragun, "Incorporating Transgender Experience"), which often receives lots of questions from academic reviewers about this "new" population, despite discussion of this population at least as early as 1993 (see Feinberg, *Stone Butch Blues*). In fact, J remembers people in support groups, even in South Carolina, in the 1990s occasionally using this language that seems new to (especially) cisgender scholars. As Collins notes (see *Black Feminist Thought*), however, this is not uncommon, as members of dominant groups often (a) do not learn or know about patterns in marginalized communities and (b) often treat such communities as new when they do begin to pay attention to them.

30. It is important to note that there were nonbinary people of color—as well as nonbinary people from all parts of the United States—in our study, but none of them raised this issue, whether or not they experienced it. Although there is no way to know if this is simply a matter of reporting or a pattern in need of investigating, at present it represents a potential pattern without analysis in current social sciences.

31. Although it was not a central focus in our survey, there have been extensive studies of the abuses and issues transgender people face in the criminal justice system and especially in prisons and jails across the country; see, for example, Jenness and Fenstermaker, "Agnes Goes to Prison"; Stanley, Smith, and McDonald, *Captive Genders*; and films like *Criminal Queers* and *Cruel and Unusual*.

32. But see, for example, Alegría, "Relationship Challenges"; Bischof, Warnaar, Barajas, and Dhaliwal, "Thematic Analysis"; Bishop, "Body Modifications"; Blumer, Ansara, and Watson, "Cisgenderism in Family Therapy"; Boenke, *Trans Forming Families*; Brown "The Sexual Relationships of Sexual-Minority Women"; Brown "Stories from Outside"; and Brown "'I'm in Transition Too.'"

33. See Ames, *Sexual Metamorphosis*; Blank and Kaldera, *Best Transgender Erotica*; Lowell, "Symbiotic Love"; Raun, *Out Online*; and Zamantakis, "'I Try Not to Push It.'"

34. See, for example, Meadow, *Trans Kids*; Pfeffer, "I Don't Like Passing"; Pfeffer, "Making Space"; Pfeffer, "Normative Resistance"; Pfeffer, "'Women's Work'?";

Stein, *Unbound*; and Travers, *The Trans Generation*. For non-US examples, see also Sanger, *Trans People's Partnerships*. It should be noted, however, that we did not ask specifically about romantic-sexual partnerships, and thus there is no way to ascertain respondents' rationale for mentioning or not mentioning such topics when discussing coming out. With this caveat in mind, we offer illustrative examples of what respondents said about coming out and romantic-sexual partnerships. Further, as no studies have done so before, we utilize specifically nonbinary transgender people's examples here, even though there are transmen and women in the sample who offered similar responses.

35. It is important to note that our respondents share similar stories in relation to families and coworkers, but since book-length social scientific works on transgender experience almost entirely focus on families or workplaces to date, here we focus on other aspects of society that receive almost no attention in existing scholarship and direct readers to, for example, Meadow, *Trans Kids*; Pfeffer, *Queering Families*; Stein, *Unbound*; Travers, *The Trans Generation*, for experiences with family; and Schilt, *Just One of the Guys?* for experiences in the workplace.

36. See shuster, "Generational Gaps." See also Stryker, *Transgender History*, for historical variations in transgender communities and meanings, and Valentine, *Imagining Transgender*, for discussion of variations within transgender populations. For further discussion of diversity within transgender populations, see also Shultz, *Trans/Portraits*.

37. In our sample, as well as some other analyses (see Darwin, "Doing Gender beyond the Binary"), such reactions come mainly from cisgender others. However, some of our respondents noted similar reactions from transmen and transwomen. (Some other studies have found this dynamic as well; see shuster, "Generational Gaps.")

38. We quote words here from many statements that offered the same verbiage in noting dangers respondents who were not out feared would befall them if they became known as transgender to cisgender others in their lives.

39. Here, again, we quote words from many statements that offered the same verbiage in relation to cisgender people.

Transgender Experience in LGBTQIA Communities

I (J) stood in a dark club in early 2018 with one of my life partners and a crowd of people who also had tears in their eyes as Andrea Gibson performed their poem about the Pulse massacre, which took place in 2016 less than two miles from where we stood.[1] As Gibson spoke, I thought about the nights I visited Pulse before the massacre, and about the text messages and e-mails the morning after as people sought to see if I was still alive.[2] I thought about the plans Lain and I made for me to take them to Pulse to dance sometime, but how instead I only got to take them to the memorial site where they cried with me over the posters, flowers, cards, letters, and other mementos left to commemorate the mostly Latinx victims of the massacre. I thought about Lain calling me a few nights after the massacre, how ze[3] had plans to see Andrea Gibson in Chicago but was scared to enter the venue. I thought about Lain calling me again after that show, telling me how Gibson spoke openly about pain and the fear of being on stage only a few nights after forty-nine people were murdered, and how ze and the audience all around zir were in tears. I thought about the mixture of sadness and joy I feel when I think about Pulse now, and how that mixture matches my experience over the years feeling either welcomed and embraced or shunned and rejected in queer spaces as a bisexual, polyamorous, nonbinary transwoman who can never be sure if queer spaces are "queer" or "just cisgender lesbian/gay only."

I thought about each of these things as Gibson somehow managed to capture such a terrible moment in such a beautiful, loving, and magical way. I remembered Lain coming out to me—first as bisexual and later as nonbinary—and asking about LGBTQIA spaces. I remember telling zir it was "complicated" and providing zir with examples of such places in northern Florida, and again later when they moved to Chicago.[4] I remembered how, like me and so many others, ze found parts of their selfhood and self-love in such places, felt the embrace and love of others who sought a place to belong without fear, and built relationships—sexual and otherwise—that cultivated zir sexual and gender identities in powerful ways. I also remembered how, like me and so many others, they encountered unexpected biphobia, transphobia, and ableism that shook them even more than usual because it came from what was supposed to be a safe place. I remembered zir talking to their own newly out bi+ trans friend and mentee in 2016 and explaining how LGBTQIA spaces are often very "complicated" for people like us.

The above examples speak to a common issue for transgender people in contemporary US society. Although the T has been regularly included in the community acronym since the 1990s, the practical integration of transgender people into such communities, movements, and spaces remains a contested issue within many LGBTQIA populations across the nation and more broadly.[5] In fact, this is sometimes even more complicated because the B is often only included in the acronym, but on surveys, younger transgender people are more likely to identify as bi+ and especially pansexual, transwomen are more likely to identify as bisexual, and transgender people overall are more likely to identify as sexually fluid in some way (i.e., most often bi, pan, and queer or often in varieties of ace and demi romantic/sexual options).[6] As such, some studies have begun investigating LG attempts to include or resist the inclusion of transgender people in LGBTQIA spaces, while other studies have focused on the ways transgender people experience such spaces.

In this chapter, we speak to these nascent literatures as well as the complexities outlined above by exploring the experiences of our respondents with LGBTQIA others. In so doing, we outline the ways that LGBTQIA spaces and people represent both the *most positive* encounters transgender people can expect in US culture and also spaces where acceptance is generally only partial, conditional, or otherwise limited. We examine these patterns by first noting the ways transgender respondents articulated overall experiences with LGBTQIA others. We then examine the ways commitment to sexual and gender binaries within some LGBTQIA communities facilitates such conflict within and between communities. As suggested in the autoethnographic accounts above, we demonstrate how LGBTQIA spaces represent both safer options for transgender people than other spaces and also replicate broader cisgender (and monosexual) realities predicated upon the absence of sex, gender, and sexual fluidity.

BRINGING T (AND BIA) INTO LGQ STUDIES

Despite the use of LGBT as an acronym since (at least) the 1990s and LGBTQIA more recently, the literature on sexual and gender minority groups mostly focuses on the experiences of lesbian and gay people. Researchers have, for example, studied the ways LG people experience religion, families, romantic-sexual relationships, workplaces, social movement organizations, sexual-based microaggressions, structural and interpersonal patterns of homophobia and heterosexism, racial conflicts within LG spaces and communities, medical science and institutions, therapeutic communities and organizations, the military, parenting, schools, colleges, sex education programs, varied sexual subcultures, and many other social contexts and issues.[7] In fact, such studies have explored these experiences and issues in a wide variety of different contexts, populations, locations, and time periods. Mirroring funding patterns and both media and religious representations in the broader US society, scholarship focused on sexual and gender minorities is overwhelmingly limited to LG populations.[8]

Readers can observe similar examples in mainstream US culture at present. It is not uncommon, for example, for commentators, politicians, social (secular and religious) movement groups, and celebrities to refer only to "gay rights" when discussing the overall community and political campaigns that also impact BTQIA people.[9] It is also not uncommon to see marketing and political campaigns calling "same-sex marriage rights" either "marriage equality" or "gay marriage" despite the interests of many BTQIA people in such marital rights and the lack of equality in marriage for poly people in the United States.[10] We could provide other examples, but ultimately the point remains the same—interest in sexual and gender minorities overwhelmingly focuses on only one (G) or maybe two (LG) parts of the acronym. This is especially striking when studies demonstrate that other parts of the population experience even more negative outcomes and face even more negative attitudes than LG people do at present, when such attitudes and outcomes were more similar in decades past.[11]

Social theorists name such patterns *homonormativity*, or a social movement strategy whereby lesbian and gay people pursue civil rights by adopting and appealing to mainstream social norms.[12] Homonormativity refers to the creation of a gay/lesbian (or even queer) subject that is acceptable to mainstream society because it is (1) white, (2) middle or upper class, (3) domesticated and reproductive (i.e., focused on family, marriage, and children), (4) religious (i.e., Christian in the American context), (5) monogamous, (6) endosex (i.e., assigned and conforming to the assignment as only male or female),[13] (7) monosexual (i.e., only gay/lesbian or straight/heterosexual—with maybe occasional flexibility or phases only—at all times), (8) cisgender, (9) patriotic (i.e., supportive of the military, government, and passive political activity), and (10) normatively bodied (i.e., rather than "differently" or "dis" abled). Put simply, homonormativity is a political strategy whereby some gay/lesbian (and even queer identified) people are accepted into mainstream society (as well as the sciences and religion) by conforming to other contemporary US social norms.

Social researchers in the past decade have extensively documented many ways that homonormativity reproduces existing race, class, sex, gender, sexual, medical, religious, political, bodily, and familial disparities throughout contemporary US society. At the same time, however, there has been less attention to how homonormativity structures both mainstream interpretations of non-LG sexual and gender minorities and interdisciplinary scientific research agendas and programs. Consistent with homonormativity, for example, mainstream interpretations and scientific literatures offer much less representation, consideration, or discussion of non-LG sexual and gender minorities and even LG people who do not neatly conform to homonormative standards.[14] Further, even studies characterized as "queer" often explore sexual and gender variation with little to no mention of, for example, transphobia, biphobia, compulsory sexuality, anti-intersex bias, compulsory monogamy, or other social factors that play powerful roles in non-LG (and some LG) queer outcomes and experiences.[15]

Recognizing such patterns and recalling prior eras when LG studies faced similar barriers and obstacles from heterosexual-focused scientific and media norms, researchers within bi+, trans, ace, intersex, poly, and other sexual and gender minority communities—as well as allies to each of these groups—have begun pushing for the expansion of such studies and representations beyond cisgender, LG-only options.[16] Here we join such endeavors by outlining some ways transgender people—many of whom are also bi+, ace, queer, lesbian, gay, intersex, and/or poly—experience LGBTQIA others in much the same way earlier scholars brought forth the ways LG people experienced cisgender heterosexual others in prior decades. In so doing, we continue the call for media, and especially science focused on sexual and gender diversity, to better incorporate the wide variety of sexual and gender populations in society as well as the conflicts, collaborations, and perspectives of such people as they navigate society.

CONDITIONAL ACCEPTANCE IN LGBTQIA COMMUNITIES

Examining cisgender heterosexual attitudes toward sexual and gender diversity, we outlined how people utilize both scientific and religious beliefs to both change and maintain prior sexual and gender assumptions to make room for LG people following recent civil rights victories.[17] In so doing, we demonstrated how such efforts rely upon both the devaluation of other sexual and gender minorities and the erasure of people's awareness of the marginalization (and even scientific, media, and religious existence) of such groups. Further, we showed how gay/lesbian people may engage in similar efforts in relation to black, bisexual, transgender, and poly populations. Drawing on prior public writing by sociologist Eric Anthony Grollman and colleagues, we named these processes *conditional acceptance*, or the ways people offer limited acceptance to others without necessarily changing overall beliefs and practices that marginalize such others. Stated another way, conditional acceptance occurs when people respond to increased social tolerance or the (somewhat visible) presence of marginalized groups by expressing acceptance of such groups in only limited or partial ways.

Although this is relatively understudied to date in existing studies of LGBTQIA community dynamics, our respondents experienced a version of such conditional acceptance in their interactions with LGBTQIA others. This was especially true for transgender people who were also racial minorities or bisexual/pansexual/queer/ace identified, and in relation to religion.[18] At the same time, however, their experiences of conditional acceptance were not only tied to LG others; they also noted occasional conflicts within and between bi+, poly, kink, queer, and ace/sexual people. Though even rarer than in relation to bi+, poly, kink, queer, and ace/sexual people, respondents even noted conflicts, as mentioned in chapter 2, between different transgender populations. Although scholarship and mainstream society often conceptualize LGBTQIA populations as a somewhat unified whole, such experiences lend weight to emerging calls for greater attention to diversity and conflict within the umbrella.[19]

Importantly, we remind readers that even in the midst of interpersonal and intergroup conflicts within LGBTQIA communities, our respondents overwhelmingly also noted positive experiences in these communities and characterized these settings and groups as generally the most welcoming and accepting they found in contemporary US society. In fact, 22 percent of our respondents noted only or almost entirely positive experiences with LGBTQIA others. However, most respondents, like the fifty-three-year-old lower-class, Native American, asexual transman quoted next, first talked about general examples of positive interactions before adding caveats like: "The only negative experiences were from gay groups of people." A twenty-seven-year-old middle-class, white, bisexual transwoman summed up the pattern: "I've had some great experiences where I was welcome, but also some bad experiences where the group was clearly geared towards the needs of cis gay white men to the exclusion of women, bisexuals, lesbians, and trans folks."

Throughout their responses, most of the transgender people who shared their stories with us noted the combination of negativity and positivity in LGBTQIA spaces while defining these mixed encounters as positive in relation to broader cisgender realities (and especially cisgender heterosexual populations) in the rest of society (a dynamic we explore in the next chapter). As a thirty-two-year-old white, lower-class, lesbian, agender person put it:

> People who are oppressed by straight people may just as easily oppress trans folks, and able-bodied people may be terribly ableist and harmful, just to name a few examples. But I do believe, being that we are lumped together and

considered deviant and unwanted by the cis straight world in power, there are struggles that we can understand in one another.

A twenty-five-year-old lower-class, black, bisexual transwoman added: "Overall I've had a positive experience with the LBGTQIA+ community, with the only exceptions being biphobia and transphobia. There are many who don't believe bisexuality is real or that it's gross. Then, there are ones who think trans people have no place in the community." Respondents regularly noted feeling at least somewhat welcomed in LGBTQIA communities, but also consistently expressed recognition that this welcome was limited at best.

Some respondents, about 15 percent, also pointed to the issue of religion as a dividing line within some LGBTQIA communities and spaces.[20] Although this divide matches patterns in cisgender heterosexual religious-secular inter-actions,[21] research into religious-secular interactions in LGBTQIA communities is almost completely nonexistent at present. As captured in the following quote from a forty-five-year-old lower-class, white, queer, spiritual-but-nonreligious transman, this may be an important issue in need of attention:

> I have not aligned myself in groups much. The closest I have come to being a regular part of an LGBTQ group is the MCC church that I have been going to for the past 11 years. I feel very comfortable in a queer spiritual community because I feel like I can bring my whole self to the worship experience.

A twenty-three-year-old lower-class, white, lesbian transwoman added: "LGBTQ rights organizations have ignored my pleas for socio-political assistance because my issues are grounded directly in religion." A twenty-three-year-old middle-class, white, pansexual transman also noted: "I've had good experiences with most, although I always feel like an outsider as a pansexual religious transgender man." Such issues, as suggested in the small amount of prior research on religious-secular dynamics in LGBTQIA communities, may be tied to historic and ongoing battles between many religious groups and the pursuit of LGBTQIA civil rights.[22] At the same time, especially as many LGBTQIA people are religious or otherwise engaged in religious organizations, while the nonreligious population in the United States continues to increase, such conflict may foreshadow coming clashes between religiosity and secularity more broadly.

There were also respondents in our sample, about 20 percent, who characterized their experiences with LGBTQIA groups as entirely or almost entirely negative. For example, a twenty-four-year-old middle-class, Hispanic, bisexual, agender person said:

> The LGBT pride group at my college has been just a negative experience for me. My community pride group has been negative due to the focus on actors and acting and disinterest in other topics. The poly community has been negative due to the sexualization of femme-presenting people and the lack of trans acceptance.

A twenty-one-year-old lower-class white, bisexual, gender-fluid person added: "A lot of the groups that are for all LGBT+ people are really just transphobic and biphobic." A twenty-seven-year-old middle-class, multiracial, queer transwoman added: "There's just an attitude where if you're not out and proud then what good are you?" In these and other examples, some respondents experienced LGBTQIA communities as only or mostly oppressive places.

It is noteworthy that all the respondents who reported entirely or almost entirely negative experiences in LGBTQIA spaces identified as sexually fluid in some manner while also identifying in varied ways in terms of race, class, gender, and religion. As such, these experiences may be tied to historical and current patterns of bi+ erasure in many LGBTQIA communities and/or the (re)emergence of (often at least implicitly biphobic) notions of hetero/homo-flexibility repeating historical discourses defining bi+/pan/queer/fluid sexualities as "phases" in a new, more marketable package without interrogation of biphobia or monosexism in both LGBTQIA and broader US culture.[23] Regardless of the source, the growing number of people who openly identify as sexually fluid or within the bi+ umbrella, as well as the tendency for transgender people to more often identify in such ways, suggests this is another aspect of LGBTQIA micropolitics that warrants systematic analysis in the coming years.

Regardless of race, class, sexuality, age, or religion, what we find here is that LGBTQIA spaces and communities are complicated for most of our respondents. Although such communities and spaces represent, as many respondents (like us) put it, the safest and most welcoming option for finding support and validation in contemporary US society, this potential safety and acceptance is only conditional for transgender people (even more so for those who identify sexually beyond the LG portions of the acronym). Even as some respondents note that LGBTQIA communities have, in some cases, provided homes and saved lives, others find only the same tension, conflict, and rejection they face in broader US society, while most find a more complicated mixture of reactions. Next, we outline some of the societal patterns that may lie at the root of this complexity in hopes of directing research, activism, and funding toward the potential of more inclusive LGBTQIA spaces.

UNDERSTANDING INTERNAL CONFLICTS WITHIN LGBTQIA COMMUNITIES

Although those within and beyond the academy often conceptualize LGBTQIA populations as outside mainstream (i.e., heterosexual, cisgender, monosexual, and monogamous) US society, this assumption does not always hold true. For instance, studies of minority experience have long noted the ways dominant social norms influence the development, operation, and organization of marginalized individuals and groups. In so doing, such research often reveals how, for example, cisgender women internalize and reproduce societal patterns of sexism, people of color internalize and reproduce patterns of racial disparity, and lower-class people internalize and adopt societal ideals necessary for continued class inequality. In all such cases, people marginalized by a given social system inadvertently reproduce aspects of the system that ultimately maintain the conditions of their disadvantage.[24]

Such patterns are rarely the result of any intentionality on the part of marginalized groups. Rather, studies show that the dominant norms exert enough symbolic influence that people adopt patterns of action, even if those patterns are ultimately disadvantageous for them, without necessarily ever becoming aware of the harmful consequences. When seeking to understand internal conflicts within LGBTQIA communities, it is important to remember that each of the letters in the acronym represents a group of people marginalized by contemporary US sex, sexual, and/or gender norms. Furthermore, each group may learn and internalize norms—regardless of any intentions—that facilitate the ongoing subordination of some or all groups that fall under the LGBTQIA umbrella. In this section, we outline three examples of how some LGBTQIA people adopt dominant US norms that facilitate internal conflicts within LGBTQIA communities but rarely find voice in even queer scholarship to date.

Cisgendering Reality in LGBTQIA Communities

Although our work outlining and extending the concept of cisgendering reality has focused primarily on cisgender and (at least potentially) heterosexual contexts to date,[25] our respondents revealed many instances where processes of cisgendering reality were at work within LGBTQIA communities. Specifically, respondents articulated many ways that commitment to and belief in distinct, binary notions of manhood and womanhood within such communities facilitate negative reactions to their presence as transgender people. As a thirty-year-old lower-class, black, queer, gender-fluid person put it, cisgender notions of manhood and womanhood in LGBTQIA communities often create hostile environments for transgender people, particularly transgender people of color:

> I've noticed that a lot of gay cis white men have really done a few gross things, like appropriating queer black culture, setting the "standard" for being gay, and there is a really gross level of trans-exclusionary radical feminism that is common among cis white lesbians. I mean, there's just an overwhelming amount of trans-misogyny, especially against trans women of color.

In this and other examples, respondents noted many ways that processes of cisgendering reality extended beyond mainstream or straight society and into LGBTQIA spaces.

Many respondents specifically mentioned that notions of toxic masculinity—or manhood predicated upon dominance, power, and control—created issues for them even in queer spaces. For example, a twenty-five-year-old upper-class, white, queer, agender person noted: "I stopped attending pride student union events and volunteering to staff the center at my university because the white cis gay dude constituency refused to stop using language such as *bitch*, *slut*, and *cunt* at a team building event which doubled as a volunteer training." Similarly, a twenty-five-year-old middle-class, white, bisexual transman wrote: "I've had trouble with gay men since I came out. They seem repulsed by the idea of a man without a penis, but they still want me to pleasure them. Even though I could still date women who treat me better, the whole experience with the gay community made me scared to date in general." In such cases, respondents outlined quintessential elements of hegemonic masculinity exhibited by gay men. These experiences confronting oppressive masculinity negatively impacted their opportunities to connect with or feel safe in LGBTQIA communities.

At other times, respondents, like the thirty-five-year-old middle-class, white, bisexual transman quoted next, expressed frustration with cisgender gay men's allegiance to limited notions of who counts as a man or belongs in men's spaces: "I have always felt unjustly excluded from gay spaces, and have had a number of experiences of cisgender gay men expressing that I should not be in those spaces when they find out I'm trans." A nineteen-year-old lower-class, white, queer transman summed up many statements about manhood in such spaces:

> I was part of a local support group, in which there was allowed a bully who was incredibly rude, invasive, purposefully dysphoria-inducing, and borderline transphobic at times, and who peer pressured me on more than one occasion. I'm not sure if he's still allowed in that group or not, but I know he's been temporarily banned more than once. I've basically decided I'm not going back because of him, which is a shame because it's one of the few safe queer spaces around here.

A sixty-year-old middle-class heterosexual transman who didn't disclose a racial identity added: "Gay men, especially, try to use a form of 'caste' system to try to keep transgender people 'in their place.'" As suggested by these quotes, many respondents (most of whom were nonbinary people and transmen) argued that oppressive notions of manhood—and interpersonal patterns among gay men—excluded them from LGBTQIA spaces. As in other cases, such observations may suggest that commitment to cisgender notions of manhood may facilitate the (at best) conditional acceptance of some transgender people in LGBTQIA communities.

At the same time, however, other respondents articulated conflicts that arose when their presence became known to cisgender lesbian/queer women committed to cisgender, essentialized notions of womanhood. For instance, a nineteen-year-old middle-class, white, gay, nonbinary person wrote: "I was gaslighted and put into uncomfortable situations by several lesbians. I feel repeatedly threatened by lesbians, due to my past abuse and also because so many lesbians are violent to trans people, especially trans women." A twenty-nine-year-old lower-class, black, pansexual, nonbinary person added: "Because of being assigned female at birth, radical feminist lesbians ask me often, why would I give up being a woman? I have to explain that I was never one to begin with, just assigned a role at birth, like a play, and that I was done acting." Although it may sound strange that lesbians, after fighting for so long for social recognition and an escape from heterosexual cisgender roles assigned to them by society would seek to force others into a specific societal role, such efforts make sense when lesbian people internalize, believe, and reproduce cisgender, essentialist norms wherein being assigned female at birth automatically equals being a woman.[26]

In fact, we see other similar examples throughout the data set, specifically among many transmen who experienced significant conflicts with lesbian women who sought to box them into the category of woman in much the same way many straight people seek to box LGBQA women into the category of heterosexual. A thirty-two-year-old lower-class, black, fluid transman notes that "[m]any lesbians disrespect trans people and call them out of their name and preferred pronouns." A sixty-year-old middle-class, Hispanic, heterosexual transman added:

> I've experienced a disconnect with a portion of the lesbian community who have real hostility towards FtMs.[27] I went to a symposium where that was the topic and it turned into a yelling match at one point. I found it vulgar that people who are part of a community that's been discriminated and beat down can turn around and do the same thing to another community.

In such examples, lesbian women committed to cisgender definitions of womanhood—like gay men invested in cisgender versions of manhood—render some LGBTQIA communities uninhabitable for transgender people.

As we will explore in more detail in chapter 4, cisgender norms and assumptions shape the entirety of contemporary US interactional and structural patterns. In the examples above, however, we recognize that entering LGBTQIA spaces does not necessarily provide relief from the enforcement of cisgender realities. Rather, gay and lesbian people—as well as others in such communities[28]—may adopt and reproduce these societal norms as easily as any other population, which impacts the ways transgender people experience—or end up avoiding—LGBTQIA spaces and communities. Though other studies suggest such patterns apply to transwomen as well,[29] it is also intriguing that within our sample, confronting exclusionary actions from cisgender lesbian/queer women was almost entirely reported by transmen and nonbinary people who were assigned female at birth. Combined with the examples above, such observations suggest there may be much to learn from examining processes of cisgendering reality in LGBTQIA communities over time.

Monosexualizing Reality in LGBTQIA Communities

As J has written elsewhere, monosexism represents another powerful societal system embedded throughout US interpersonal and structural norms that may be found both within and beyond LGBTQIA communities.[30] Put simply, *monosexism* is an ideology that requires all people to only be attracted to others of one sex or gender, at a time or over the life course, and disadvantages those who experience and/or express attraction to people of multiple sexes and/or genders.[31] Utilizing experiences from her own life and constructions of bisexual people drawn from in-depth interviews in two separate projects, J outlined how monosexism is constructed and reproduced when people engage in activities she named *monosexualizing reality*, or the process whereby people create an imaginary world devoid of sexual fluidity while punishing—or labeling in derogatory ways—any signs of sexual fluidity in others. The examples above as well as the following quotes from respondents illustrate such processes in LGBTQIA communities.[32]

While discussing a multitude of issues they faced in LG-focused groups and organizations, for example, a twenty-two-year-old white, queer, genderqueer person who did not disclose a class identity wrote: "I always felt out of place because it was mainly monogamous, cisgender, gay-or-lesbian-only people. There were very few who identified as bisexual or pansexual; there were very few transgender members; there was never any mention of nonbinary gender." A twenty-three-year-old middle-class, white, bisexual transwoman added:

> I have had many people explain to me that bisexual people cannot like transgender people because bi means two. I have been in arguments with them before, as many people's views depend on the belief that transgender people

are neither male nor female, but some third category that requires a special sexuality to like. When I have said that I am bisexual and that I also like transgender people, because I view them as the sex they identify with, I was told that I am not bisexual, and that I am trying to enforce the gender binary by being a binary trans person.

A twenty-three-year-old lower-class, black, ace-pansexual transman added: "Because I'm pan and asexual, I'm often excluded or forced to 'prove' that I'm queer because of my romantic partners or my gender, and that I have to 'pick one' instead of being pan. I tend to stay away from 'queer' groups." Such cases reveal biphobic and monosexist assumptions and beliefs about sexually fluid transgender people—and likely cisgender ones as well—from LGBTQIA community members who put their faith in monosexual realities.

Especially because transgender people—alongside some estimates concerning younger people in general—are more likely than other groups to openly identify in sexually fluid ways, processes whereby people monosexualize reality in LGBTQIA communities may become an ever more salient topic in the coming years. This is further complicated by transwomen being more likely to identify as bisexual than any other sexual identity in large-scale surveys, and, as suggested in the second of the three quotes above, ongoing conflicts between non-bi+ identified people seeking to define what *bisexual* means (i.e., in relation to a gender binary they likely believe in as part of their own internalization of cisgender realities) against how most bisexual-identified people—transwomen and others—define the term themselves (i.e., [1] bodies like mine and [2] bodies not like mine across multiple genders). These observations again suggest there may be much to learn from more inclusive studies of LGBTQIA communities over time.

Othering the Other: Conflicts within Transgender Communities

As noted in the last chapter, there are also internal conflicts that emerge between different groups of transgender people. As shuster notes, conflicts often emerge between different generations of transgender people as well as between transgender people who transition from one part of the gender spectrum to another (i.e., transwomen and transmen) and nonbinary transgender people.[33] In fact, such conflicts are not surprising considering earlier trans-focused scholarship exploring boundaries some transgender people drew around "what constitutes transness" and "what is really trans" in the 1990s.[34] Much like internal conflicts between lesbian, gay, and bisexual populations at different points in history, such conflicts, as shuster puts it, can be described as "othering the other," or the process whereby members of a given group define other members of their own group as other or less valuable than themselves.[35] Here, we outline examples of such othering processes between transgender people that emerged in the stories our respondents shared about their interactions in LGBTQIA communities.

Although there were relatively fewer examples of this process within our overall data set compared to the ones we mentioned above (about 8 percent of respondents), the examples respondents shared often focused on boundaries concerning who is "really trans" or "trans enough."[36] As a twenty-six-year-old lower-class, white, queer, nonbinary person put it: "Being nonbinary sometimes alienates me from binary trans-focused groups." Stated more explicitly, a twenty-year-old lower-class, white, queer, gender-fluid person added: "I've been told over and over by transgender groups that I do not count because I sometimes, though rarely, align with my assigned gender." A thirty-year-old upper-class, queer, nonbinary person who did not disclose a racial identity summed up the majority of the nonbinary examples: "Some binary transmen are really cis men trapped in the wrong bodies. They see me, a nonbinary person not trapped in the wrong body, as only aspiring to be male; as long as I haven't changed my body it's only an aspiration. Even though my body, no matter how it's configured, is still male to some extent." In such cases, respondents noted tensions around what counted as transgender.

At the same time, a few nonbinary respondents and transwomen, such as the twenty-nine-year-old lower-class, black, pansexual, nonbinary person quoted next, pointed out how expectations from others that did not align with one's own economic resources could also lead to conflict:

> Sometimes, I get from other trans folks that you should put transition first, but when you're poor like I am, and others are, transition has to take a back burner to other life problems, like "where am I gonna live?" Even explaining this to them, I get told that I'm not really trans, and it irritates me, and seems a bit classist to me as well.

In such cases, emerging discourses emphasizing the importance of transition (often tied to medical recognition, as we discuss in chapter 6) create tensions between those who could and those who could not afford such care. Further, examples like this one highlight the importance of resources in defining and determining where one fits within a given transgender community.

Alongside these cases, there were also a few examples where transgender people—almost entirely transmen and transwomen—ran into issues wherein other transgender people—also, again, almost always other transmen and transwomen—expressed hostility toward their gender identities, pronoun preferences, and/or bodily desires. The following quote from a thirty-year-old lower-class, black, ace transman offers a typical case of such a scenario:

> My experiences in the trans community have been mostly positive, though I've had issues in the past with transwomen—mostly older ones—being clueless, or downright disrespectful toward my (mostly) male gender identity when I was first coming out. They'd use as many incorrect pronouns and forms of address as your average cis person, and it was really aggravating. It caused me to avoid mixed-gender trans groups, and to only attend trans male or transmasculine groups because of the behavior of some of the transwomen I encountered. I mean, I don't go into trans spaces to be misgendered, especially by other trans people!

Whether offered by a transman or transwoman, each of these types of cases involved someone on another part of the gender spectrum who was almost always older and defined as "clueless," "disrespectful," or, in other cases, "hostile" toward people transitioning in a different direction along the spectrum. Further, in each case, the respondent noted the tendency to focus more on gender-segregated groups after such experiences, which ultimately reproduced widespread patterns of sex and gender segregation throughout US society.

Although mostly contained within historical accounts and scholarship undertaken in different generational contexts at present, these dynamics suggest boundary-making processes, like shuster's analysis of "othering the other," at work in contemporary transgender communities and LGBTQIA spaces. Especially with the elevation of some forms of transgender experience as ideal in recent years—specifically forms of transgender existence that fit transnormative narratives and the medical science model of transgender identity— this may be an incredibly important aspect of transgender experience in the coming years, just like it was in the 1990s.[37] Like shuster, our examination of "othering the other" processes may provide a baseline for efforts to better document and understand both the diversity of transgender populations and potential internal conflicts within such populations.

OUTSIDERS WITHIN

In this chapter, we have illustrated some ways transgender people experience LGBTQIA communities. On the one hand, LGBTQIA communities generally offer transgender people the safest, most welcoming, and most affirming spaces to exist freely as we are in contemporary US society. On the other hand, our acceptance into these communities is often fraught with tension, conditional or partial at best, and complicated when we also occupy other social locations marginalized within LGBTQIA communities (such as non–middle/upper class, nonwhite, nonmonosexual, nonmonogamous, and nonsecular). Put simply, transgender people are simultaneously members of LGBTQIA communities and also not necessarily part of these communities in practice due to the issues our genders and/or other social identities create for the cisgender and monosexual norms often prioritized by other members.

This type of situation, where one is both a member of a group and also not a full member of the group in practice, is almost a textbook definition of what Collins calls an *outsider within*.[38] Examining the ways that black women (cis, trans, or otherwise) were both part of the broader category woman but also often separate from the political efforts, daily concerns, and even lives of white women, Collins demonstrates how people occupying outsider-within social locations in relation to a given group could often illustrate aspects of that group not as easily recognized by others. We see this same type of process play out throughout this chapter when transgender perspectives illuminate often unmentioned, sometimes harmful, aspects of LGBTQIA communities. In the next chapter, we extend this line of analysis even further as we examine the ways transgender people experience and shed light upon the norms of cisgender realities beyond LGBTQIA contexts, communities, and populations.

NOTES

1. This poem is on Andrea Gibson's album *Hey Galaxy*.

2. For J's writing on Pulse, see Sumerau, "Embodying Nonexistence," and Sumerau, *That Year*. See also Lampe, Huff-Corzine, and Corzine, "The Pulse Scrolls"; www

.pulsescrolls.org and www.onepulsefoundation.org; and Gutiérrez et al., "Systemic Violence" for more reflections on the Pulse massacre.

3. Throughout the text, "ze/zir" and "they" pronouns are used interchangeably when referring to Lain.

4. See Mathers, "What Team?"

5. See Stryker, *Transgender History*; Stone, "More than Adding a T"; Stone, "Flexible Queers"; Hagen, Hoover, and Morrow, "A Grounded Theory"; and Marine and Nicolazzo, "Names That Matter."

6. See Movement Advancement Project, "A Closer Look."

7. See, for example, Ahlm, "Respectable Promiscuity"; Coley, *Gay on God's Campus*; Hartless, "Questionably Queer"; Jones, *Queer Utopias*; Schrock, Sumerau, and Ueno, "Sexualities"; Steele, Collier, and Sumerau, "Lesbian, Gay, and Bisexual Contact"; and Vidal-Ortiz, Robinson, and Khan, *Race and Sexuality*.

8. See Monro, Hines, and Osborne, "Is Bisexuality Invisible?"; San Francisco Human Rights Commission, "Bisexual Invisibility"; and Schilt and Lagos, "The Development."

9. More recently, many refer to gay and transgender rights, but even this leaves out bisexualities and asexualities, which becomes even more apparent if one asks someone on the street—as we and others now often do—who uses such language, for example, "What about bi or ace?" as the reaction is usually very negative.

10. See Eisner, *Notes for a Bisexual Revolution*; Schippers, *Beyond Monogamy*; and Wolkomir, "Making Heteronormative Reconciliations."

11. See Badgett, Durso, and Schneebaum, *New Patterns of Poverty*; Barringer, Sumerau, and Gay, "Examining Differences"; Cragun and Sumerau, "The Last Bastion"; Cragun and Sumerau, "No One Expects a Transgender Jew"; Davis, *Contesting Intersex*; Gorman, Denney, Dowdy, and Medeiros, "A New Piece of the Puzzle"; Movement Advancement Project, "A Closer Look"; and Mize, "Sexual Orientation."

12. See Bryant, "In Defense"; Duggan, *The Twilight*; Ferguson, "Race-ing Homonormativity"; Mathers, Sumerau, and Cragun, "The Limits of Homonormativity"; Rosenfeld, "Heteronormativity and Homonormativity"; Seidman, "From Identity"; Stryker, "Transgender History"; and Ward, *Respectably Queer*.

13. For discussion of endosex, see Costello, "Nonconsensual Intersex Surgery"; Costello, "Understanding Intersex Relationship Issues"; and Davis, *Contesting Intersex*.

14. See Monro, Hines, and Osborne, "Is Bisexuality Invisible?"; and Schilt and Lagos, "The Development," for reviews.

15. It is important to note that we are in no way saying that the relative absence of bi+, ace, and other sexual and gender populations is intentional on the part of researchers or movement organizers. Rather, we would argue that this is likely the same kind of oversight seen historically when populations less well known in existing academic circles are then left out when new study areas emerge. For example, a recent example of this type of omission can be seen in an incredibly well-crafted methodological text focused on queer studies of sexualities and gender in sociology (where we happen to know there are bi+ and ace allies among the authors in the volume) that goes beyond prior volumes by including chapters on transgender people and issues but also leaves out issues of bi+ and ace communities in the process (Compton, Meadow, and Schilt, *Other, Please Specify*). An important and well-crafted book like this, for example, breaks new ground by focusing on the difficulties of research for LGT queer people and with such populations, but at the same time it mirrors broader patterns in society and the sciences by focusing on only these members of queer populace and subject matter (though nonmonogamy, ace populations, and bisexualities are mentioned in the introduction). As scholars impressed by this work in many ways, we recommend it widely to others and applaud the incorporation of at least three identifiable transgender voices (i.e., three authors explicitly identify themselves within the transgender umbrella) in the volume, but also must warn bi+, ace, and other queer colleagues and friends that unfortunately their experiences are still erased or missing even in this type of groundbreaking queer research text.

16. See, for example, Davis, *Contesting Intersex*; Monro, Hines, and Osborne, "Is Bisexuality Invisible?"; Moon and Tobin, "Sunsets and Solidarity"; Pfeffer, "'I Don't Like Passing'"; Schilt and Lagos, "The Development"; Schippers, *Beyond Monogamy*; Sumerau and Cragun, *God Loves (Almost) Everyone*; and Vares, "My [Asexuality] Is Playing Hell."

17. See Cragun and Sumerau, "The Last Bastion"; Cragun and Sumerau, "No One Expects a Transgender Jew"; Mathers, Sumerau, and Ueno, "This Isn't Just Another"; Mathers, Sumerau, and Cragun, "The Limits of Homonormativity"; Steele, Collier, and Sumerau, "Lesbian, Gay, and Bisexual Contact"; Sumerau

and Cragun, *God Loves (Almost) Everyone*; Sumerau and Grollman, "Obscuring Oppression," 322–37; and Sumerau, Grollman, and Cragun, "'Oh My God.'"

18. Discussions of encounters—positive or negative—with intersex people never emerged in our data. Although there is no way to explain why intersex people were never mentioned in respondents' discussions of LGBTQIA spaces and communities, this observation may provide an opportunity for future research concerning relationships between transgender and intersex communities as well as relationships between these communities and broader LGBTQIA populations.

19. See Cragun and Sumerau, "The Last Bastion"; Eisner, *Notes for a Bisexual Revolution*; Jones, *Queer Utopias*; Moss, "Alternative Families, Alternative Lives"; Schippers, *Beyond Monogamy*; Stryker and Aizura, *Transgender Studies Reader*, vol. 2; Stryker and Whittle, *Transgender Studies Reader*, vol. 1; and Worthen, "An Argument."

20. This observation mirrors early work on religious-secular interactions (see O'Brien, "Wrestling the Angel") wherein many nonreligious LGBT respondents had difficulty understanding any interest in religiosity, and religious LGBT people had concerns about the morality of other LGBT people. See also, Sumerau, "'They Just Don't Stand.'"

21. See, for example, Cimino and Smith, *Atheist Awakening*.

22. See Moon and Tobin, "Sunsets and Solidarity"; and Sumerau, "'Somewhere between Evangelical and Queer.'"

23. At present, most work on fluidity or nonmonosexuality involves scholars within the social sciences, intentionally or otherwise, reproducing patterns of bi+ erasure in their examinations. For example, in some of the recent work on the topic (work that has garnered significant attention, won awards, or been otherwise lauded in the social sciences), there has been little to no mention of bisexual stigma or monosexism, and how these systems of inequality may influence one's experiences with sexual fluidity or even produce the patterns in the data captured within such work. In this way, the social sciences, regardless of intention, reproduce these patterns of monosexism and biphobia when talking about nonmonosexualities (see, Diamond, *Sexual Fluidity*; Silva, "'Helpin' a Buddy'"; and Ward, *Not Gay*, for examples of this type of scholarly erasure). It is also important to note, however, that there is nothing intrinsically wrong with studying homo/hetero flexibility or phases (as there are people who identify in such ways), but studying these dynamics without attention to biphobia and

monosexism is equivalent to prior decades where closeted gay/lesbian people were studied without attention to homophobia or heterosexism.

24. See, for example, Bonilla-Silva, *Racism without Racists*; Collins, *Black Sexual Politics*; Connell, *Gender and Power*; Garcia, *Respect Yourself, Protect Yourself*; Mathers, Sumerau, and Ueno, "'This Isn't Just Another'"; Schrock, Sumerau, and Ueno, "Sexualities"; and Schwalbe et al., "Generic Processes."

25. See Mathers, "Bathrooms, Boundaries, and Emotional Burdens"; and Sumerau, Cragun, and Mathers, "Cisgendering Reality."

26. See Pfeffer, *Queering Families*, for a similar observation.

27. FtM is an abbreviation for "female-to-male," sometimes used to refer to transmen. While some transgender people still use FtM on a regular basis, this abbreviation, as well as the counterpart MtF to refer to transwomen, has fallen out of favor among others.

28. We point this out because, while seemingly rarer at present even though research focusing on such communities could impact this impression, our experiences and those of other transgender people we interact with—within and beyond the academy—reveal that there are bi+ (bi, pan, ambi, queer, etc.), ace (across the spectrum), intersex, and poly people who also internalize and enforce cisgender realities at the expense of transgender people. This was only mentioned by ten of our respondents, but even these few examples beyond our own experiences point out that such issues occur and also require critical discussion and examination within and beyond LGBTQIA populations and settings.

29. See, for example, Schrock and Reid, "Transsexuals' Sexual Stories," 75–86; Schrock, Reid, and Boyd, "Transsexuals' Embodiment," 317–35; and Stryker, *Transgender History*.

30. Lain is also currently finishing zir dissertation, which focuses on how bi+ people navigate monosexism in their daily lives. See Mathers, "Sibling Relationships," for an analysis from these data.

31. See Eisner, *Notes for a Bisexual Revolution*.

32. Sumerau, "Embodying Nonexistence"; Sumerau and Cragun, *God Loves (Almost) Everyone*.

33. shuster, "Generational Gaps."

34. Hines, *TransForming Gender*; Schrock, "Transsexuals' Narrative Construction," 176–92; Schrock and Reid, "Transsexuals' Sexual Stories," 75–86; Schrock, Reid, and Boyd, "Transsexuals' Embodiment," 317–35; Stryker, *Transgender History*; and Valentine, *Imagining Transgender*.

35. This process is also an example of what some scholars have referred to as *defensive othering*. See Ezzell, "'Barbie Dolls,'" 111–31; Finley, "Skating Femininity," 359–87; Schwalbe et al., "Generic Processes," 419–52; and Suen, "Older Single Gay Men's Body Talk," 397–414, for more on defensive othering.

36. See also Garrison, "On the Limits of 'Trans Enough,'" 613–37, for more on this topic, as well as our discussion of how one becomes medically (and legally) recognized as transgender in the United States in chapter 6.

37. *Transnormativity* refers to an ideology wherein people adopt ideal expectations of what "good" or "real" transgender people look and act like in search of necessary medical care, medical and legal recognition, and other resources. For more on transnormativity, see Johnson, "Transnormativity," 465–91; LeBlanc, "Unqueering Transgender?"; McIntyre, "'They're So Normal,'" 9–24; Ruin, "Discussing Transnormativities," 202–11; and Stone, "The Empire Strikes Back," 337–59.

38. See chapter 1 for more discussion on this topic.

4

Transgender Experience in Cisgender Realities

When I (Lain) was an undergraduate student, I became fascinated by the ways my own gender socialization influenced how I acted, thought about, and experienced the world.[1] Like most people, this was not something I had consciously considered before, but rather, I was trained in the cisgender norms of my society as a child and often unintentionally reproduced lessons from such cultural teachings in daily life. As I became more aware of such processes in my journals, classes, and interactions with other people from different backgrounds, I sought to ascertain distinctions between (1) what I did because I was taught it was what I was supposed to do and (2) what I actually believed in, wanted to do, and felt as a person. To this end, I remember going to see J during their office hours and asking them to help me notice whenever I did things that could be examples of simply repeating the gendered lessons I received in my life so that I could think about these unconscious, taken-for-granted aspects of my existence.

J agreed to help with my project, and over the next year she pointed out every time I did something around her that could be considered "doing gender," or acting, thinking, and/or presenting myself in line with existing masculine or feminine behavior expectations. As this process continued, I developed the ability to critically consider what aspects of my behavior were of my own choosing and what aspects I was performing because I had been taught that people like me (i.e., people assigned female at birth and then expected to become girls and then women over time by learning and practicing societal notions of femininity) were supposed to do. After getting fairly good at asking such questions about my own and others' gendered behaviors over time, I remember asking J, "How did you learn to notice these things?" Chuckling, J said, "I didn't really have a choice, when you live in this world surrounded by cisgender folk and all their beliefs, you just kind of learn quick what the rules are and how to survive any time you demonstrate an exception to those rules."

The above example speaks to the common thread running throughout this book: the ways transgender people experience cisgender realities.[2] Although the bulk of this book involves transgender people's experiences interacting with cisgender people, organizations, and belief systems in specific contexts, here we focus attention on overall patterns that emerge when transgender people encounter cisgender others. This is especially important because cisgender people make up the bulk of the American population, and as a result, they are the main demographic group transgender people of any social location frequently encounter.

In this chapter, we thus provide a broader portrait of transgender experiences dealing with cisgender people in contemporary US society to complement discussions of coming out and experience in LGBTQIA communities and to set up the specific analyses focused on experiences with religious people and medical providers in the next two chapters. As such, we seek here to provide examples occurring throughout society that may facilitate further in-depth study of the construction, maintenance, and operation of cisgender realities throughout the interpersonal, organizational, and institutional structures of the nation.

OUTSIDERS WITHIN CISGENDER REALITIES

As we discussed at the end of chapter 3, transgender people currently occupy a curious social location in US society. On the one hand, we exist within families, schools, religious traditions, cities and towns, and other social groups throughout the nation and in every religious, racial, class, and sexuality population. On the other hand, we exist outside the knowledge, understanding, and often conceptualizations of "what reality looks like" for the vast majority of our fellow citizens, who, whether consciously or not, occupy cisgender or otherwise nontransgender social locations. As a result of greater visibility to the broader cisgender public in recent years, however, we also currently watch as (mostly cisgender) people debate our place in society, how to make sense of us, and what we mean for their existing race, class, gender, sexual, and other belief and/or scientific systems. We also watch as they seek to maintain prevailing systems by pretending that we are something new rather than a population active within this nation—and others—throughout recorded history.

As we will return to in the conclusion, we are not the new part of this equation.[3] Whether we look all the way back to sex/gender variation observed in the Stone Age or simply to discussions of sex/gender variations at the emergence of Western science, what we now refer to as intersex and transgender people have been part of the overall story of human development.[4] What is new, however, is the way cisgender realities and authorities within cisgender-dominated societies are responding to us at present. Put simply, our existence is not the new revolution some scholars claim is taking place in society;[5] the new revolution is cisgender people—due to our social movement activities and other factors—having to pay attention to our existence (and to sex/gender variation itself) in more open, and in some cases more welcoming, ways. Just as the Americas were not newly discovered when European colonizers conquered them, we are not a new population simply because cisgender people have started to pay attention to us.[6]

Since we are not new and, even in US society, have a long and complex history as a population named in many ways at different times,[7] it is important to understand how we became so unknown—or able to be seen as new—to our fellow citizens. As Collins notes[8] in the case of people of color, such a scenario generally arises from societal discourses that erase aspects of a given social reality over time to create a specific narrative about how the world works and what reality looks like. In such cases, people who occupy spaces both outside the dominant narrative and within empirical social reality may direct attention to the operation of such social forces. In this section, we outline this type of mechanism in the case of transgender people.

Cisnormativity as an Organizing Force in Society

Seeking to understand the creation and maintenance of cisgender reality throughout present-day interpersonal and structural patterns in societies, researchers have demonstrated the construction and operation of a master narrative most people are taught about the nature and function of sex/gender/sexualities in the world.[9] Whether looking at scientific, political, religious, or media authorities over the last century or more, such endeavors reveal an ideology named *cisnormativity*, which, as discussed in chapter 1, posits an imagined social world wherein all people are cisgender, should conform to cisgender assumptions and norms, and should maintain cisgender assumptions and norms throughout the life course. At the same time, cisnormativity defines non-cisgender people (whether transgender identified or otherwise) as unnatural, and—in different terms depending on the social authority in a given case or context—problematic/deviant/diseased/sinful due to sex/gender nonconformity.[10] In so doing, people promoting and/or believing in cisnormative stories about the nature of the world create and maintain the symbolic resources necessary for the ongoing marginalization of sex/gender variant others.

Although almost entirely missing from the sciences until the last decade or so,[11] researchers have begun outlining the construction, operation, and maintenance of cisnormativity in a wide variety of settings. Specifically, qualitative case studies undertaken all over the United States reveal some ways entire religious traditions, norms about what a family is and how it works, assumptions about reproduction and childrearing, official identification for government recognition, public spaces like bathrooms and airport security lines, scientific surveys and labs, educational settings and classrooms, marital rights and licensing, applications for jobs and housing, and clothing stores are built upon cisnormative requirements for the segregation of social life into options for two—and only two—mutually exclusive sex/gender groups.[12] Further, researchers have revealed many ways such structural patterns find voice in people's construction and experience of narratives, interpersonal interactions and relationships, and attitudes concerning different political, religious, and scientific issues. The consistency and widespread nature of such findings suggest cisnormativity is a primary organizing feature of contemporary US society that people across the country will either resist or conform to in their daily lives.

The Effects of Cisnormativity

Alongside qualitative case studies documenting the operation of cisnormativity in contemporary US society, the emergence of large-scale surveys detailing transgender people's experiences demonstrates the significant impacts this system has on the lives of sex/gender-variant people. The USTS, for example, reveals the "pervasive mistreatment and violence" transgender people face within cisgender realities across the nation. For example, the USTS finds that almost half of respondents were verbally harassed, 9 percent were physically attacked, and 10 percent were sexually assaulted in the year prior to the survey. However, this was not just a bad year for transgender people; almost half have been sexually assaulted at some point in their lifetime. As activists and researchers have been noting at least since the 1970s, being identified as transgender in US society often makes one a target for violence, harassment, and other forms of harmful treatment.[13]

We can also see the bird's-eye view of such patterns across the United States when we look at findings from the USTS. As noted in chapter 2, for example, transgender people are much more likely than cisgender people to live in poverty, despite often having more educational attainment, and we are much less likely than cisgender Americans to own homes. Moreover, our unemployment rate is five times as high as that of US society as a whole, and about one-third of USTS respondents had been homeless at some point in their lives. Further, as in cisgender populations, these patterns are even more dire in the case of transgender people of color and/or transgender people occupying other marginalized statuses.

We also see the impact of cisnormativity in other social spheres. For example, almost two-thirds of USTS respondents did not have an identification that matched their name or sex/gender. This may seem odd to some cisgender readers, but it is a common issue for many transgender people that impacts, for example, applications for jobs and homes, the ability to attend school or acquire medical care, and treatment in interactions with police or other authorities.[14] Identification, however, can come with its own costs. For example, more than three-fourths of USTS respondents who were known or perceived as transgender in schools were bullied, with more than half experiencing harassment and another quarter experiencing assault. In another arena, more than half of respondents faced harassment from police, and 57 percent noted that they would not feel comfortable asking police for help if they were in trouble due to past experiences.[15] Finally, more than half of the respondents in the USTS reported avoiding public restrooms because of experiences with harassment, assault, and denial of access in such settings during their lives.

Although we could continue with many other examples from the USTS and even look to the special reports on transgender people of color and sexually fluid transgender people for even more examples,[16] the pattern remains the same. Put simply, the social construction and enforcement of cisnormativity turns almost any aspect of the social world into a potentially hostile and traumatic situation for transgender people. As we did in chapter 2, here we add the statements from our respondents to shed light on the ways they navigate these cisgender realities in their own lives. In so doing, we highlight how transgender people—as outsiders within a cisgender reality—are required to constantly educate and survive cisgender people to navigate life in contemporary US society.

EDUCATING CISGENDER PEOPLE

As suggested in the discussion above, one of the primary effects of cisnormativity involves the erasure of non-cisgender people from history, media, science, religion, and everyday life. This process is, of course, what allows many cisgender people (and even some transgender and otherwise gender-identified people) to redefine their lack of information about us as the result of our being a new issue or population. This situation, however, is not limited to transgender populations and history; rather, it is similar to the ways that systemic racism relies partially on the absence of historical examples of antiracism and positive accomplishments of people of color. It is also similar to the ways LGBQIA people's and cisgender women's historical accomplishments and lives are often absent, downplayed, or otherwise marginalized in mainstream representations of US history, media offerings, and K–12 (and often college) curricula. As has been and continues to be the case with the aforementioned populations, there is no *lack* of transgender history, accomplishments, arts, or other phenomena that could be shared with society; rather, such information is *excluded* from mainstream representations of the United States as part of the operation of cisnormativity.

Of course, cisgender people could do the work independently to better inform themselves about our histories and experiences. Especially considering that they were likely the ones to delete us in the first place, this would seem like the fairest approach to (re)incorporating transgender experience into cisgender people's awareness of the nation and world we share. However, as the examples of other marginalized populations suggest, this not very likely (save for the few people who truly wish to support transgender people).[17] Rather, absent the infrastructure providing education on various marginalized histories across the United States, transgender people often have to take on the work of educating cisgender people about our lives, histories, and needs. As has been the case with other marginalized populations, historically and at present, this educational work occupies a central element of our respondents' experiences with cisgender people.

As suggested above, transgender experiences with cisgender people are often reminiscent of nonreligious people's experiences with (more conservative) religious people,[18] people of color's experiences with white people,[19] and LGBQA people's experiences with heterosexual people.[20] This is because many of our interactions require us to withstand cisgender attempts to convert us to their own faith system and worldview: cisnormativity. Put simply, cisgender people have been allowed to believe their reality is the only reality. As a result, they often try to convert transgender people to their own belief in the rightness or normality of cisgender realities.[21] As such, our respondents—across racial, class, sexual, and religious identities—regularly had to explain to cisgender people that their own (cisnormative) way of living was not the only way.

A nineteen-year-old lower-class, white, asexual romantic, transgender person summed up the limits of cisgender people's awareness about gender in many cases: "Cisgender people have a hard time understanding any gender besides 'man' and 'woman.'" Echoing this and other respondents' frustration with the ignorance of cisgender people, a twenty-one-year-old lower-class, white, pansexual transman added:

> Many cis people just tend to be aggressively ignorant and many of them seem to feel that they don't have a responsibility to learn about experiences that aren't their own. I experience a lot of difficulty communicating with many cis people. They won't respect pronouns or names, and they seem to think that my gender identity is somehow harder for them than for me. I've also found that cis people tend to do a lot of gatekeeping (defining who is "trans" and who is not). My father, for example, has decided that only trans people who have gone through extensive medical transition are valid.

Whether dealing with family, friends, or strangers, respondents noted regularly encountering cisgender people who adopted a form of (cis)gender fundamentalism (i.e., my way is the only way that exists).

The second part of the above quote also mirrors many heterosexual people who try to tell gay/lesbian/bisexual/ace/queer people who they really are, and in so doing often define gay/lesbian/bisexual/ace/queer identities as problematic.[22] It also mirrors many monosexuals who try to tell bi+/pan/queer/ace people who or what they really are, what the *bi* or *pan* means, and that their identities are problematic.[23] In such cases, people are so committed to their own view of the world that they feel comfortable forcing that view on others. Most respondents—like the thirty-one-year-old middle-class, white, queer, nonreligious transwoman quoted next—reported constant attempts by cisgender people to define who and what transgender people are as well as their own experiences trying to correct or do their best to ignore such nonstop proselytizing:

> They want to decide who we are. Most of the times I've offered to describe my experience about what I feel like being trans to cisgender folks, they get really curious and hung up on whether or not I've had surgery; conflate drag, crossdressing, homosexuality, and being trans; and are generally not aware of anything beyond their life.

A twenty-year-old middle-class, black, queer, genderqueer person added:

> You just have to educate cis people all the time. Many cisgender people believe transgender people have to pass as their gender as well as have the "proper" sex organs. This is based on society's rules that many cisgender people just are not willing to examine closely for its flaws.

As suggested in these examples, cisgender people—like other members of privileged social groups—are not required to learn anything about transgender people in most schools, media, or other settings. This allows them to see us as new and to be surprised by our appearance in their reality. Based on the sex/gender lessons cisgender people receive, many are even able to explicitly argue that we do not exist when they encounter us. At the same time, this allows cisgender people—once again, like members of other privileged groups in relation to those marginalized by their advantage—to avoid recognizing their own privileges within the current structure of contemporary (cisgender) US society. A twenty-six-year-old middle-class, white, bisexual, nonbinary person illustrated this dynamic:

Most cis people are transphobic, the same way that white people are racist. I am white and my society raised me to be racist. It is my job to unlearn everything to be a better person. Cisgender people have to do the same thing with us. They have to educate themselves in order to stop being transphobic. I have yet to meet a cisgender person who is really interested in learning, for more than five minutes, but I don't give up on them.

After noting that she always has to educate cisgender people over and over again, a thirty-year-old middle-class, black, asexual aromantic transwoman added: "It's a recurring negative experience with cisgender people. They misunderstand my gender identity. Once they find out I'm trans, they start using the wrong pronouns, calling me a man, implying I'm not actually a woman."

In fact, most of our respondents—as illustrated in the following quote from a thirty-year-old upper-class multiracial, queer, nonbinary person—noted that even cisgender people who tried to be supportive often had to be taught a lot in the process: "Every day, the usual transphobic bullshit about transmen being women who want to be men, and well-meaning but misguided cis people who accept you're trans but don't consider you a man until after medical transition." A thirty-three-year-old middle-class, white, queer, intersex transman added: "The main thing is having to explain what *intersex* means, and people immediately ask if that means I have a penis and a vagina. It's intrusive and inappropriate, but you'd be shocked how often people ask."

Overall, the transgender people who shared their stories with us (like both of us in our own lives within and beyond the academy) are required to constantly serve as the entire US education system for most of the cisgender people we encounter in our lives.[24] This pattern also transcends any given location where our respondents reside and any given setting wherein they encounter cisgender others. Further, this pattern shows up regardless of the race, class, sex assigned at birth, gender, sexual, or religious characteristics of the respondents, and regardless of where they fall on the age spectrum. The same way such patterns in prior studies have revealed endemic norms concerning whiteness, hetero- and monosexuality, monogamy, reproductive expectations, and other inequitable social systems embedded throughout the fabric of US society, our respondents reveal that cisnormativity serves alongside these other systems as a foundational component of life in the United States today.

SURVIVING CISGENDER PEOPLE

Social theorists exploring other systemic patterns of "normalness" that facilitate ongoing privileges for some and oppression for others have long noted that social life for members of the groups marginalized by such systems is often an exercise in survival.[25] This is because the affirmation, support, opportunities, and acceptance associated with positive health and other social outcomes is almost nonexistent and/or something one must acquire on one's own. This is also because every moment of each day can be a reminder that one is not necessarily welcome, safe, or respected within society. As we discuss in more depth in chapter 6, mental and physical health scholars have shown that the combination of these factors results in dramatically disparate outcomes between people in more privileged groups, people in marginalized groups, and people occupying multiple marginalized social locations.[26]

Exploring the ways such dynamics play out in the lives of people occupying varied unequal systems of social knowledge and behavior, researchers have shown that members of marginalized groups are othered (i.e., defined and treated as deviant, deficient, and dangerous) and policed (i.e., held to dominant norms that benefit others at their expense) in many social settings and contexts.[27] Further, numerous studies demonstrate how these patterns play out in relation to systems of race, class, sex, gender, sexualities, age, and other social systems of inequality. Although such patterns can play out in a wide variety of ways, researchers consistently find that members of marginalized communities must continuously be prepared for and manage negative actions and reactions from others throughout their daily lives. Here, we outline the ways cisgender realities create the same requirement for transgender people.

Discursive Aggression

Examining narratives of transgender people in the midwestern United States who identify in a variety of ways within the broader transgender umbrella, shuster shows how transgender people experience regular verbal taunts, slights, harassment, and other forms of aggression in interactions with cisgender people.[28] These experiences often involve cisgender people commenting on or questioning transgender people in ways that implicitly or explicitly challenge their rights, safety, lives, or well-being. Mirroring observations in the last section, where members of more privileged groups seek to define marginalized others, these forms of what shuster calls *discursive aggression* rest upon cisgender people's lack of knowledge, care, concern, or sensitivity for transgender people.

A thirty-nine-year-old middle-class, white, pansexual, transgender person offered an illustrative example of this type of experience: "They attack us; cis people seem less sensitive or considerate of others and more likely to be abusive." Such discursive aggression tactics—as a nineteen-year-old upper-class, Hispanic, asexual romantic, transgender person who echoed many respondents put it—generally involve cisgender people insulting or otherwise denigrating transgender people they encounter: "They are often very close minded, they are very angry about people being different from them. People called me *tranny* and other slurs before I even knew what they meant, because I looked different." A forty-five-year-old lower-class, white, queer transman added: "Cis male gay guys say I might be on hormones, but 'technically' I'm not male because of chromosomes, instead of just accepting me as I am."

As the last quote shows, cisgender people's discursive aggression often involves utilizing cisnormative understandings of the world to belittle transgender people. When someone talks about chromosomes, for example, it is telling that they either are not aware of or are simply ignoring the fact that almost no one is tested to ascertain chromosomal content in the United States, which means many cisgender people might not be male or female based on beliefs about these characteristics despite their pervasive chromosomal essentialist beliefs about their own and others' bodies. It is further telling that, as intersex scholars have noted and historical studies of the development of genetic fields demonstrate, there are a wide variety of chromosomal possibilities (i.e., not just two) that can be assigned to people of any sex/gender in practice.[29] Rather than being based in empirical realities concerning the biological diversity of humankind, such statements—like biological arguments utilized in the past to define people of color, cisgender women, and lesbian and gay people as inferior—rely upon biological fiction utilized to construct and assert a cisgender reality.[30]

At the same time, our respondents demonstrated some ways the discursive actions of cisgender people reveal cisgender people's own lack of concern for others who do not share their cisgender reality. For example, a thirty-year-old lower-class, black, heterosexual, gender-neutral person added: "It's a regular part of life, misgendering, being referred to as 'it' and blatant disrespect, family rejection, mockery everywhere." A twenty-nine-year-old middle-class, white, asexual romantic, nonbinary person drew an important comparison between what cisgender people value and what they do not when it comes to language: "Cisgender people think pronouns are important when it's a dog; they don't think it's so important when it's a trans person."

As suggested above and sometimes noted in other studies, cisgender people's dismissal of transgender realities is often accompanied by attempts to demean or control transgender people. As a twenty-eight-year-old lower-class, white, pansexual, transgender person put it:

> They just want to control everything. *Oh boy*, so many things cis people do, using the wrong pronouns repeatedly, disagreeing with cold hard facts about trans and nonbinary discrimination, using cissexism casually, like saying they believe there are only two genders and only women can have vaginas, assuming someone's gender based on how they look and telling people they/them isn't a pronoun when it is—learn some history or look at the goddamn dictionary; I could go on all day.

Similarly, a twenty-three-year-old lower-class, white, lesbian transwoman wrote: "They don't respect boundaries, like asking about if I want a sex change in public and a professor asking about my genitals in public."

Rather than seeking to learn something beyond cisgender realities, cisgender people often try to force transgender people into these ideological belief systems. For example, a twenty-three-year-old lower-class, multiracial, asexual panromantic transman added: "The worst is when they ask, 'What are you?' and then try to convince me that I am wrong." A twenty-year-old lower-class, white, asexual romantic transman summed up a lot of the observations of cisgender others' attempts to exercise discursive control over whether or not transgender people could exist in their cisgender reality: "Cis people will say genderfluid people are seeking attention, trans people aren't real, asexual people are just celibate, and all kinds of other stuff to try to limit who other people can be to what they want and nothing else." Rather than embracing the diversity of transgender people's actual realities, such examples reveal cisgender people's constant attempts to limit what can be allowed in "their" world.

Broader Forms of Aggression

As researchers have consistently noted in relation to gender as an overall concept and social norm as well as meetings between the privileged and marginalized in other social systems, aggressive language often demonstrates at least the possibility of further attacks.[31] Stated another way, one who talks about harming other types of people may easily expand such talk to physical violence, voting behaviors that harm others, and other forms of maltreatment beyond verbal harassment. As a result, members of marginalized groups must be prepared each time they face discursive aggression for at least the possibility of other types of hostility from more privileged people they encounter in the course of their lives.[32]

This preparation is even more necessary in the case of transgender people because many of us face violence and other forms of aggression from cisgender people. As noted in the USTS, for example, transgender people—and especially those of color and transwomen—are much more likely than other members of society to face sexual violence, physical harassment and violence of varied types, and forms of domestic abuse at the hands of cisgender romantic/sexual partners and family members. Transgender people are also among the populations most likely to face structural violence from police, organizational and institutional sectors (such as employment and housing), and even healthcare providers. These concerns are also complicated by cisgender people in positions of authority who may characterize transgender and other gender-nonconforming people as defensive, overly emotional or sensitive, or otherwise problematic when we express fears about interactions with cisgender people at work, in the home, or in broader social environments.

The combination of these factors can lead the "normal" or everyday social world inhabited by cisgender people to appear more like a potential battlefield or danger zone for many transgender people. Our respondents, for example, often noted the role of the public (or the presence of an audience) in responding to the potential of more extreme forms of aggression from cisgender people. This, as symbolic interactionists have long noted, may be due to the possibility that at any time, any member of a given audience may become part of a mob or other form of danger once an individual of a marginalized group becomes visible to members of more privileged groups.[33] As a result, transgender people navigating US society often must remain prepared for potential violence anytime we encounter cisgender others.

In fact, our respondents shared many situations wherein they felt unsafe in their interactions with cisgender people regardless of our respondents' other social identities. For example, a forty-three-year-old upper-class, white, queer transwoman noted: "An LGBT group rejected me because I was both queer and trans and they were focused on just gay and lesbian experiences. Another group wouldn't listen to my ideas unless I had a gay male friend put them forward." While this quote reveals implicit marginalization and dismissal within a specific context or community, echoing our findings outlined in chapter 3, the following quote from a nineteen-year-old middle-class, white, asexual romantic transman offers more explicit examples that occur in many contexts:

> My health teacher taught us about "the transgenders" and referred to transmen as "she" and transwomen as "he." Every person in the class other than me was cisgender, and all the boys said it was disgusting. My therapist told me transmen don't exist; everyone my age questions gender. Her close-mindedness pushed my coming out back about a year.

Although it is difficult enough to continuously manage potentially dangerous conversations with a given cisgender person, encounters with cisgender people become even more fraught in cases where marginalization is compounded by, for example, facing this kind of treatment in groups where one may be the only trans person, or from social authorities (i.e., bosses, parents, police, doctors, teachers, professors, etc.) with the capability to shape and influence the minds of others and/or one's economic standing. In such cases, discursive aggression blends with existing power structures and hierarchies to limit transgender people's chances for resistance to or departure from such encounters.

Especially considering historical and current violence against transgender people,[34] it is not surprising that our respondents reported many such experiences at the hands of cisgender people.[35] These reports included bullying in schools, clubs, and religious organizations; physical attacks in public and private settings; abuse within prisons and jails; forcible removal from businesses and academic settings; assaults in medical settings; and sexual assault within and outside of relationships. As a fifty-year-old middle-class, white, lesbian transwoman noted after disclosing she had been sexually assaulted: "Most cis men do not understand or like women. Multiply that times a factor of eight for transwomen." A twenty-five-year-old lower-class, white, lesbian nonreligious transwoman added: "So many things: I've had slurs yelled at me, so much unwanted touching, glass bottles thrown at me by cis people; it's a lot." A sixty-year-old lower-class, heterosexual transman who did not disclose a racial identity summed up many of the statements:

> Because of cisgender people I have PTSD. I have lived in fear most of my life because of America's predetermined view on gender-variant individuals. American society with their transphobic rules, regulations, laws, and cisgender hatred toward anything that is nonbinary has made trans people victims.

As the examples throughout this section reveal, transgender people often must endure constant aggression—verbal, physical, structural, and otherwise—simply to survive in the cisgender reality of contemporary US society. Importantly, as in the continuous requirement to educate cisgender people, this is a pattern that transcended variations in the overall data set.

THE FOUNDATIONS OF CISGENDER REALITIES

In this chapter, we have expanded our earlier discussion of the experiences of transgender people in LGBTQIA communities to explore the overall experiences our respondents reported with cisgender people throughout the United States. At the same time, the illustrations in this chapter demonstrate how US society looks to transgender people who must live within a cisgender reality. In so doing, we note the ways that the systematic erasure of transgender people from the belief systems of most cisgender people in the United States results in widespread, ongoing marginalization of transgender people throughout the nation. As stated earlier in this chapter, however, it is important to remember that our existence is not what is new about this equation. Rather, the new component many scholars, reporters, and individuals more broadly are referring to is this: People who have only known and accepted cisgender realities are becoming more and more aware of our long-standing presence within the nation and world.

This observation suggests a question we examine in the next two chapters: Since our presence is not actually a new thing, how have so many Americans developed such devout faith in cisgender realities? How have they become so convinced of this fictional version of the world they live in that we are able to appear new to them? To answer these questions, we turn to what attitudinal scholarship often finds are two of the most—or the two most—powerful types of stories that shape what social beings believe to be real, natural, or true about the world they inhabit: religion and science. Specifically, we explore the ways transgender people experience interactions with members of these traditions and the ways such experiences shed light upon the operation of these foundational forms of cisgender reality construction and maintenance throughout US society.

NOTES

1. See Connell, "Doing, Undoing, or Redoing"; Hollander, "'I Demand More'"; Lucal, "What It Means"; Pfeffer, "Bodies in Relation"; West and Zimmerman, "Doing Gender."

2. See Sumerau, Cragun, Mathers, "Cisgendering Reality." See also Johnson, "Beyond Inclusion."

3. See Bellwether, *Fucking Trans Women*; Ekins and King, "Towards a Sociology"; Feinberg, *Transgender Warriors*; Hines, "What's the Difference?"; Stone, "The Empire"; Stryker, *Transgender History*; Stryker and Aizura, *Transgender Studies Reader*, vol. 2; and Stryker and Whittle, *Transgender Studies Reader*, vol. 1.

4. This rhetorical device (i.e., something newly noticed by the mainstream is, in fact, new) is also reminiscent of arguments decades prior about the "new" same- and multiple-sex sexualities (i.e., LGB sexualities) that had been erased from heterosexual and monosexual based accounts of US and world history previously; see, for example, Warner, *The Trouble with Normal*; Katz, *The Invention of Heterosexuality*; Foucault, *History of Sexuality*.

5. For examples of scholars talking about the new gender revolution of transgender communities, see Meadow, *Trans Kids*; Stein, *Unbound*; and Travers, *The Trans Generation*, as well as much media coverage of recent transgender-related events and celebrities such as *National Geographic*'s 2017 issue "Gender Revolution" and *Time* magazine's 2014 issue "The Transgender Tipping Point."

6. See Loewen, *Lies My Teacher Told Me*; and Omi and Winant, *Racial Formation*.

7. See Rosenberg, *Jane Crow*; Snorton, *Black on Both Sides*; and Stryker, *Transgender History*.

8. See Collins, *Black Feminist Thought* and *Fighting Words*; see also Foucault, *Archaeology of Knowledge*.

9. See Butler, *Gender Trouble* and *Bodies that Matter*; Foucault, *History of Sexuality*, vols. 1, 2, and 3; and Plummer, *Telling Sexual Stories*.

10. People who subscribe to religious beliefs are likely to say "god" or "deity" created cisgender realities and to define nonconformists as sinful/deviant/ problematic for the designs of the supernatural, whereas people who place their faith in science or secular logics are likely to say "nature" created cisgender realities and define nonconformists as diseased/deviant/problematic for the designs of physical and social sciences since the 1800s. In both cases and others where media and political authorities utilize these narratives, such groups cherry-pick existing history, science, and theologies to make the world (i.e., their reality) conform to their own cisgender assumptions, norms, and beliefs (i.e., cisnormativity).

11. As noted in chapter 1, earlier studies of transgender experience typically sought to locate such experience within existing cisgender man/woman gender binaries without much consideration of the overall ideology that created and maintained such systems in the first place; see again Schilt and Lagos, "The Development."

12. See nn. 54 and 55 in chapter 1.

13. Stryker, *Transgender History*.

14. See also Davis, *Beyond Trans*.

15. This is often because, as J has written elsewhere (Sumerau, "Embodying Nonexistence"), even mundane interactions with police can turn dangerous or violent if one is perceived to be sex/gender variant in appearance.

16. See n. 12 in chapter 2 for relevant sources. See also de Vries, "Intersectional Identities."

17. See Collins, *Black Feminist Thought*; hooks, *Teaching to Transgress*; Sedgwick, *Epistemology*; Smith, *The Everyday World as Problematic*; and Warner, *The Trouble with Normal*.

18. Cragun and Sumerau, "The Last Bastion."

19. Bonilla-Silva, *Racism without Racists*.

20. Eisner, *Notes for a Bisexual Revolution*.

21. Serano, *Excluded*.

22. Barton, *Pray the Gay Away*.

23. Eisner, *Notes for a Bisexual Revolution*.

24. We use the word *most* here because there are exceptions in our own lives and in the lives of our respondents. Among our respondents, for example, 3 percent

(i.e., 14 people out of our 469 respondents) noted only positive interactions with cisgender people.

25. See nn. 13 and 16 in this chapter.

26. Collins, "Intersectionality's Definitional Dilemmas"; Grollman, "Multiple Disadvantaged Statuses"; Grollman, "Multiple Forms of Perceived Discrimination"; Link and Phelan, "Fundamental Causes"; Phelan and Link, "Is Racism."

27. See Chen, "Everywhere Archives"; Collins, "Intersectionality's Definitional Dilemmas"; Ridgeway, *Framed by Gender*; Schrock, Sumerau, and Ueno, "Sexualities"; and Schwalbe et al., "Generic Processes."

28. shuster, "Punctuating Accountability."

29. Almeling, *Sex Cells*; Costello, "Nonconsensual Intersex Surgery"; Costello, "Understanding Intersex Relationships"; Davis, *Contesting Intersex*; Karkazis, *Fixing Sex*.

30. Somerville, *Queering the Color Line;* Washington, *Medical Apartheid.*

31. See Bonilla-Silva, *Racism without Racists*; Ezzell, "Lad Mags"; Martin, *Rape Work*; Jasinski, Weekly, Wright, and Mustaine, *Hard Lives*; Schilt and Westbrook, "Doing Gender, Doing Heteronormativity"; Schilt, *Just One of the Guys?*; and Warner, *The Trouble with Normal.*

32. Jooyoung Lee refers to this psychological state (i.e., constant preparation for potential violence and danger at the hands of others) as "existential urgency," which requires members of marginalized groups to maintain a heightened sense of preparation within encounters with members of privileged groups, see Lee, *Blowin' Up.*

33. See Edgley, *The Drama of Social Life*; and Goffman, *The Presentation of Self.* See also work on people of color's experiences in predominantly white spaces, such as Bonilla-Silva, *Racism without Racists;* Collins, *Black Corporate Executives*; and Gay, "Navigating Marginality."

34. See Brown, Kucharska, and Marczak, "Mental Health Practitioners' Attitudes"; James et. al, *Report of the 2015 U.S. Transgender Survey*; Schilt and Westbrook, "Doing Gender, Doing Heteronormativity"; Stryker, *Transgender History.*

35. The quotes of this type from our respondents of color pointed out an experience (i.e., I was kicked out of school; I was disowned by family; I was assaulted by a cis person) without much explanation beyond stating what occurred, and thus we present such information as part of the list, as white respondents often offered similar short responses to the question.

5

Transgender Experience with Religion

When I (J) attended support groups as a scared teenager in the 1990s, a regular theme involved the ways we transgender folks sought to make sense of religious teachings that suggested either that we did not exist or that we were a perversion of God's creation. Most of the attendees present at any given meeting were heavily focused on figuring out lessons learned in (almost entirely) Christian churches and finding some way to integrate religious and gendered selves. Sermons promising that God made only women and men and stories of religious-based discrimination against LGBTQIA people in general were regular topics. All of us knew that openly identifying as transgender—and in most cases also as sexual minorities—meant risking scorn, violence, and dismissal from religious organizations, families, and God's love. Like many other transgender people in support groups then and now, all of us in these meetings, at different times, expressed a debilitating surety of eternal damnation as well as social and religious ostracism and isolation.[1]

On the other hand, Lain grew up in a household where religion was almost entirely irrelevant.[2] In fact, their earliest experiences navigating relationships between religion, gender, and sexuality came when I was teaching zir how to do ethnographic fieldwork at an LGBTQIA Christian church while they were in college. Although I spent most of my young adulthood unlearning negative religious lessons while some friends remained religious and others (like me) left religion, Lain experienced religion as an abstract, distant thing that influenced politics rather than as a visceral part of zir life. For Lain, even the existence of deeply committed LGBTQIA religious people was something that was hard to wrap zir mind around, but for me, the possibility of growing up without constant consideration of religion was entirely foreign.

In the years since, these differing standpoints have provided fuel for our individual and collaborative work exploring the religious experiences of sex/gender/sexual minorities throughout contemporary US society.[3] In this chapter, we combine our prior work with the observations provided by our respondents to explore the ways religion serves as a foundational component in the construction and maintenance of a cisgender reality, as well as the myriad ways transgender people experience religion in contemporary US culture. As we have elsewhere, we continue to join others in calling for a greater focus on religious studies among scholars focused on sex, gender, and sexualities as well as more specific attention to sex, gender, and sexualities studies among scholars focused on religion.[4] In so doing, we highlight the complexity of both sexual-gender-religious politics in contemporary US society and the religious experiences found in the case of transgender people across the United States.

SEX, GENDER, SEXUALITIES, AND RELIGION IN AMERICA

As Dawne Moon and Theresa Tobin point out, US conceptualizations of sex, gender, and sexualities are inextricably linked to the religious past and present of the nation.[5] Specifically, Western Christian[6] authorities created and enforced beliefs in *complementarity* (i.e., the assertion that two sexes/genders were created by God as counterparts to each other in reproductive heterosexual communion) as part of the rise of European power during colonization. This belief system was then used as justification for conquering Native nations throughout the world that believed in more diverse notions of sex, gender, sexualities, bodies, and religious options. Put simply, complementarity rests on the assumption that God created humans in only two sexes, that these two sexes complement each other as oppositional halves of a whole, and that such halves can become whole only through heterosexual activity that results in reproduction. Within this framework, LGBTQIA experience is defined as oppositional to the will of God as well as God's design of nature and humanity. Likewise, this framework relies upon cisnormative notions of male/man and female/woman as fundamentally different, static, and separate forms of humanity created with divergent abilities, desires, and needs.

As noted in earlier chapters in this book, complementarity requires the construction and maintenance of a cisgender and monosexual reality enforced alongside and via the construction and operation of white, heterosexual, masculine, reproductive, able bodied, and capitalist class systems that privilege some groups at the expense of others.[7] Put simply, the original segregation of the world into only cisgender women and men who are also only reproductive monosexual heterosexual people provides a foundational form of "doing difference"[8] created, required, and sanctified by God. From this ideological source, Western Christian authorities within and beyond the United States developed beliefs and practices that allowed for—and continue to provide justification for the maintenance of—the devaluation of people of color, LGBTQIA people, and cisgender women who were deemed lesser, nonexistent, or otherwise problematic according to the natural will and design of the supernatural.[9]

In fact, even a casual glance at historical reactions to openly LGBTQIA people, as well as movements for cisgender women's and people of color's rights, reveal continuous utilization of complementarian beliefs by those who oppose such movements. However, we also often see mobilization of more expansive notions of God's will in movements allied with various populations marginalized in social spheres.[10] At the same time, scholars continue to note the common tendency for studies of sex, gender, and sexual experience to operate completely separate from religious studies, and for religious studies to often operate without much incorporation of insights from sex, gender, and sexualities studies.[11] As a result, unlike other social systems that define some people as lesser, religion itself is rarely studied as an axis of social inequality like race, sex, class, gender, sexualities, ability, or nationality.[12] As Orit Avishai notes, this is especially troubling since most people cannot create or do identities and practices related to these other systems of inequality without also doing or undoing the religious norms that exist at the heart of what it means to be or have a race, sex, class, gender, sexual identity, ability, or other identification in practice and daily life throughout contemporary US society.[13]

In this chapter, we focus on and take seriously such observations by exploring religious politics related to sex, gender, and sexualities in recent decades. Specifically, we outline the ways transgender people occupying a variety of social locations experience religious others in their lives. However, this effort requires exploring the complex relationships between religion and LGBTQIA experience that have become a staple in the social sciences since the 1990s. In the case of our respondents—as it was for J and others growing up in very religious parts of the country years ago—these relationships are complicated and often shifting in wide-ranging ways alongside broader social attitudes, policies, and movements by LGBTQIA groups, religious groups, and LGBTQIA religious groups active across the United States.

COMPLICATED RELATIONSHIPS BETWEEN RELIGION AND LGBTQIA POPULATIONS[14]

Examining the rise of the Religious Right alongside increasing social movement activity by lesbian and gay organizations, sociologist Tina Fetner[15] demonstrates how religious opposition to homosexuality—especially since the 1940s[16]—dramatically impacted the experiences of LGBTQIA[17] people in the United States over the past five decades. Specifically, she explains how conservative Christian movements employed depictions of "the dangerous homosexual" that became increasingly popular in the 1940s and 1950s to justify religious and political attacks on families, employment opportunities, marital potential, recognition in society, educational chances, and other arenas of everyday social life. Further, her analysis shows how lesbian and gay groups responded by adopting discourses first popularized by LG-Christian organizations in the 1960s to define homosexuality as inborn (i.e., born this way), and gay/lesbian people as normal, moral, and safe in the eyes of heterosexual Americans.[18]

At the same time, the shift of lesbian/gay movements away from more radical and nonconformist approaches to a politics of emulating straightness both fueled the ongoing development of specifically LG-Christian organizations and provided a defense against the rising power of ex-gay/ex-lesbian movements on the other side of the religious/political spectrum. For example, LG-Christian organizations like Dignity and the Metropolitan Community Churches built congregations and support groups for LG (and later BTQIA as well) religious people who sought an alternative to the damnation of homosexuality found in mainstream religious organizations.[19] This occurred alongside the emergence of ex-gay/ex-lesbian organizations throughout the nation, which promoted the fallacy that lesbian/gay and other sexual "sinners"[20] could be forced or converted into hetero- and cisnormative systems of masculine and feminine complementarity through religion.[21] During the last three decades of the twentieth century, both sides of this debate operated and spread within the context of ongoing LG civil rights movement battles with (mainly) religious-based movements opposed to sex, gender, and sexual diversity.[22]

The combination of lesbian/gay similarity, or assimilation politics, alongside rising specifically LGBTQIA religious organizations and explicitly anti-LGBTQIA religious organizations pushed political debates about family and marriage into the cultural spotlight. It is important to remember, however, that such shifts made sense at a time when LGBTQIA families, communities, and non–legally recognized marriages and partnerships were under constant, systemic attack from both religious political operations and the broader US government.[23] Put simply, families, lovers, and communities were being torn apart, and this reality created the conditions for adopting any political strategy that could, at least in the moment, blunt the unrelenting state-sanctioned assault on LGBTQIA existence. As noted in chapter 2, this homonormative politics of similarity has created its own problems, but it rose in response to the devastation of our communities at a specific historical moment and in response to massive society-wide conflicts we faced at the time.[24] As marriage is often constructed as the central element of normative complementarity, it is not surprising that this became the focal point for religious and LGBTQIA interaction at this time.

In fact, sociologist Melanie Heath has shown the ways that marriage itself became the central concern of many Americans, within and beyond LGBTQIA communities, throughout the 1990s and into the new century.[25] As she notes in her analyses of marriage promotion campaigns, this foundational tenet of normative complementarity-based Western Christianity also became the central element of what it meant to be an American. Thus marriage became a core component in determining who was or was not welcome in US society.[26] At the same time, marriage promotion relied explicitly upon attempts—by religious organizations as well as the US government—to reinforce socially accepted *and* expected forms of hetero-, mono-, and cisnormative and reproductive complementarity across the United States. Put simply, governmental and religious authorities constructed the legally married, cisgender, monogamous, monosexual/heterosexual focused on reproduction, family, and economic accomplishment as the ideal image of what a "real American" was and should be.

However, these constructions of complementarity as the ultimate American norm developed at the same time that non-LGBTQIA religious organizations were losing members in large numbers and specifically LGBTQIA religious organizations—as well as pagan, spiritual, and other religious traditions—were gaining some of these members. This was also a period when US religious institutions more broadly began to witness falling membership levels as more Americans openly adopted and formed nonreligious identities, politics, and communities.[27] The combination of these developments led some—and later more—previously non-LGBTQIA religious organizations to begin welcoming a few LGBTQIA people back into their traditions, local churches, and political endeavors.[28] Although many LGBTQIA people preferred to remain in specifically LGBTQIA religious groups or lead nonreligious lives, many others accepted these invitations and began to have influence within mainstream religious traditions.

As of the writing of this book, these dynamics continue to play out in contemporary US society.[29] Although the work of secular and religious LGBTQIA people and allies accomplished the legalization of same-sex marriage in 2015, for example, this accomplishment was automatically met with attempts from the other side of the political/religious spectrum to overturn the incremental victory of same-sex marriage. These attempts took the form of efforts to challenge same-sex marriage rights in US courts, ban transgender people from public spaces, pass "religious liberty" laws that allow overt discrimination against LGBTQIA people in public spaces, and deny LGBTQIA civil rights pursuits beyond marriage. In fact, as Fetner put it in 2016, opposition to LGBTQIA people following the legalization of same-sex marriage is in many respects the "same as it ever was."[30] Specifically, much of the rhetoric utilized against LGBTQIA civil rights in 2018 mirrors examples of rhetoric used against our communities as early as the 1940s.

This does not mean, however, that nothing has changed. Although attitudes about homosexuality among the most conservative Christians have remained relatively stable in the past four decades,[31] broader social attitudes concerning lesbian/gay people, homosexuality itself, and same-sex marriage have changed dramatically. Additionally, even though the foundational commitment to complementarity and (monosexual/monogamous) heterosexuality focused on reproduction has remained constant in conservative Christian teachings, the ways leaders of these traditions conceptualize and make sense of gay/lesbian people have become somewhat less hostile since the 1970s.[32] Likewise, whereas it was almost impossible to find any discussions of bisexual, transgender, asexual, polyamorous, or intersex religious experience or of religious people's attitudes about such populations as recently as a decade ago, early studies and conversations about these populations and experiences have at least begun to appear in the mainstream and within interdisciplinary scholarship.[33] These developments suggest that at least some religious opposition has been softening over time alongside continued religious-based attacks on LGBTQIA civil rights.

As we previously discussed in relation to homo-, cis-, and mononormativities in LGBTQIA communities,[34] however, such softening is not equally distributed. Recent attitudinal studies suggest that even as some religious opposition to lesbian/gay people softens, it is coupled with even more hostile reactions to bisexual, transgender, and poly populations.[35] Put simply, even people who have found ways to include lesbian/gay people within normative frameworks of hetero/cis/mono complementarity now turn damnation—formerly focused on LGBTQIA people as a whole—onto bisexual, transgender, and polyamorous people specifically.[36] In fact, survey results demonstrate that these are presently three of the most (or even the three most, in some surveys) hated groups in the United States.[37] Studies that reflect this pattern of hatred toward transgender, bisexual, and polyamorous people suggest the ongoing conflict between religious-based complementarity and LGBTQIA populations within US society remains as complex as ever.

ECHOES OF THE PAST IN TRANSGENDER PEOPLE'S EXPERIENCES WITH RELIGIOUS OTHERS

In the USTS, transgender people were much more likely than the average American to identify as nonreligious.[38] Although we find the same pattern among our respondents (i.e., 50 percent of our respondents who identified a religious identity were nonreligious), we can also extend this observation since we not only asked what respondents' religious identities were now, but also what religion they identified with at age twelve. As shown in table 5.1, a comparison of these two time points reveals that Christianity lost members while other religious and nonreligious traditions all gained members as our respondents aged. Considering the complexity of the relationship between religious and LGBTQIA communities in recent decades, this pattern raises

Table 5.1. Religious Identities Now (*n* = 290) and at Age 12 (*n* = 299)

Religious Identity at Time of Survey	Number of Respondents	Religious Identity at Age 12	Number of Respondents
Nonreligious or None	145	Nonreligious or None	93
Christian	55	Christian	171
Pagan	37	Pagan	14
Muslim	25	Muslim	12
Jewish	14	Jewish	8
Buddhist	12	Buddhist	1
Sikh	1	Sikh	0
Hindu	1	Hindu	0

critical questions for discussions about religion in US culture, especially as transgender people gain more mainstream attention and begin to become integrated in scholarship concerning both religious and secular populations.

Our work here speaks to some of these questions and also extends the statistical patterns in the USTS by outlining the experiences our respondents had with religion. We explore the ways their own discussions of religious experience reflect both positive and negative aspects of the past few decades of conflict between LGBTQIA movement groups and mainstream (and especially conservative Christian) religious organizations in the United States. Much like early studies of lesbian/gay religious experience in the 1990s, we provide a baseline for the continued emergence and expansion of scholarship exploring transgender religious experience within and beyond specific religious traditions.

When Sheila's a Transgender Person

The title of this section is a reference to a classic discussion in social scientific studies of religion.[39] In the 1990s, scholars expressed curiosity upon witnessing the rise of people who adopted individual notions of religion and spirituality rather than versions of these beliefs specifically and necessarily tied to a given religious tradition or organization. This notion of individual religion as a choice—defined as an exercise in shopping for community in varied religious, spiritual, or secular places, and a journey over the life course rather than a specific commitment of faith—became associated with the pseudonym Sheila Larson in early studies on religious identities.[40] Exploring this issue in 2002, however, religious studies scholar Melissa M. Wilcox noted that in some populations—and especially LGBTQIA ones—interpretations of religious life as an individual journey in search of the right community should be expected in most cases. Wilcox suggests this is because believers who experienced negative reactions from early religious communities might be as likely to leave religion altogether as they are to pursue their religion on their own terms and with new communities.

The majority of our respondents shared religious experiences that reflect the journeys Wilcox outlined from cases of LG people in 2002 and LBT women in 2009. As Wilcox discusses at length in these and other works, many LGBTQIA people experience religion as an ongoing journey wherein one searches for accepting religious communities before, during, and/or after navigating negative experiences in other religious communities.[41] For example, a thirty-nine-year-old middle-class, black transman who identified as a nondenominational Christian but did not provide a sexual identity shared the following: "I am a pastor and my journey has not been that great with the church. I was told that I was an abomination, so I hid it for most of my life. I had to leave church as I knew it and took a break from ministry for about three years. But I have a renewed relationship with G-d and I am back in ministry." A fifty-year-old middle-class, white, lesbian transwoman who identified as pagan added: "You have to search because there are some that have the capacity to experience and comprehend basic humanity."

A fifty-eight-year-old middle-class, gay transman who identified as Jewish but did not disclose another racial identity[42] summed up the comments of many who wrote about seeking religious welcome over time: "Over the years, I have had very positive experiences with Rabbis on all occasions, but very negative experiences with Christian ministers who have told me that I am going to hell." A thirty-year-old lower-class, black, asexual transman who identified as pagan added: "I've dealt with homophobic and otherwise bigoted pastors, especially in my early adulthood, and it's made me largely cynical toward Christianity. I've only really had positive religious experiences as an adult, when I started attending pagan rituals." Similarly, a twenty-seven-year-old middle-class, Hispanic, bisexual transwoman who identified as Episcopalian noted: "I attended a very transphobic church as a child and had a hard time hearing about going to hell. However, I've now had positive experiences with some priests in my current denomination and the priest who married my wife and [me]; that was a very healing experience for me with regard to religion."

Although the above examples come from transgender people who remain religious, this was also the most common pattern among respondents who left religion. For example, a twenty-five-year-old lower-class, white, lesbian transwoman who identified as agnostic wrote:

> I have had lots of negative experiences with religious leaders in the Baptist church I attended as a child—conservative political views, anti-science rhetoric, not the best views towards differing opinions; but I have had many positive experiences at a Unitarian Universalist church, and positive experiences with a progressive Christian church where TDoR[43] was held this year.

A thirty-year-old middle-class, white, queer, nonbinary person who identified as an atheist added: "The humanist[44] religious leaders I have met are amazing, wonderful people who have helped me become a better person. The Christian leaders may have wanted to help me, but could not actually do so given the things they wanted me to believe that were actually self-destructive." In such cases, respondents reported a journey that involved first facing significant marginalization in (almost always Christian) religious communities but often finding more acceptance in other religious organizations or traditions at later points in life.

The Problem of Christianity

Echoing some nonreligious people who leave the Christian traditions in which they were raised,[45] most of our respondents shared negative experiences with Christian organizations, leaders, and lay people. Especially considering the number of our respondents who were raised in some denomination of Christianity only to leave it for either nonreligious identification or other religious traditions, such examples reveal that despite its elevation in contemporary US culture, Christianity itself may be a major social problem for certain populations.[46] In fact, it is especially noteworthy that we received very few responses that pointed out negative experiences in other faiths in which our respondents either grew up or are now active. Although the examples above shed light on some of these experiences with Christian others, here we outline the main recurring patterns in our respondents' statements about harmful experiences with Christianity throughout the survey and across sociodemographic and regional locations.

In some cases, as revealed in the following statement from a sixty-seven-year-old middle-class, black, heterosexual transwoman who identified as a Lutheran, these negative experiences were coupled with violence and abuse: "I was coerced into inappropriate sexual relationships with several ministers during my early preteen and adolescent childhood." A thirty-nine-year-old lower-class, white, asexual, bigender person who did not report a current religious identity added: "I was discriminated against because of being transgender and trauma related to my past (I was sexually abused as a foster child) by quite a few people who called themselves Christians." A twenty-five-year-old upper-class, white, queer, agender person who identified as agnostic noted: "As a sixteen-year-old, I had my youth pastor tell me if I didn't repent for my nonheterosexual feelings I was going to go to hell. He said this while another youth minister poured fake blood on a large wooden cross in a room where all of the lights had been exchanged for red lightbulbs. I never entered that church again and have only entered one church since."

Respondents also shared experiences of being dismissed from families and churches. For instance, a twenty-two-year-old lower-class, white, bisexual transwoman who identified as a Mormon wrote: "I had to deal with transphobia, ignorance, and lack of understanding or compassion with my bishop, which eventually led to him recommending I be excommunicated." Similarly, a twenty-six-year-old lower-class, white, pansexual, nonbinary person who identified as an atheist shared: "My dad ran a men's group at his church and completely disowned me when I came out at sixteen." A forty-nine-year-old middle-class, Native American, pansexual transwoman who identified as pagan and recounted a history of abuse at the hands of cisgender people recalled: "At thirteen years old, my parents surrendered their parental rights over me to the minister and membership board of the local church." A twenty-three-year-old lower-class, white, lesbian transwoman who identified as a Christian added: "Religious leaders in my life stopped talking to me when I came out, and one congregation tried to 'pray the gay demon away.' When it didn't work, I was blamed for not having enough faith."

Although we could continue to outline examples of negative experiences our respondents had with Christian groups, the majority of the other statements are very similar to the ones above. Commenting on the specter of (especially conservative) Christianity in the lives of transgender Americans, for example, a forty-eight-year-old middle-class, white, lesbian transwoman who identified as pagan summed up the most pervasive patterns in our data and observations by other scholars:

> Just a perspective, but on my way to and from work every day, I drive past no less than ten churches. Some of which, like Southern Baptist, have leaders who espouse my death. Right now, the Salvation Army collections outside the doors, but behind their red hats and jingle bells is an anti-LGBT religious organization. My life is besieged by those who wish to visit injustice and harm upon me.

As Bernadette Barton aptly points out, Christianity operates as a kind of all-seeing, panoptic force for lesbian and gay people in the southeastern United States, one that pressures them to adjust their behavior to anticipate negative interactions with religious neighbors, coworkers, and family members.[47] Responses like the one above suggest that perhaps a similar Christian panopticon impacts the lives of transgender people across the United States. Echoing case studies of a multitude of lesbian/gay people living in heavily Christian parts of the nation and in the face of continuous Christian influence in national politics, our respondents—across race, class, sex assigned at birth, gender (throughout the transgender umbrella), age, and religious identity—were well aware that Christian commitments to complementarity could translate into visceral harm, including but not limited to violence and discrimination.

It Doesn't Have to Be This Way

Although the examples above mirror many of the negative experiences and complex religious journeys outlined in prior studies of LG religious people, they are not the only echoes of the past revealed by our respondents. Rather, our respondents also demonstrate an important fact increasingly witnessed in studies of lesbian/gay religious experience within and beyond Christian (and even evangelical Christian) traditions: The danger, violence, and marginalization transgender people face from many (especially conservative Christian) religious people is not necessary or automatic. Stated another way, religious people do not have to be transphobic in their religious activities, beliefs, or other endeavors.

This observation comes to light in the stories of positive religious experiences shared by almost 20 percent of our respondents. As a twenty-five-year-old lower-class, white, gay transman who identified as spiritual noted, religious people are capable of including and welcoming transgender people into their rituals and groups:

> Every time I get heated about trans or gay issues at or after our discussion group, the next time the guy that runs it sees me he asks to make sure that he didn't offend me. One time, someone else was being sort of homophobic and after a bit the same leader figure said, "There is no place for homophobia or racism in our religion." That made me very comfortable. I'm impressed by this because I'm pretty sure I'm the first queer person to even be close to them.

A thirty-three-year-old middle-class, white, queer transwoman who identified as a Quaker added: "My meeting has been as supportive as they could be, and another meeting hosted the Philadelphia Trans Health Conference for several years. My Quaker school was also broadly supportive, if a little ignorant on specifics." Much like the variation in lesbian/gay experiences of religious organizations, such examples reveal the possibility of religious organizations embracing transgender people.

Other respondents also noted the impact of supportive religious leaders who made them feel both welcome and safe within Christian and other religious organizations. For example, a forty-five-year-old lower-class, white, queer transman wrote:

> I have been fortunate to have primarily positive personal experiences with religious leaders as an adult. The most positive experiences I had was when I had been working at a Presbyterian church as a pianist for about three months before I began my transition. Although I thought the pastors (a cis heterosexual married couple) would be okay with me, I was ready to be let go when I asked to meet with them to talk about it. In that meeting, these two pastors were overjoyed for me and promised to do whatever they could to make the transition on the job as smooth as possible. They kept that promise. They made me feel not just accepted but celebrated.

A fifty-five-year-old lower-class, white, asexual, aromantic agender person who identified as a Presbyterian added: "When I was finally ready to admit who I am, my pastor was very supportive. When I was ready to let others know, she read my statement to the congregation. My church is the one place where I am completely accepted as me."

In fact, the theme of leadership within Christian organizations was a consistent part of most of the positive experiences with Christianity reported by our respondents. For example, a thirty-three-year-old middle-class, white, heterosexual, genderqueer person who identified as an agnostic recalled: "The church my mom and I started attending when I was about eight had an absolutely wonderful pastor. She was so kind, understanding, and helpful. It was her, more than anything, that made me comfortable with Christianity." A twenty-two-year-old lower-class, white, queer, genderqueer person who identified as pagan added:

> I bonded with the pastor through discussions about theology and life and by serving side-by-side during the services. I no longer identify as Christian or attend services regularly, and I have picked up a number of pagan traditions instead, but I keep in touch with my pastor, and he is one of a handful of people I know who seem to experience religion and spirituality in the same way that I do, even though we have different mythologies and perform different ceremonies.

A nineteen-year-old lower-class, white, asexual romantic transman who identified as pagan added: "I'm good friends with my youth leader from high school youth group. He is one of the kindest, good-hearted people I know. Not as common as one would think for Christians. He has always praised my talents and been a part of my support system."

Across these examples, our respondents also emphasized—as suggested in the last quote—the possibility for religious leaders and organizations to act in unexpected ways. Further, they noted that being transgender and religious often required educating others about their religious location and experience (with and without the help of religious leaders). However, as demonstrated by a twenty-eight-year-old lower-class, multiracial, intersex transman who identified as a Muslim, this was even more common for non-Christian respondents:

> I often get the question, "How can [you] be Muslim and trans?" Many have severe misconceptions of Islam, and being trans is not a sin in Islam since it's the way the Lord made us and our true nature, not something we do for perverse reasons. I wish there were more truthful facts about my religion in this country; it's hard being in a country that exclusively shames and attacks one religion based on the actions of a few people.

Like many LGBTQIA Christians, a handful of respondents pointed out that many cisgender/heterosexual/monosexual religious people had difficulty understanding that one could be transgender and also be Christian, pagan, Muslim, or a member of another religion. This type of education, as illustrated by a twenty-five-year-old lower-class, white, heterosexual transman who identified as Methodist, also involved correcting assumptions that religious groups would automatically be anti-LGBTQIA: "Despite growing up in a small conservative town, the Methodist church was home to quite the budding queer community, and this continued into my undergrad years with many of the Methodists (Presbyterians as well) who were super-progressive and outspoken with social justice issues." A twenty-eight-year-old middle-class, white, queer, gender-fluid person who identified as an atheist added: "I have to explain it to people, but a friend is a clergy member, and she transformed her flock into a more inclusive space and then left the church to teach white people about white supremacy."

These experiences—as well as the number of transgender people in our study and the USTS who ultimately found supportive religious communities after a period of searching—reveal that religion does not *have* to be a cisgender reality built upon the enforcement of complementarity. This is an important consideration, both because religious traditions play a powerful role in broader social norms and assumptions and because religions can have a dramatic impact on the lives of people within them. Just as the respondents quoted above were deeply harmed in many religious contexts, religion can function as a powerful source of affirmation, as noted by a fifty-five-year-old middle-class, white, lesbian transwoman who identified as a Christian and echoed a handful of other respondents with similar experiences:

> My church saved my life when I was outed. I had to own the unavoidable fact that I was transgender, and I was not entirely able to do that. My church dragged me through a couple of years when the notion of not living was in the forefront of my mind, without regard to whatever pressing matter I had to attend to. They opened up and embraced me. The elderly women who helped me herd my kids scolded me for not reaching out sooner. When I transitioned, it was a nonevent and a collective sigh of relief. I have been blessed beyond belief.

Though much rarer than both journeys between traditions and explicitly negative experiences with religious people, organizations, and traditions, cases
like this demonstrate that religion—Christianity-based or otherwise—does
not have to be a negative force in the lives of transgender people. Rather, it is
up to the ways the people within various religious contexts interpret and act
upon their beliefs concerning the supernatural, the world they inhabit, and
other people.

At the same time, however, it is noteworthy that the transgender people
of color who shared their religious experiences with us were much less likely
to report only or mostly positive experiences. Although their voices emerged
equal to those of white transgender people in terms of journeys through and
between religious traditions and negative experiences with Christianity, only
a handful were among the respondents who reported mostly positive experiences.[48] Although this observation does not change the overall point that religious organizations can become more transgender inclusive, it does indicate
that the position of transgender people of color within religious organizations
may be even more complicated than that of whites.[49] This suggests that there
may be much to learn not only from analyses of transgender religious experience but also from specific aspects of such experience within and between
different racial populations.

CONTINUITY AND CHANGE

Although studies of lesbian/gay religious experience have proliferated in the
past thirty years, revealing a complicated relationship that both changes in
some ways and remains stable in other ways over time, studies of transgender
religious experience are only beginning at present. This is the same situation
with such studies focused on bisexual, asexual, intersex, and poly populations,
which often intersect with transgender communities much like they do with
cisgender ones. Here, we have continued the process of integrating transgender people into such studies while demonstrating how contemporary transgender religious experiences echo patterns of the past in both positive and
negative ways. Put simply, Christianity itself can become a dangerous system
of inequality for transgender people, but religion more broadly also has at
least the potential to be a source of affirmation and welcome for us. Overall,
however, transgender religious experiences are characterized by patterns of

searching for a faith tradition that feels comfortable over the course of many years, in much the same way that such patterns were found in earlier studies of LG religious people.

These observations speak to long-standing studies about the continuity and change of religious and other ideological systems of knowledge.[50] Scholars have long noted that mainstream (and thus privileged) social institutions and sources of knowledge production do not typically change or stay the same in any absolute manner; rather, such structures typically shift just enough to keep pace with mainstream society while maintaining enough continuity to appeal to a particular niche or population segment that might become disgruntled or otherwise problematic if too much transformation occurs. Religious traditions within the United States provide an example wherein change has occurred (at varied levels and to varied extents) in response to LGBTQIA populations, but at the same time, many things remain the same. In the next chapter, we outline a similar pattern of continuity and change in medical science.

NOTES

1. For work on transgender support groups, see Schrock, "Transsexuals' Narrative Construction"; and Schrock and Reid, "Transsexuals' Sexual Stories." For similar dynamics in gay Christian support groups, see Wolkomir, *Be Not Deceived.* For studies on ex-gay Christian support groups see Erzen, *Straight to Jesus;* and Ponticelli, "Crafting Stories."

2. In Lain's case, some of zir first meetings between LGBTQIA life and religion came in their twenties when people in Chicago and Florida, at different times, sought to save zir due to zir presentation of gender/sexual nonconformity.

3. Mathers, "Expanding on the Experiences"; Mathers, Sumerau, and Cragun, "The Limits of Homonormativity"; Sumerau, Cragun, and Mathers, "Cisgendering Reality"; Sumerau, Mathers, and Cragun, "Incorporating Transgender Experience."

4. See, for example, Aune, "Feminist Spirituality"; Avishai, Jafar, and Rinaldo, "A Gender Lens"; Barrett-Fox, *God Hates;* Barton, *Pray the Gay Away;* Burke, *Christians under Covers;* Gerber, "Grit, Guts, and Vanilla Beans"; Khurshid, "Islamic Traditions of Modernity"; Prickett, "Negotiating Gendered Religious Space"; Rodriguez and Follins, "Did God Make Me"; Wilcox, *Queer Women;* and Zion-Waldoks, "Politics of Devoted Resistance."

5. Moon and Tobin, "Sunsets and Solidarity." See also Barrett-Fox, *God Hates*; Barton, *Pray the Gay Away*; Burke, *Christians under Covers*; Erzen, *Straight to Jesus*; Jordan, *The Invention of Sodomy*; Moon, *God, Sex, and Politics*; Sumerau and Cragun, *God Loves (Almost) Everyone*; Fetner, *How the Religious Right*; Heath, *One Marriage*; Wilcox, *Coming Out in Christianity*; Wilcox, *Queer Women*; Wilcox, *Queer Nuns*; and Wolkomir, *Be Not Deceived,* for similar observations over time and within different religious-sexual-gender traditions. See also El-Rouayheb, *Before Homosexuality*; Rinaldo, *Mobilizing Piety*; and Najmabadi, *Women with Mustaches,* for discussions related to Islam. See also Dzmura, *Balancing*; and Schneer and Aviv, *Queer Jews,* for discussions of gender and sexuality related to Judaism. See Pattanaik, *The Man,* for examples from Hinduism. See Fuhrmann, *Ghostly Desires,* for examples from Buddhism.

6. While there are varied LGBTQIA histories and relationships in every religious tradition, here we focus our discussion on Christianity, as it holds the place of most power and privilege among the many religions practiced in contemporary US society; see also Barton, *Pray the Gay Away*; and Barrett-Fox, *God Hates*.

7. See discussion of similar concepts beyond the religious case in chapters 1 and 3.

8. West and Fenstermaker, "Doing Difference."

9. See Davidman, *Rootless World*; and Kleinman, *Equals before God*, for discussions of relationships between Western religious development and patriarchy. See Perkinson, *White Theology*, for discussion of relationships between Western religious development and white supremacy.

10. See McQueeney, "We Are God's"; Moon, *God, Sex, and Politics*; Wolkomir, *Be Not Deceived*; and Wilcox, *Coming Out in Christianity*.

11. Although unmentioned in work to date, part of this issue may arise in the tendency for queer, sexualities, and/or LGBTQIA scholarship to focus more on cities, college towns, and regions (i.e., West, Northeast) buffered or otherwise disconnected from the heart of the Bible Belt. In such cases, many people, like Lain, experience religious forces in more abstract ways or tied to national politics and often witness a combination of many moderate, liberal, and non-Christian traditions in the same social space. Especially considering that demographic evidence suggests the largest regional population of LGBTQIA people in the nation is in the Bible Belt and specifically the southeast heart of the Bible Belt (see Compton, *Other, Please Specify*; Stone, "The Geography"), coupled with observations of how religion operates as a form of panopticon in the Bible Belt in ways that are far more visceral

and ever-present than other parts of the nation (see Barton, *Pray the Gay Away*), scholars from and working in other parts of the nation may be more easily (like Lain) able to think about sex/gender/sexuality without considering religion at the same time that people who grew up in the Bible Belt have trouble thinking about these topics without consideration of the role of religion (like J). There is no way to know, at present, if such geographic factors play a role in the development of these interrelated though usually separate fields, but it presents an interesting theoretical question for further study.

12. But see Barton, *Pray the Gay Away*; Mathers, Sumerau, and Cragun, "The Limits of Homonormativity"; and Sumerau and Cragun, *God Loves (Almost) Everyone*.

13. See Avishai, "'Doing Religion'"; Sumerau, Mathers, and Cragun, "Incorporating Transgender Experience."

14. Although we offer a snapshot of the complexity of recent religious-sexual-gender history specifically focused on LGBTQIA communities here, it is worth remembering that there are many events not contained in this snapshot as well as ongoing tensions and collaborations between religious groups and other marginalized communities within US society; see the citations throughout this section for more information on the breadth and depth of this topic over the last century.

15. Fetner, *How the Religious Right*. See Barrett-Fox, *God Hates*, for a more recent analysis of the Religious Right.

16. See also Wilcox, "Of Markets," for examples of this over time.

17. Although such patterns impacted the entire community in varied ways, most research to date focuses only on the experiences and movement organizations of LG people in relation to religion and US policy.

18. For examples of this history, see Wilcox, *Coming Out in Christianity*, and Dignity newsletters published by DignityUSA since the end of the 1960s.

19. For studies focused on these groups see, for example, Loseke and Cavendish, "Producing Institutional"; Sumerau, "Mobilizing"; Sumerau, Cragun, and Mathers, "'I Found God'"; Thumma, "Negotiating"; Wilcox, *Coming Out in Christianity*; and Wolkomir, *Be Not Deceived*.

20. For discussion of sin see Sumerau, Mathers, and Cragun, "'Can't Put.'" For discussion of sexual sin, see Sumerau, Cragun, and Barbee, "'This Incredible Monster.'"

21. For examples of these groups, see Erzen, *Straight to Jesus*; Ponticelli, "Crafting Stories"; Robinson and Spivey, "The Politics"; and Wolkomir, *Be Not Deceived*.

22. For more examples of LG experience in religious groups not necessarily tied to Dignity, the Metropolitan Community Churches, or other specific organizations as well as studies of such experience among people of color, see also Moore, "Articulating a Politics"; Pitt, "'Killing'"; Pitt, "Still Looking"; Rodriguez, "At the Intersection"; and Thomas and Olson, "Beyond the Culture War."

23. Barrett-Fox, *God Hates*; Chambre, *Fighting*; Fetner, *How the Religious Right*; France, *How to Survive*; Sontag, *Illness*.

24. It also rose as a result of societal patterns of cisnormativity, mononormativity, patriarchy, white supremacy, middle-class respectability, and other systems with religious support that also find voice, as noted in chapter 3, in LGBTQIA communities embedded within broader US sociocultural norms and socialization processes at specific time points; see Duggan, *The Twilight*.

25. See also Kruse, *One Nation*; and Bernstein and Taylor, *The Marrying Kind?*

26. See also Fetner and Heath, "Studying the 'Right,'" for discussion of experiences they had studying members of these movements and groups.

27. See again Wilcox, *Queer Women*.

28. See again Moon, *God, Sex, and Politics*.

29. There are at least three other elements of these conflicts that we do not specifically discuss here—Parents, Families, and Friends of Lesbians and Gays (PFLAG), ally groups like gay/straight alliances, and sex education programs. We do not address these movements (1) for clarity in the narrative and (2) because while they often involve religion, they are not necessarily tied to religious domains in their varied incarnations. For information on PFLAG or other similar groups throughout this time, see Broad, "Coming Out"; and Fields, "Normal Queers." For information on ally groups during this period, see Fetner and Kush, "Gay-Straight Alliances"; and Mathers, Sumerau, and Ueno, "'This Isn't Just Another.'" For information on sex education programs and debates, see Fields, *Risky Lessons*; and Garcia, *Respect Yourself, Protect Yourself*. Finally, recent years suggest another role played in such dynamics by the emergence of atheist movements and churches, which may play a greater role in future years. For information on such movements and churches, see Cimino and Smith, *Atheist Awakening*.

30. Fetner, "Same as It Ever Was." See also Stone, "Gender Panics."

31. For a review of such attitudinal studies, see Adamcyzk, *Cross-National*, on public opinion regarding homosexuality; for more examples beyond studies of religion and LGBTQIA experience, see Worthen, "An Argument," for a review.

32. See Cragun, Williams, and Sumerau, "From Sodomy"; Sumerau and Cragun, "'Why Would'"; and Thomas and Olson, "Beyond the Culture War."

33. See Sumerau and Cragun, *God Loves (Almost) Everyone*, as well as n. 3 in this chapter.

34. See chapter 3.

35. See Mathers, Sumerau, and Cragun, "The Limits of Homonormativity"; Sumerau and Cragun, *God Loves (Almost) Everyone*; Sumerau, Grollman, and Cragun, "'Oh My God'"; Cragun and Sumerau, "The Last Bastion"; and Cragun and Sumerau, "No One Expects a Transgender Jew."

36. This may also be the case for asexual, queer, and intersex people, but as of this writing, there are no studies examining this question that we could locate.

37. See n. 34 in this chapter.

38. See James et al., *Report of the 2015 U.S. Transgender Survey*. Also note the similar pattern in bisexual populations; see, Sumerau, Mathers, and Lampe, "Learning from the Experiences."

39. Wilcox, "When Sheila's a Lesbian."

40. Bellah et al., *Habits of the Heart.*

41. Wilcox, *Queer Women*; see also Creek, "'Not Getting Any,'" 119–36; and Wolkomir, *Be Not Deceived*. For more on the journey some folks go through, see Sumerau, Cragun, and Mathers, "'I Found God.'"

42. We use *another* here as Jewish is sometimes used as a racial and religious identity, though we do not know whether or not this was the case for our respondent.

43. For cisgender readers who are not familiar with TDoR, the acronym refers to the annual Transgender Day of Remembrance, which transgender people observe in recognition of the lives lost to transphobia and the lives that continue into the future; see https://tdor.info and Lamble, "Retelling."

44. Humanism currently occupies a curious place between religious and nonreligious communities as it is sometimes conceptualized as a religion, as nonreligious, and even as a combination of the two in practice.

45. Sumerau and Cragun, "'I Think Some People.'"

46. Similar observations have been made in relation to LGB people, especially in the Bible Belt; see Barton, *Pray the Gay Away*, for such discussion and reviews.

47. See n. 45 in this chapter.

48. This pattern is another place where our respondents mirror the findings from the USTS, which notes journeys between faith communities and a combination of rejection and affirmation among transgender people of color in each of the breakout reports. See n. 12 in chapter 2 for information on the USTS breakout reports.

49. See Pitt, "Killing"; and Pitt, "Still Looking," for similar findings among LG people.

50. See, for example, Foucault, *History of Sexuality*, vol. 1; Kuhn, *Scientific Revolutions*; Stryker, *Transgender History*; Katz, *The Invention of Sodomy*. For specifically religious cases, see Ammerman, *Congregation and Community*; and Becker, *Congregations in Conflict*.

6

Transgender Experience with Medical Science

I (Lain) still find myself feeling surprised sometimes when I visit my doctors. Usually I'm surprised that I feel safe, comfortable, understood, and affirmed. This is because I still occasionally have nightmares about terrible experiences with other doctors, years ago, and how such experiences led me to avoid mental and physical healthcare providers for years. I remember my body being treated like an anomaly or simply an object. I remember being misgendered and told that transgender wasn't a real thing. I remember shaking with fear any time I thought about going to a doctor for any reason. I shake a little bit thinking about it right now. Even more so, however, I remember—as noted in the last chapter in relation to religion—realizing that it didn't have to be that way. I can still see my current doctors asking about my pronouns, providing me with transgender-specific guidance and resources, and asking me questions so they could better understand my needs and body as a nonbinary transgender person seeking medical care.

I also understand that even given the terrible experiences I had with doctors before finding my current medical providers, I am somewhat fortunate when I think about J's experiences with medical science. I wasn't told I was an abomination by doctors. I didn't have doctors try to diagnose me as mentally or physically disabled due to my gender identity. I have not been refused service or had police called on me by doctors. I haven't had a doctor tell me that I got what I deserved after being assaulted by people who did not take kindly to my outfit. But even these and other terrible experiences are not the whole story in J's case, either. Although she would not have believed me if I or anyone else tried to tell her so in the 1990s or 2000s, she has also more recently seen that it doesn't have to be this way. Rather, thanks to the help, expertise, and protection provided by her legal spouse,[1] Dr. Alexandra (Xan) C. H. Nowakowski, even J has now encountered medical scientists capable of stepping outside of cisgender realities enough to treat her with kindness, compassion, and competence. In fact, alongside Xan, J now often interacts and sometimes works with medical scientists to foster more transgender- and LGBQIA-inclusive approaches to medicine and bodies.

These examples speak to broader patterns in transgender people's experiences with medical science. As medical sociologist Austin Johnson shows,[2] medical science wields tremendous influence upon both the experiences of transgender people in relation to health, law, education, family, and overall social standing, and the ways cisgender Americans know about (or don't know about) and interpret transgender people in their own lives, political decisions, and development of social attitudes.[3] Put simply, medical sciences are currently in a period of transition after historically (and, for the most part, presently) relying upon and reproducing cisnormativity[4] in much the same way scholars have demonstrated their role in historical patterns of racism, sexism, ableism, and heterosexism.[5] In this chapter, we extend this emerging work by revealing transgender experiences with cisnormative—as well as some transgender-inclusive exceptions—medical science in the United States to date.

MEDICAL SCIENCE AND THE CISGENDERING OF REALITY

Much like dominant US religious traditions, Western medical science was founded on complementarity. As historical studies of the formation of scientific disciplines in the United States and Europe demonstrate, early Western scientists utilized dominant beliefs and norms among colonial authorities to reduce the biological diversity of humankind into two and only two sexes that complemented each other in reproductive heterosexuality.[6] Echoing (or maybe inspiring) their religious counterparts at the time, these newly created "natural laws" or "laws of nature" were utilized to justify the conquest and destruction of Native nations, people of color more broadly within and beyond colonial territories, and a variety of sex/gender/sexual nonconformists. They further supplemented scientific racism at the time as a collaborative justification for the enslavement of people of color regardless of—and sometimes justified by beliefs about—sex/gender/sexualities.[7] Likewise, medical science played a powerful role in the justification of scientific sexism that supported the subordination of cisgender women to the control and often violence of cisgender heterosexual men. By the end of the 1800s, these simplified renditions of nature were broadly accepted as objective statements of fact and truth throughout US and European physical, social, and medical sciences.

In many ways, much of the past century has involved the efforts of cisgender women, LGBQA people, intersex people, people of color, people with disabilities, and transgender people to correct these early scientific falsehoods (and dominant religious teachings) in pursuit of more empirical understandings of the world and the acquisition of civil rights.[8] At the same time, the past century includes massive numbers of cisgender women, LGBQA people, intersex people, people of color, people with disabilities, and transgender people who were institutionalized, criminalized, killed, assaulted, or otherwise devastated by people utilizing scientifically backed beliefs in sex/gender/sexual complementarity to justify their religious, scientific, and/or political goals.[9] Although it appears unlikely that anyone could now empirically ascertain whether political, scientific, or religious authorities adopted these cisgender realities first, such notions of complementarity continue to be promoted (to varying degrees) through each of these institutional power structures, to the detriment of racial, sexed, gendered, sexual, and (dis)ability civil rights movements today.

Such patterns within historical and contemporary scientific practice reflect what social theorists have referred to as "sciences of oppression."[10] Specifically, sciences of oppression are those that developed within and after the Enlightenment period to justify the marginalization and disenfranchisement of minority populations that were considered to be a potential threat to the rise of rational, hierarchical, and capitalist restructuring of social, political, religious, and economic relations. Put simply, these forms of science legitimize the status quo and/or dominant religious norms rather than documenting empirical biological and social conditions. In such cases, scientific disciplines—intentionally or otherwise—ultimately serve to define some things (i.e., the existing power structure) as biologically and socially natural, and other things (i.e., minority groups) as biologically and socially unnatural. In much the same way religious traditions define what constitutes morality or immorality, oppressive sciences distinguish between which parts of bio- logical and social experience are recognized (or *how* they will be recognized) and which parts are not in a given society, at a given time, and in relation to prevailing political structures.

It is important to note, however, that any scientific tradition can become an oppressive science or move away from oppressive patterns over time. Scientific traditions, like all human-made beliefs, objects, and communities,[11] rely upon ongoing processes of interaction, interpretation, and affirmation (or accep- tance) by and between people. Thus, any type of science can take a multitude of forms, shift and change in a wide variety of ways, and serve any number of functions. For example, an oppressive science could be transformed into a more empirical or explicitly social justice–focused endeavor, just as empirical or explicitly social justice–focused sciences could become oppressive ones. In fact, scientific disciplines generally possess among their ranks practitioners who are seeking to accomplish each of these options, explicitly or not, inten- tionally or not. The distinction between these options, however, rests upon the beliefs and actions of scientists at work in a given field, at a given time, and in relation to a given set of political factors and circumstances that influence scientific endeavors, norms, literatures, and assumptions.

As a result of these factors, it is not surprising that historical relationships between medical science and LGBTQIA populations are at least as compli- cated as relationships between these populations and religion.[12] Early medical science, for example, defined all sex/gender/sexual variant people (i.e., every- one in the acronym) as abnormal, diseased, and in need of medical interven- tion.[13] Put simply, these endeavors rested on the belief that non-cisgender selfhood, nonheterosexual selfhood, and a host of other forms of sex/gender/ sexual diversity resulted from a biological and/or psychological inversion wherein one failed to develop proper sex/gender performances and sexual desires complementary to the assumed nature of a given set of genitals. Until the early 1970s (and in some cases, much more recently), these beliefs were used by scientific, religious, and governmental authorities to pathologize and criminalize same- and multiple-sex attractions, desires, and practices.[14] While beliefs like these continue to find voice in US society,[15] they have become much rarer in recent medical science.[16]

At the same time, sex/gender complementarity in US medical science has remained firm throughout the past century. In the case of sex, for example, medical scientists utilize their own discipline's creation of a two-sex system, which emerged in relation to various religious traditions, to justify unnecessary surgeries on children born with ambiguous genitalia.[17] Although such practices have no medical benefit and result in tremendous harm to the children in question, commitment to complementarity-based cisgender realities continues to justify such practices while contemporary intersex movements throughout the world push for an end to them.[18] In other words, the suggestion that one should "first, to do no harm" does not seem to apply when harm is required to maintain the sex/gender binary necessary for the existence and perpetuation of cisgender realities built upon complementarity. As intersex scholar Georgiann Davis shows, the surgical alteration of intersex children serves no purpose other than the reproduction of the long-standing fantasy (or supernatural belief) that there should only be two sexes allowed to exist within human populations.[19]

In the case of gender, the process is not the same; however, the intention to force people to fit within a two—and only two—sex/gender system persists.[20] Specifically, medical science controls whether or not one may receive gender-affirming care and whether such care involves transition resources (i.e., hormones, surgeries, and other medical options) or recognition of one's gender identity, relationship to the body, and conception of self as a person.[21] In so doing, medical science enforces a "scientific" narrative that limits what will or will not be recognized as transgender in terms of medical, legal, and other forms of recognition.[22] People who are able to adopt this narrative (because it fits their experience or for other reasons) may gain medical care, legal standing, and other forms of social recognition as transgender people. By the same token, people who are unable or unwilling to adopt this narrative (for whatever reason) become ineligible for the same resources and recognition.

In fact, many studies of transgender populations in the 1990s and early 2000s focused specifically on how transgender people learned to tell the life stories required by medical gatekeepers to gain access to care, and how the acquisition (or not) of medical recognition could exacerbate in-group tensions within transgender communities (see chapter 3 for more discussion on such tensions).[23] Then and now, the narrative necessary for medical recognition requires transgender people to pass through the same three general steps.[24]

First, one must express their experience of discomfort and distress about their gender throughout the life course. Then, one must acquire a psychiatric diagnosis attesting to one's discomfort/distress due to gender variance. Finally, one must access gender-affirming medical intervention. If one completes these steps—under the supervision of medical scientists, that is—then one can be medically recognized as transgender.[25]

It is noteworthy that this process has not really changed much at all in recent decades. Although the language and terminology have become less damning, explicitly transphobic, and pathologizing in incremental steps over time, the process continues to rely upon diagnosis of gender variation as a medical disorder that can be overcome only by submitting to the power of medical authorities and interventions. Importantly, this narrative is useful for many transgender people, as it both legitimizes the discomfort many of us feel in relation to sex/gender and also provides a medically affirmed path for transgender people who seek gender-affirming medical procedures, hormones, or other care at some point in their lives. At the same time, however, it is also problematic for many transgender people, since it delineates what medical science will recognize as transgender in very narrow terms, necessitates medical control over transgender people as a requirement for healthcare services and medical recognition, and defines the source of our discomfort as located within our own bodies and minds instead of the cisgender realities we are forced to inhabit.[26]

As we have shown throughout this book, however, transgender people are a much more diverse community than medical science acknowledges at present.[27] At the same time, the historical mistreatment of transgender people by medical science—and other social institutions—leaves many of us understandably fearful about granting any kind of access to or control over our bodies or lives to medical professionals unless absolutely necessary. Further, much of our discomfort and distress comes from having to navigate the cisgender realities of the rest of contemporary US society and dominant US religious norms. Although it is certainly possible that people could still face similar discomfort and distress in a more gender-expansive society,[28] there is no way to know that without first creating such a society to test this option in an empirical manner. In fact, as we show below, medical science practitioners themselves often cause many of us discomfort and distress related to our sex, gender, and bodies via their attempts to maintain cisgender realities at the expense of our healthcare access and needs.

HEALTH DISPARITIES AMONG TRANSGENDER POPULATIONS

Before proceeding to our respondents' experiences with medical scientists and other providers within the healthcare system, it is important to contextualize these experiences in relation to broader knowledge concerning transgender health. Quantitative researchers have begun to demonstrate significant health disparities in survey comparisons of transgender, gender-nonconforming, and cisgender populations.[29] Put simply, transgender people—and especially transgender people of color and LGBQIA transgender people—navigate significantly worse experiences and outcomes with medical science in the United States than other populations. Exploring this topic in the USTS, for example, the authors of the survey note the significant impact of violence, discrimination, and prejudice on transgender people's reported psychological and physical well-being. In fact, almost half (40 percent) of respondents (and J)[30] had attempted suicide at some point in their lives in response to their experiences in US society over time.

The USTS also outlines the current standing of its respondents in relation to medical access and other patterns of health disparity. More than half of the respondents, for example, had been refused medical care in the year prior to the survey, another one-fourth of respondents avoided doctors due to fear of mistreatment, and 33 percent did not see doctors because they could not financially afford to do so. This number—33 percent—was also the percentage of respondents who experienced negative treatment when they did go see doctors, and these patterns were again even worse for racial minorities and for transgender people with disabilities. Further, the USTS reveals that respondents were living with HIV/AIDS at nearly five times the rate of the US population, and such patterns were also starker among transwomen and even more so among black, Hispanic, and Native American transwomen. Additionally, compared to 5 percent of the broader US population, 39 percent of USTS respondents experienced serious psychological distress based on current medical and psychological measurements of such experience.

These patterns point to significant inequalities in health outcomes and healthcare experiences within transgender populations. At the same time, it is noteworthy that within both the USTS and our own sample, the majority of respondents did have health insurance, a resource often assumed to grant people access to proper medical care. In the USTS, for example, 86 percent of respondents had health insurance: 53 percent got health insurance from their employer and 33 percent purchased or received health insurance from the US government. In our sample, 82 percent of respondents had health insurance: 48 percent received from employers and 34 percent through governmental options. At the same time, about one-fourth of USTS respondents reported problems attempting to use insurance for their health care, and about 10 percent of our respondents mentioned these issues in their statements. Put simply, the acquisition of insurance may or may not lessen existing medical inequalities faced throughout contemporary US transgender populations.[31]

NAVIGATING CISGENDER MEDICAL SCIENCE

As we have done throughout this book, here we focus on the ways transgender people experience the cisgender realities created and maintained throughout US interactional and structural patterns of activity. In the case of transgender people's interactions with medical science, prior survey findings and case studies reveal both systemic health disparities in transgender populations compared to cisgender others as well as attempts of medical providers in specific local settings to embrace—or, more often, resist—the appearance of transgender people in their (most often) cisgender realities and cisnormative conceptions of medical science. Below we utilize the qualitative responses from our respondents to show how these patterns influence the lives of transgender people across the United States.

Refusal of Service

Although the USTS demonstrates that transgender people often experience refusal of service from medical providers specifically related to gender-affirming care, our respondents noted that such refusal impacts *all* facets of transgender people's health care. After writing about seeking a routine medical checkup, for example, a fifty-two-year-old lower-class, Hispanic, queer transman shared: "It didn't matter what for; I was refused just for being trans." A thirty-nine-year-old lower-class, black transman who did not report a sexual identity expressed the sentiments of many respondents in relation to both specifically transgender-related and broader medical care: "It has been hard to find a doctor that will deal with me." A twenty-six-year-old lower-class, white, heterosexual transwoman provided one of many startling cases of such issues: "I have been turned away in the ER while bleeding because 'I can't treat a trans person' even though my injury had nothing to do with being trans; I just needed stitches after being attacked."

Respondents also noted occasions when both transgender identities and medical scientific categorizing of transgender people as needing a "different type of medicine" created struggles in finding healthcare providers who would not refuse them service. A thirty-year-old lower-class, black, queer, genderfluid person, for example, wrote about the difficulty in even locating competent healthcare providers: "It's been near impossible for me to find a therapist who is LGBT friendly, that is, a therapist who doesn't feel like my past trauma shaped my sexuality and gender identity." A twenty-five-year-old middle-class, white, asexual aromantic, nonbinary person offered examples of many of the experiences respondents noted in relation to being refused or unable to find service:

> A reproductive health clinic told me I could only schedule an appointment with their trans specialist (who was only in the office once a month), even though I was looking for a basic pelvic exam that has nothing to do with my transition. I went to my university clinic for help with chronic pain, but instead of addressing my pain, the doctor spent the entire appointment telling me that as a trans person, I should be seeing a therapist. In the end, I got a referral to the counseling center and no help for my severe chronic pain. When I was twenty years old, a psychiatrist refused to help me with my anxiety because in her opinion I was "just a whiny, immature girl who wants to be a boy." She told me her twelve-year-old nephew was more mature than me.

Summarizing this and many other examples, a thirty-year-old upper-class, queer, nonbinary person who did not disclose a racial identity added: "I just could not get past the gatekeeping."

Although respondents who shared their interactions with medical providers who were unwilling to provide them services spanned racial, class, sex assigned at birth, gender, sexual, and religious identity groups, broader statistical portraits of these issues suggest similar patterns are even more pronounced among transgender people of color and transwomen. At the same time, however, our respondents who experienced medical service refusal, like those in the USTS, lived all over the United States and were not concentrated in any specific more liberal, moderate, or conservative region. Thus, these findings call for consideration of what, if anything, transgender people can do or where else they can go—regardless of the type of health care they are seeking and/or if they can even access the transportation and other resources necessary to pursue medical service—when medical professionals may not even be willing to see us as people, much less as patients in need of care.

Scientific Ignorance

As noted by the Institute of Medicine seven years ago (as of this writing), one social dynamic that exacerbates the patterns noted above is the lack of education scientists often receive about transgender people.[32] Put simply, commitment to cisgender realities throughout most physical and social sciences means that medical doctors, nurses, and nurse practitioners as well as others, often trained in the social sciences, who operate medical organizations, can complete their entire educational experience without having to learn about the bodies or lives of transgender (or intersex) people. This form of scientific ignorance creates conditions where transgender people—as noted in relation to broader cisgender realities in chapter 4—have to educate and survive the profound misinformation of medical care providers as part of seeking health care.

Rather than isolated incidences in specific locations, many of our respondents, like the fifty-nine-year-old middle-class, white, asexual romantic transwoman quoted next, shared experiences where they "[h]ave to educate almost everyone in health care." Such education, as illustrated in the following quote from a sixty-year-old middle-class, white, heterosexual, transgender person, often involves answering transphobic questions from medical scientists: "For example, I had a doctor actually ask me, 'So, you had it cut off or something?' Now, I just try not to go to healthcare 'professionals' if I can avoid it." Our respondents also noted that cisgender people—even medical providers who claim to prioritize care and empiricism in their work—were not very good students. For example, a twenty-eight-year-old middle-class, white, queer, genderqueer person stated: "They are fine with being ignorant; for example, mine always call me 'Ms.' or use my legal name even after I've repeatedly asked them not to and explained why. I also hate that I have to explain one hundred times, at least, why I can't be pregnant, because my husband is a transman."

In fact, some respondents shared experiences where it appeared that medical providers sought to protect and maintain the ignorance among their colleagues. Such cases involved doctors, nurses, and other healthcare practitioners explaining why it was okay that their colleagues didn't know things about anatomy or hormonal options or why they could not be expected to keep up with new information. As illustrated by the following quote from a thirty-five-year-old middle-class, white, bisexual transman, maintaining medical ignorance sometimes involved ignoring confidentiality expectations to warn other providers about transgender people seeking medical care:

> Most providers take it on themselves to "warn" other providers that I'm trans without asking my permission. Many providers ask questions about what it's like to be trans, when this information is completely irrelevant to the reason I've sought medical attention. Every single time a provider has to deal with my genitals I have to reassure them at length and repeatedly that the appearance of my genitals is normal for me. In general I have to say "That's normal for me" a lot.

Such ignorance on the part of medical providers concerning the biological and social diversity of the world they inhabit sometimes manifests in attempts to deceive transgender patients. A nineteen-year-old middle-class, white, asexual transman, for example, shared a common example that emerged in our data: "My doctor told me that trans men do not exist and that everyone my age questions their gender. She told me not to change my appearance because there was no reason to." Additionally, a twenty-year-old middle-class, asexual aromantic, nonbinary person who did not disclose a racial identity was one of the respondents who shared a common myth promoted by many conservative and religious political commentators over the years: "I had to stop seeing my 'doctor.' I said something to the effect of 'I don't identify as female,' and she said, 'Oh, don't tell me you're transgender; you know they stopped doing sex changes because all the people who got them kept going back and saying they wanted their old sex back.'"

As others have noted, the ignorance of medical scientists and others in the business of health is not surprising considering the significant influence of cisgender realities in shaping historical and contemporary forms of medical and broader scientific education in the United States.[33] Our respondents, as illustrated in the following quote from a twenty-seven-year-old lower-class, white, queer transman, recognized the ways medical practice had been built as a specifically cisgender reality:

> The system is structured towards confining people in their birth sex. There are so many gatekeepers it is difficult to ever feel like you have agency, and even after acquiring care, on medical forms you are still referred to by birth sex as if nothing has changed. It's been really problematic that I need several diagnoses and my mental status questioned and pathologized just to receive the health care I need.

A nineteen-year-old middle-class, white, asexual, nonbinary person added: "The medical system is just cis people who don't care about the rest of us. I am forced to misgender myself on intake forms, and everything else is about only M or F." In fact, as revealed in the next quote from a fifty-five-year-old middle-class, white, lesbian transwoman, even when medical scientists seemed supportive of our respondents, their own ignorance about our communities often created problems: "I had to teach my primary doctor about trans health care. Initially, she told me she didn't know of any doctors in our network who did hormone therapy, but then I found some and let her know who they were. She wanted to help me but just didn't seem to know anything."

Surviving Cisgender Medical Providers

In chapter 4, we outlined the ways cisgender people's attempts to maintain their own cisnormative beliefs and customs required transgender people to experience much of social life as a form of survival. Although we focused on cisgender people overall in that chapter, here we demonstrate that this is not simply an uneducated or otherwise exceptional occurrence; even the most educated people in the United States, with the most—or at least some of the most—scientific training, such as doctors and other medical providers, embrace beliefs and practices that facilitate the ongoing operation of cisgender realities at the expense of transgender lives, bodies, and needs. In this section, we demonstrate these broader social patterns of survival in the context of our respondents' experiences with medical providers.

Our respondents' negative interactions with medical professionals mirrored the examples they shared about broader encounters with cisgender people. For example, a fifty-three-year-old lower-class, Native American, asexual transman echoed many who experienced verbal or discursive aggression[34] in medical settings: "I went to the VA to enroll in health care there. The person I had to hand the paperwork to loudly exclaimed to the entire lobby, *'Did you have the sex change surgery?'* loud enough for everyone to hear." A thirty-two-year-old middle-class, black, fluid transman added: "A doctor told me they needed to see my genitals when they heard I was trans, even though I only went in for a sinus infection." A thirty-year-old lower-class, black, asexual transman added: "Doctors and nurses constantly use the wrong pronoun, and assistants trying to empathize with my pain after a procedure say, 'It's a female thing; it'll be okay,' when I am a transman/male presenting, and at an LGBT clinic at that." A forty-six-year-old middle-class, Native American, pansexual transwoman summarized what many of our respondents said: "I receive judgmental bashing over 90 percent of the time from medical professionals. The doctors, nurses, and staff routinely and purposefully misgender me or delay and deny treatment."

The need to survive and manage the aggression of cisgender medical providers was not, however, only expressed by transgender people of color. Like the people of color quoted above, a fifty-two-year-old middle-class, white, pansexual transman echoed many across racial identities by sharing: "Doctors will make it very clear that they don't want to treat people like me. I will constantly get dirty looks and rudeness from the staff as well." A twenty-nine-year-old middle-class, white, asexual, nonbinary person added:

> I've had nonconsensual physical exams performed on me by medical professionals who wouldn't take no for an answer. I've been misgendered and told I couldn't possibly need services since I'm an X. I've had them assume I'm a cis man and my partner a cis woman, without asking or meeting my partner. I've been assumed to be a cis gay man who only has receptive anal sex.

Additionally, a twenty-nine-year-old middle-class, white, bisexual transwoman wrote: "I run into very biphobic, sexist, and transphobic healthcare providers, for example, the therapist who said that she didn't 'buy' that I was bisexual, and medical doctors who don't feel like they can see me because I'm transgender." A twenty-two-year-old lower-class, white, bisexual transman added: "I came close to death because a doctor chose to belittle my symptoms when he learned of my transgender status. I was dying, and he was interested in my genitals instead."

Medical Science Also Doesn't Have to Be This Way

As we discussed in chapter 5 in relation to religion and earlier in this chapter while discussing the development of medical science over time, our respondents also demonstrate that healthcare provision does not have to rely upon and reproduce cisgender realities.[35] In fact, about 40 percent of our respondents (including some of those quoted above) reported similar journeys to the ones people take from one religion or religious organization to the next in search of transgender-inclusive medical care. Like Lain and J, the respondents who shared these journeys reported finding healthcare providers with whom they had positive interactions, though often only after much searching. In fact, there were respondents—only about 5 percent—who reported only positive experiences with providers, which demonstrates that it is at least possible to do medical science without cisnormativity.

Transgender people who reported entirely positive experiences, like the forty-seven-year-old lower-class, white, lesbian transwoman quoted next, generally noted feeling "blessed" or "fortunate" since they were likely aware of how rare such experience is: "I have been very fortunate to have had accepting and supportive healthcare providers. All my providers refer to me by my correct gender and have changed all my forms to match." Further, as illustrated by a twenty-five-year-old lower-class, white, lesbian transwoman, these respondents pointed out that wholly positive experiences could occur even when medical providers were ignorant about transgender people and issues: "I have a very trans-friendly doctor and therapist. My experiences have been 100 percent positive. My psychiatrist (different from my therapist) has always been accepting, but when I initially came out to her in 2012, she had no knowledge of trans issues and couldn't help me much. She has more experience now and has remained supportive for me the entire time." A nineteen-year-old middle-class, white, gay transman added: "My general practitioner was very supportive when I came out to her. She offered to use my chosen name and does use my he/him pronouns. She and I talk about it, and she makes sure I have resources for sexual health and know my options." Although exceptional, such cases reveal that medical science—and the delivery of it to transgender populations—can leave behind its cisnormative heritage.

At the same time, however, it is important to note that all of the people who described entirely positive experiences in our sample were both white and monosexual. In terms of race, this observation echoes statistical and qualitative portraits finding that transgender people of color—like their cisgender peers—are more likely to have negative and/or complicated experiences with medical science and practitioners due to implicit or explicit racial patterns among providers and within healthcare settings.[36] At the same time, however, it is hard to draw any conclusions here when the majority of our sample consists of white transgender people, and the majority of our sample did not report entirely—or even mostly—positive experiences with providers. As such, we point this out to once again join calls for more systematic examination of the myriad ways race may influence, impact, and potentially shape aspects of transgender experience.

Although there is much scholarship on relationships between race and medicine,[37] the second part of this observation raises questions without answers in existing studies of sexualities, gender, and health. Especially since transgender people—more broadly and within our sample—are much more likely to identify as nonmonosexual (i.e., not lesbian/gay/straight/ heterosexual), it is intriguing that only monosexual respondents reported entirely or mostly positive healthcare experiences, and that bi+/pan/queer/ fluid and asexual (across the romantic spectrum) respondents provided the vast majority of the negative experiences—within and beyond explicitly LGBTQIA healthcare settings—about interactions with medical science. It is not possible to tease out this observation with our current data, although we can speculate about potential mechanisms at work that systematic study of health experiences across gender/sexualities might examine over time.[38]

For example, this pattern could arise as part of the tensions within LGBTQIA communities discussed in chapter 3. Specifically, the processes of monosexualizing reality noted by our respondents in such settings may extend to both explicitly LGBTQIA and broader healthcare organizations. At the same time, this pattern may arise from recent advances in the social recognition and acceptance of lesbian/gay people that have not been shown to extend to bi+/pan/queer/fluid populations or transgender people more broadly. Stated another way, it could be another example of the conditional acceptance of only those who fit the homonormative ideal. Finally, considering limitations in scientific work and our sample itself, this could be a pattern that might not appear in another future systematic study of transgender experiences with medical providers. In any case, the pattern itself raises interesting questions about transgender—as well as nonmonosexual—experience that, at present, escapes explanation in the literature.

It is also noteworthy that while transgender people's experiences with medical science reveal similar journeys (i.e., shopping for acceptance) to the religious experiences in chapter 5, our respondents were more likely to mention exceptions to the general pattern of cisnormativity in the case of religion than they were in the case of medical science. This is an important pattern considering that many people argue that science is likely to shift and change in relation to new information at a faster rate than religion.[39] Although it is beyond the scope of our data to explore the veracity of this argument at present, the case of transgender experiences with medical science in comparison to such experiences with religion suggest this may be an important question for both the ongoing development of science and societal understandings about differences and similarities between science and religion as mechanisms of "official" knowledge production.

CONTINUITY AND CHANGE REVISITED

Similar to our discussion of religion in chapter 5, the above examination of US medical science through transgender eyes reveals patterns of continuity and change. In terms of continuity, we see both sustained commitment to cisgender realities on the part of medical science that contribute to ongoing negative experiences and barriers to access among our respondents. In terms of change, we again see examples that reveal that medical science does not *have* to conform to the cisgender realities of its historical foundation. Overall, however, our respondents report overwhelmingly negative experiences with medical professionals, wherein medical settings and providers tend to offer more officially sanctioned (based on the norms and educational practices in medical sciences) forms of the marginalization, harassment, and discrimination transgender people face in the broader US society.

These observations speak to emerging studies focused on transgender health experiences and the ways medical sciences are adjusting to greater transgender visibility. They also, unfortunately, reveal that many aspects of the medical models and the disenfranchisement transgender people faced in 1990s medical settings continue today. Although many health programs have suggested—and even begun to implement—greater recognition of sex/gender/sexual diversity in undergraduate and graduate medical curricula, such efforts will take time to achieve significant change and will most likely benefit younger, more so than older, transgender populations. In the meantime, however, transgender people of varied ages are already in need of proper, competent health care, and our respondents' examples suggest that one of the hardest—if not the hardest—parts about accessing health-related resources involves finding medical providers capable of practicing medical science beyond the limitations of cisgender realities.

NOTES

1. As noted in chapter 2, J has multiple life partnerships, but only one of them is legally recognized due to continuing marital inequality that only allows one legal marital partner at a time.

2. See Johnson, "Transgender People"; and Johnson, "Normative Accountability"; Johnson, "Rejecting." See also Erickson-Schroth, *Trans Bodies*; Pearce, *Understanding Trans Health*; shuster, "Uncertain Expertise"; Vincent, *Transgender Health*; and Xavier et al., "Transgender Health Care Access."

3. See also Bolin, *In Search*; Miller and Grollman, "The Social Costs"; Nowakowski and Sumerau, "Out of the Shadow"; and Schleifer, "Make Me Feel."

4. Bennett, "'Born this Way'"; Denny, "The Politics"; Drescher, "Queer Diagnoses"; Johnson, "Normative Accountability"; Rubin, "The Logic"; Stryker, *Transgender History*; and Walters, *The Tolerance Trap*.

5. See Collins, *Black Sexual Politics*; and Washington, *Medical Apartheid*, on race. See Katz, *The Invention of Sodomy*; and Scarce, *Smearing*, on heterosexuality and heterosexism. See Chrisler and Caplan, "The Strange Case"; and Calasanti and Selvin, *Gender, Social Inequality*, for sexism.

6. See citations in n. 2; see also, Butler, *Gender Trouble*; Foucault, *Archaeology of Knowledge*; Foucault, *History of Sexuality*, vols. 1, 2, and 3; Samuels, *Fantasies of Identification*; Somerville, *Queering the Color Line*; Warner, *The Touble with Normal*.

7. Somerville, "Scientific Racism."

8. Samuels, *Fantasies of Identification*.

9. Samuels, *Fantasies of Identification*; Somerville, *Queering the Color Line*; Washington, *Medical Apartheid*.

10. Foucault, *Discipline and Punish*; Foucault, *The Order*; Lynch, "The Power"; Sweet and Decoteau, "Contesting Normal"; and Marx, *Capital*.

11. See Blumer, *Symbolic Interaction*; Butler, *Gender Trouble*; Goffman, "The Arrangement"; Kleinman, *Feminist Fieldwork*; and Washington, *Medical Apartheid*.

12. See Burke, "Resisting Pathology"; Castañeda, "Developing Gender"; Davis, *Contesting Intersex*; Eyssel et al., "Needs and Concerns"; Gehi and Arkles, "Unraveling Injustice"; Johnson, "Normative Accountability"; Karkazis, *Fixing Sex*; Khalili, Leung, and Diamant, "Finding the Perfect Doctor"; Kosenko, Rintamaki, Raney, and Maness, "Transgender Patient Perceptions"; Poteat, German, and Kerrigan, "Managing Uncertainty"; Redfern and Sinclair, "Improving Health"; shuster, "Uncertain Expertise"; Stroumsa, "The State"; Stryker, *Transgender History*; Torres et al., "Improving Transgender"; and Unger, "Care."

13. Foucault, *History of Sexuality*, vol. 1; Somerville, *Queering the Color Line*.

14. Bryant, "In Defense," 455–75.

15. Erzen, *Straight to Jesus*; Gerber, "Grit, Guts, and Vanilla Beans"; Robinson and Spivey, "The Politics"; Wolkomir, *Be Not Deceived*. See also Sumerau and Cragun, *God Loves (Almost) Everyone*.

16. There are many more aspects of LGBTQIA life impacted by medical science; for reviews, see France, *How to Survive*; MacDonald et al., "Transmasculine Individuals' Experiences"; Mamo, *Queering Reproduction*; More, "The Pregnant Man"; Ramirez-Valles, *Queer Aging*; Scarce, *Smearing*; Schrock, Sumerau, and Ueno, "Sexualities"; Somerville, *Queering the Color Line*; Trotsenberg, "Gynecological Aspects"; and Warner, *The Trouble with Normal*, for examples.

17. Fausto-Sterling, *Sexing the Body*.

18. For more information on intersex populations, movements, and studies, see, for example, Davis, *Contesting Intersex*; Kessler, *Lessons*; Karkazis, *Fixing Sex*; Costello, "Not a 'Medical Miracle'"; Costello, "Trans and Intersex Children"; and Costello, "Understanding Intersex Relationship Issues."

19. Davis, *Contesting Intersex*; see also Samuels, *Fantasies of Identification*.

20. Califia, *Sex Changes*; Hughes, "Beyond the Medical Model of Gender Dysphoria"; Prosser, *Second Skins*; Roen, "Transgender Theory"; Romeo, "Beyond a Medical Model."

21. See Johnson, "Normative Accountability," for a breakdown of such protocols in transgender medical cases as well as the diagnostic shifts that have occurred since 1980 in relation to transgender identities, medical services, and psychological definitions. For debates concerning the role of medicine in transgender lives, see also Burke, "Resisting Pathology." For information on the history of psychological reactions to sex/gender variance and diagnostic terms, see Stryker, *Transgender History*.

22. For readers unfamiliar with these dynamics between medicine and other social institutions, at present, one often requires medical recognition of transgender status to acquire legal standing and recognition; to acquire potentially better treatment from families, coworkers, and others in society; and to be recognized—and again seek potentially better treatment—in schools, colleges, and governmental offices. As such, the relationships between transgender (and intersex) people with medical science are not simply about medicine or medical care but also often tied to their broader social experiences with cisgender US institutions, populations, and norms; see Johnson, "Normative Accountability," for more discussion on these issues.

23. In fact, J remembers crafting her narrative in relation to lessons from others in the 1990s (she can still recite it by heart). See also, Gagné and Tewksbury, "Conformity Pressures"; and Gagné and Tewksbury, "Knowledge and Power."

24. We say *general* because such narratives can contain many elements and more or less exposition (required by a given medical provider or not), but the overall pattern of the story necessary for medical recognition remains the same. In fact, there are and long have been worksheets people may acquire that tell them how to craft their narratives for the purposes of convincing medical scientists to recognize our humanity and medical needs.

25. Arlene Stein's recent book *Unbound* follows four transmasculine people as they work through this process over time.

26. See n. 20 in this chapter. See also Dewey and Gesbeck, "(Dys)Functional Diagnosing."

27. For examples of diverse medical needs among transgender people, see, Cruz, "Assessing Access"; Peitzmeier et al., "Health Impact"; Rebchook et al., "The Transgender"; Rosh, "Beyond Categorical"; Scheim et al., "Inequities in Access to HIV"; Sevelius, Patouhas, Keatley, and Johnson, "Barriers and Facilitators"; and Spicer, "Healthcare Needs."

28. For example, many transgender people experience so much tension and conflict with their bodies (that may or may not be tied to social norms or interactions) that

gender-affirming hormones and surgeries can mean the difference between healthy living and, to name a few possibilities, suicide, self-harm, and/or recurring physical and/or psychological breakdowns and conflicts. Put simply, even if we created a more gender-inclusive social structure or more safe spaces for gender variance, access to affirmational healthcare services would likely still be a very important need for many who need such care for survival, and even more so, for transgender people regardless of the types of healthcare needs and desires we have over the life course.

29. See, for example, Giblon and Bauer, "Health Care Availability"; and James et al., *Report of the 2015 U.S. Transgender Survey.*

30. Lain has not attempted suicide, but they have thought about it passively at times in zir life.

31. For more on issues related to health insurance in the United States, see Quadagno, *One Nation.*

32. Dewey, "Challenges of Implementing."

33. See Davis, Dewey, and Murphy, "Giving Sex," 490–514; Denny, "The Politics," 9–20; and Johnson, "Normative Accountability." See also n. 10 in this chapter.

34. shuster, "Punctuating Accountability."

35. See also Reisner et al., "Comprehensive Transgender Healthcare."

36. Quadagno, *The Color*; Washington, *Medical Apartheid.*

37. For reviews and examples, see Carter and Anthony, "Good, Bad, and Extraordinary"; Link and Phelan, "Fundamental Causes"; Phelan and Link, "Is Racism"; Quadagno, *The Color*; Stewart, Cobb, and Keith, "The Color of Death"; and Washington, *Medical Apartheid.*

38. See Chasin, "Making Sense"; Eisner, *Notes for a Bisexual Revolution*; Gorman, Denney, Dowdy, and Medeiros, "A New Piece of the Puzzle"; Gupta, "'And Now I'm Just Different'"; Przybylo, "Crisis and Safety"; Shearer et al., "Differences"; and Walters, Chen, and Breiding, *The National*, for more information on inequalities bi+ and asexual individuals experience.

39. See Cimino and Smith, *Atheist Awakening*, for a review.

7

Conclusion

As with most other book-length qualitative research projects, we began this discussion with observational data from our experiences in a specific social context—common interactions occurring every day in contemporary US society.[1] In fact, we followed other researchers by sharing situations and interactions that appear odd, curious, or otherwise questionable for us based on our social locations within US society.[2] Further, we used only interactional examples that have both led to violence and/or harassment at times in our lives and have not resulted in any violence or harassment at other times. We selected interactions of this variety to specifically exhibit the specter of violence we, as transgender people, navigate on a daily basis, even when such violence doesn't always come to fruition. As we discussed in chapter 1, the difference between these two outcomes—and many others in between—emerges as a result of whether or not (mostly cisgender) others seek to reassert the cisgender realities they are comfortable with, realities predicated upon the erasure and marginalization of transgender people.

It would not be surprising, however, if cisgender readers did not see anything special, unusual, or potentially dangerous about the examples at the beginning of this book.[3] In fact, echoing the experiences of scholars from other marginalized communities over time, we even had early cisgender readers (before we submitted it to presses) of the introduction ask, for example, (1) what was the significance of these examples, (2) why didn't we start the book with what they defined as "data" based on their social locations within US society, and/or (3) why we didn't just focus on one setting instead of utilizing the United States itself as a case study.[4] As feminist, queer, and critical race scholars have noted for at least the past thirty years, such responses demonstrate how some people are allowed to see interactions and situations that appear strange or difficult for others as unworthy of consideration or critique.[5]

Following in the footsteps of such scholars, here we flipped the usual script wherein researchers seek to make sense of transgender people from a cisgender perspective.[6] We did this by examining cisgender people and social structures from a transgender perspective. Put simply, we expanded on the work of Smith and others over the past three decades by demonstrating how the everyday (cisgender) world is problematic through our transgender eyes.[7] As Collins suggests, we did so by focusing on how dominant patterns appear from a marginalized perspective to reveal the far-reaching operation of a societal system that benefits some people at the expense of others.[8]

To this end, we began with autoethnographic examples of stressful situations for us and many other transgender people, and a broad introduction situating our work in existing scholarly, activist, and artistic literatures. Then we focused on the most common areas of scholarship where our perspectives find some recognition and voice (coming out and LGBTQIA communities) in chapters 2 and 3. As early feminist, critical race, and queer scholars did before us, we then turned our eyes to broader social patterns across the United States in chapter 4, and to the dominant religious and scientific lessons cisgender people learn before they ever meet one of us in person, in the media, or otherwise in chapters 5 and 6. In so doing, we utilized our own and our respondents' experience to demonstrate what the United States can look like from a transgender perspective and how people contribute to this version of the United States by enforcing, intentionally or otherwise, cisgender realities.

As we show throughout this book, the enforcement of cisgender realities is not an isolated practice limited to only one or another specific population, setting, or context. Rather, such efforts—like the autoethnographic examples we began with in chapter 1—are everyday, foundational, and continuous aspects of contemporary life within the United States, and these dynamics transcend sociodemographic populations and scientific or religious lessons about the way the world is and should be. However, as we also note throughout this book, the enforcement of cisgender realities can vary in many ways in relation to different racial, class, sex, gender, sexual, age, generational, scientific, and religious populations and contexts.[9] As has been revealed in prior endeavors by marginalized scholars to problematize seemingly normal patterns in US society,[10] our analysis here reveals the operation of a systematic pattern of inequality that may escape the attention of people who benefit from this system.

As we conclude this book, it is important to note that nothing we have demonstrated here is new for most transgender people living in the United States. In fact, the experiences we highlight are eerily reminiscent of lessons J and many of her peers learned decades before Lain and zir contemporaries came out in the current period of increased attention to and visibility for transgender people. This, of course, is also similar to the observations of feminist, queer, and critical race scholars decades ago. At the same time, however, we recognize—from our own lives and from the experiences shared by such scholars in prior decades—that these insights may *feel* incredibly new, disorienting, and potentially even alarming for many cisgender people and social scientists today.[11] As a result, we utilize this conclusion to point out four specific areas where researchers, activists, artists, and anyone else may join the ongoing work, presently done mostly by transgender people, to transform US society from a cisgender reality to a more equitable and inclusive society for everyone, regardless of sex/gender/sexual identities.

DOING CISGENDER

The same year Smith demonstrated the problematic patterns of cisgender womanhood and manhood upon which everyday life was built, Candace West and Don Zimmerman revolutionized scientific—and over time, broader social—understandings of sex/gender/sexuality with their article "Doing Gender."[12] Rather than an immutable element of human bodies, brains, or other biological characteristics, West and Zimmerman demonstrated how gender arose from (1) the lessons people learned about how this or that type of person should behave, particularly based on one's sex category (or assumed body type in relation to sex); (2) the ways people then sought to conform to and/or reject these lessons in their daily interactions with other people, with social structures, and within themselves; and (3) the ways people sought to enforce conformity to these lessons upon others. Put simply, their work, and much scholarship since, demonstrates the importance of problematizing how people learn, perform, and force others to conform to existing gender norms throughout social life, and how these processes serve as a mechanism for understanding and potentially changing any given set of sex/gender/sexual inequalities.

As we note in chapter 1 and other work elsewhere, we utilized this framework to elaborate the construction and enforcement of cisgender realities.[13] Specifically, cisgender realities rely upon people engaging in what we would call "doing cisgender." People "do cisgender" by (1) conforming to lessons that suggest only cisgender people exist or matter in the world, (2) conforming to current norms concerning cisgender manhood and womanhood, and (3) enforcing their own conformity upon others who deviate from cisgender norms and expectations. The same way that recent studies have demonstrated how people like J, Lain, and others learn to "do transgender" or "do nonbinary"[14] through lessons gained from other non-cisgender people and/or medical requirements, cisgender people similarly learn to do cisgender selves. However, the primary emphasis so far, both in social science scholarship and in US society more broadly, on the ways transgender people learn to embody and assert their genders shows just how unmarked processes of doing cisgender are in the present social context (and thus why these processes warrant further investigation).

Any of these doings may ultimately undo or redo broader gender inequalities within and between cisgender, transgender, and otherwise gendered populations, now or in the future. The possibility of more equitable gender relations, however, requires attention not only to how people do gender as a whole, or transgender selfhood/nonbinary selfhood specifically, but also to how people *do* cisgender selfhood. Such possibilities for greater gender equity also require systematic attention to the ways religious, scientific, and other social authorities create and enforce specific rules for what it means to do cisgender, do transgender, do nonbinary, and otherwise do gender within and between specific settings and populations. Finally, as suggested in our discussion of othering the other in chapter 2, such possibilities require analyses of conflicts that develop within specific gender populations about what counts as doing cisgender, doing transgender, doing nonbinary, or doing any other form of gender the "right" way.

Although this may sound the same as existing studies of "doing gender" to many cisgender readers, we urge such readers to consider examples from the past to better understand the distinction we are outlining here. For example, would you feel the same way if researchers focused only on the ways people do race, do black, do Hispanic, do Asian, or do Native American as if these processes were interchangeable? Likewise, would you feel the same way if researchers said people do sexuality, do gay/lesbian selfhood, do bi+/pan/queer selfhood, or do ace selfhood, and suggested that such processes all point to identical social dynamics? Finally, would you see it as unworthy of critique if researchers said people do gender or do womanhood as if these gendered accomplishments are synonymous? In each case, the dominant group is left unmarked while only the systematically marginalized group(s) are treated as problematic or in need of more analysis. Echoing scholars focused on other previously unmarked dominant populations,[15] we suggest the next step in the evolution of gender studies involves marking the processes whereby people do cisgender in ways that challenge and/or reproduce the marginalization of transgender people.

At the same time, however, we also show here that cisgender people do not have to do cisgender in ways that require the marginalization of transgender people. As has been the case in prior scholarship, this finding points to unanswered theoretical questions in existing literature and broader social debates. For example, what types of cisgender selfhood might be formed in opposition to or in support of gender equality for all? What factors facilitate these different forms of doing cisgender? Although such questions could be answered only through future systematic research, our work in this book reveals the importance of these theoretical questions as well as some ways transgender perspectives can shed light on societal notions of gender more broadly. We thus ask readers: What might be found through analyses of the ways people do cisgender in confirmation and/or opposition to broader processes of cisgendering reality?

DOING SEXUAL AND MONO NORMATIVITIES

Building on societal observations of doing gender, researchers have more recently focused increasing attention on the relationships between sex, gender, and sexualities in US society and more broadly.[16] In so doing, scholars have outlined many ways people do sexual identities within and between varied populations, settings, and identity categories.[17] At the same time, studies demonstrate that much of existing social life in the United States involves the ways people do heteronormativity or the enforcement of heterosexuality at the expense of other sexual practices, desires, and identities.[18] In fact, such studies have even noted links between cis- and heteronormative systems in the case of violence against transgender people, transgender people's workplace interactions, reactions to cisgender partners of transgender people in public settings, and the use of religious/scientific condemnations of same-sex sexualities in previous years to oppose transgender rights at present.

At the same time, however, this work notes that doing heteronormativity relies upon the limitation of human sexualities to only genital/gender specific notions of homo/hetero sexual desire, practice, and identity.[19] Specifically, the interactional and structural enforcement of heteronormativity—as well as homonormativity—in everyday life relies first upon the assumption that everyone is only gay/lesbian or straight at all times, and only sexually involved with one other person at a time. Although this aspect of heteronormativity receives much less attention, emerging poly, bi+, and transgender studies point out that if these assumptions make sense to people, then such people have already defined sexualities as only monogamous and only monosexual. Further, ace studies point out that such patterns also rely upon the assumption that all people are sexual, and therefore one may guess the (already assumed to exist) monogamous and monosexual identities of another person without any need to find out if the person in question has any interest in sexual activity or relationships in the first place.

As bi+, poly, and ace activists and scholars have pointed out in recent decades, the assumption that people have only one sexuality and one partner at a time relies upon systemic patterns of sexual and mono normativity. As noted in chapter 3, however, sexual and mono normativities—like cisnormativity—have received much less attention both in mainstream US scholarship and society and in specifically queer communities and scholarship to date. Especially since emerging studies thus far suggest transgender people are less likely to conform to either sexual or mono normativity than cisgender people, this may be an especially problematic gap in public and academic knowledge in the years to come. Luckily, emerging interdisciplinary bi+, poly, and ace studies do provide guidance for moving mainstream and queer assumptions beyond mono and sexual normativities.

As we have elsewhere,[20] here we join such work by suggesting that scholars, activists, and others who seek to foster greater inclusion of transgender people—as well as ace, bi+, and poly populations—begin directing systematic attention not only to the ways people do hetero/homo normativities but also the ways they do mono and sexual normativities, whether or not they necessarily mean to do so. As in the case of doing gender, such attempts may allow us to shed light upon the foundations of sexual inequality and to generate possibilities for more equitable sexual relations throughout US society. Once again, however, we recognize that only empirical and theoretical attention to these systems will tell us both how they operate and how they may be transformed. Even so, we ask readers to consider what might be accomplished—for transgender people or more broadly—by examining the sexual and mono normativities that underlie societal patterns of gender and sexual inequality.

DOING ENDOSEX

Alongside increased attention to and debate about sexual and gender diversity, more equitable social relations require serious attention to the ways social authorities do or construct the sex categories that provide the basis for doing gender and sexualities.[21] Although many endosex people—regardless of gender or sexual identity—treat sex as something people possess as a straightforward categorization of genital shape and appearance, these beliefs rely upon a simplification of biological diversity that negatively impacts the lives, bodies, and broader experiences of intersex people. Put simply, scientific and religious teaching about complementarity manifests in the assignment of all humans to one of only two socially allowable sex categories at birth (i.e., doing endosex or creating two sexes). At the same time, people whose bodies do not fit into this human-made model (i.e., intersex people) are subject to unnecessary genital surgeries utilized to make their bodies conform to endosex norms.

Although sex categorization is integral to the construction, enforcement, and otherwise doing of both (trans, nonbinary, and cis) gender as well as sexualities, most scholarly and mainstream discussion treats sex as a stable, static assignment and often conflates sex and gender (i.e., female is woman). Such patterns simultaneously erase and maintain the marginalization of intersex people in relation to broader endosex and cisgender norms. Furthermore, reinforcing cis- and endosex normativities provides excuses for people who seek to reject or dismiss transgender experience by appealing to sex as an unmalleable biological reality created by nature and/or god. Despite these patterns in mainstream and scholarly work, however, the experiences of intersex people clearly reveal that sex is something people *do* rather than something people *have*. Put simply, social authorities in medicine, law, and other institutions do endosex by forcing all humanity into two—and only two—sex categories, and people more broadly do endosex by assuming and enforcing beliefs about a two and only two sex system.

Rather than natural, such efforts—like the doings of race, gender, sexualities, and other social systems—rely upon the ongoing efforts of human beings and result in the marginalization of anyone who does not fit into the normative system. Emerging studies of intersex people, however, demonstrate that this population is just as diverse, broad, and varied as any other in US society. Such studies also demonstrate that many intersex people also do gender and sexualities in both normative and nonnormative ways and, like other sex/gender/sexual minorities, face continuous interactions with endosex others who often do not even know they exist. Further, intersex-inclusive scholarship—like emerging transgender studies—demonstrates complex relationships between sex, gender, and sexualities as well as significant marginalization intersex people face within and beyond different settings in contemporary US society.

If we seek to pursue sex/gender/sexual equality for all, such insights demonstrate the importance of problematizing societal notions of static or natural sex categories. To this end, researchers and others more broadly could examine, for example, the ways people do endosex by spreading and affirming beliefs in two and only two sexes; erasing intersex experiences from scientific, religious, and other representations of US society; and/or deconstructing the legal, medical, and religious norms that allow for the continued violation of intersex children's bodies. We could further seek to ascertain how intersex people do gender and sexualities as people who do not necessarily fit neatly into transgender, cisgender, or other existing gender options. Such efforts could dramatically transform US attitudes about sex categorization, and in so doing, work toward broader movements for sex/gender/sexual equality for all. As such, we ask readers to consider the ways people do and affirm the doing of endosex, and what could be learned from systematically examining these efforts within and between varied social contexts.

DOING EDUCATION

As of this writing, we have been asked a recurring question throughout our careers (and this question has come up in the reactions of some scholars to this project). Although it is phrased in many ways, the question seeks to ascertain why we devote attention to institutions like religion and science when most LGBTQIA scholarship focuses on other arenas.[22] As noted in chapter 1, the answer to this question is simple: Religious and scientific (formal and informal) educational endeavors are generally among the most (or the most) likely social forces to influence, create, and maintain US attitudes about and reactions to every aspect of social life, including the ones most often focused on in other LGBTQIA scholarship.[23] In fact, history demonstrates the powerful roles religious and scientific educational systems have played in the experiences and outcomes of LGBTQIA people within and beyond any specific setting or demographic group.

We thus focus on religious and scientific meaning systems—as suggested by Michel Foucault, Karl Marx, Max Weber, W. E. B. Du Bois, Patricia Hill Collins, Michael Warner, Judith Butler, and others[24]—to deconstruct the foundational systems of knowledge that create and maintain sex/gender/ sexual inequality. As we show in chapters 5 and 6, these institutions were built upon and (in most cases) continue to enforce cisgender realities at the expense of those wo do not fit neatly into existing normative expectations about sex/gender/sexuality. In fact, considering the influence of these systems upon US attitudes and beliefs, the patterns of transgender experience outlined throughout this book are not entirely surprising. Rather, they are predictable examples of people doing—or putting into practice—the lessons they have been taught by religious and scientific authorities. As a result, we often ask why more LGBTQIA scholarship is not focused on these institutions, the lessons they teach that influence sex/gender/sexualities, and the ways such lessons show up in studies of other major US institutions.

Rather than seeking to answer this particular theoretical question, we join others calling for more systematic and integrated analyses of the ways scientific and religious traditions do sex/gender/sexual education throughout the contemporary United States.[25] Considering that it is often possible to acquire educational credentials—from high school diplomas to doctorates—without ever having to learn anything about transgender people in the United States today, it is not all that surprising that sex/gender/sexual variation may seem new to even some of the most educated people in society. Likewise, considering that the vast majority of major US religious traditions are based upon a world in which God only created endosex cisgender people, it is not surprising that many religious people respond negatively to these seemingly new possibilities.

If the experiences of lesbian/gay people, people of color, and cisgender women have taught us anything over the past few decades, however, it is that incorporating populations who have been marginalized and/or erased in dominant religious and scientific traditions can facilitate massive societal changes. In fact, scientific and religious traditions have been on both sides of each major social movement toward racial, gendered, and sexual civil rights throughout the past two centuries, and have often played important roles in the outcomes of such endeavors. We thus ask readers to consider what US society would look like if transgender history and experience—as well as broader LGBTQIA topics—became a more common part of the education most people depend upon to understand the nation and the broader world.

CONCLUDING REMARKS

As we complete this book, it is interesting to think about a conversation five years ago that may have begun this project as well as our other work integrating transgender (and poly and bi+) perspectives more fully into social science. We were sitting at a table outside a hotel in the Midwest having coffee with another transgender person who was in search of reading materials by and for members of our community. J provided them with a list of options off the top of her head, many of which appear in the bibliography of this book. Afterward, Lain asked why it was so hard to find work about our communities more broadly and especially by researchers, artists, and others in our communities.

The work we've done elsewhere and the examples throughout this book provide some answers to this question, but such insights also reveal many more questions. It is our hope that alongside the increased mainstream visibility of our communities in recent years, this work will become one of many empirical portraits of the nation we encounter in our lives, and only one of many more accessible options for transgender people seeking to see our experiences reflected in scientific and other representations of the world. As we noted in chapter 1, our goal throughout this book has been (1) to present a transgender perspective on contemporary US society through our own and our respondents' experiences of the nation at present and (2) to demonstrate some ways more incorporation of transgender perspectives can expand existing scientific, religious, and broader social discussions about sex/gender/sexualities.

At the same time, however, we recognize that this is only one book, and our perspectives—as well as those of our respondents—are not by any means the only transgender perspectives in existence. In fact, our own experiences suggest that the variations and diversity within our communities make it impossible for any single project or viewpoint to adequately speak to the wide variety of transgender experiences in the United States in a holistic way. We thus submit this work as one portrait of transgender experience in the United States from a transgender perspective while continuing our own and others' ongoing calls for greater transgender inclusion throughout the scientific, media, artistic, religious, governmental, and other facets of contemporary US society. We further ask readers to consider what US society might look like if we move beyond cisgender norms and embrace the sex/gender/sexual diversity and potential of us all.

As we demonstrated throughout this book—in both the text and the bibliography we provide for readers in search of more information—we are not new, even if cisgender reactions to us are newly changing in some cases. We are an incredibly diverse and multifaceted population occupying a wide variety of sociodemographic and contextual locations. For the ones among us who, like many younger transgender people and like ourselves in the past, might not know it and may especially need to know it on the hardest days: You are not alone; there are many, many, many of us throughout the world both similar to and different from you in a multitude of ways. Like members of other marginalized groups have done throughout history, we thus end this book by calling for a reconsideration of existing systems of social organization in hopes of both greater recognition of transgender people and experiences in the United States and beyond, and the potential of more equitable sex/gender/sexual relations for us all.

NOTES

1. For examples of this pattern in qualitative books about transgender experience, see, for example, Meadow, *Trans Kids*; Pfeffer, *Queering Families*; Schilt, *Just One of the Guys?*; Stein, *Unbound*; and Travers, *The Trans Generation*. For examples of this pattern in other qualitative books see also, Acosta, *Amigas y Amantes*; Bonilla-Silva, *Racism without Racists*; Davis, *Contesting Intersex*; and Garcia, *Respect Yourself, Protect Yourself*.

2. See examples in n. 1 for this pattern.

3. See, for example, Collins, *Black Feminist Thought*; Compton, Meadow, and Schilt, *Other, Please Specify*; and Smith, *The Everyday World as Problematic*, for similar patterns in other scholarship related to minorities.

4. We also received this reaction from a couple of transgender prereaders, but most transgender prereaders understood what we were doing in the introduction, and a couple cisgender prereaders caught it too. We also received similar comments in reviews of the proposal when we submitted it to presses, though we do not know if such reviewers were cisgender, transgender, or otherwise identified.

5. Smith, *The Everyday World as Problematic*. See also n. 3 in this chapter.

6. For recent examples where researchers seek to flip dominant scripts or patterns in the literature, see Pfeffer *Queer Families*; see also Pascoe, *Dude*, and n. 3 in this chapter.

7. Smith, *The Everyday World as Problematic*.

8. Collins, *Black Feminist Thought*; see also Crenshaw, "Mapping the Margins"; hooks, *Teaching to Transgress*; Sedgwick, *Epistemology*; and Warner, *The Trouble with Normal*, for more examples.

9. See also the survey and case study research discussed and cited throughout this book, particularly in chapters 2–4.

10. See again nn. 3 and 8 in this chapter. It is also important to note that although these texts were considered controversial and disruptive at the time of their publication, most of them have since become citation classics.

11. For more evidence on the fact that transgender existence is not new, see chapter 1. See also Stryker, *Transgender History*; in sociology specifically, see Vidal-Ortiz, "Transgender and Transsexual Studies."

12. West and Zimmerman, "Doing Gender." See also,West and Fenstermaker, "Doing Difference"; and Connell, "Accountable Conduct."

13. Mathers, "Bathrooms, Boundaries, and Emotional Burdens"; Sumerau, Cragun, and Mathers, "Cisgendering Reality."

14. Connell, "Doing, Undoing, or Redoing"; Darwin, "Doing Gender beyond the Binary."

15. Such studies, for example, reveal that people also do whiteness, do heterosexuality, do monosexuality, and do manhood, and understanding race, sexuality, and gender requires also deconstructing the doing of these identities. See,

for example, Bonilla-Silva, *Racism without Racists*; Pascoe, *Dude*; Eisner, *Notes for a Bisexual Revolution*; and Schrock and Schwalbe, "Manhood Acts."

16. See, for example, Ahmed, *Queer Phenomenology*; Barringer, Sumerau, and Gay, "Examining Differences"; Cromwell, *Transmen*; Dozier, "Beards, Breasts, and Bodies"; Garcia, *Respect Yourself, Protect Yourself*; Lucal, "What It Means"; McCabe and Sumerau, "Reproductive Vocabularies"; Pascoe, *Dude*; Pfeffer, "'I Don't Like Passing'"; Schilt and Westbrook, "Doing Gender, Doing Heteronormativity"; Schippers, *Beyond Monogamy*; Schrock, Sumerau, and Ueno, "Sexualities"; Somerville, *Queering the Color Line*; Sumerau, Cragun, and Mathers, "'I Found God'"; Vidal-Ortiz, "Queering Sexuality"; Westbrook and Schilt, "Doing Gender, Determining Gender"; and Zamantakis, "'I Try Not to Push It.'" See also Pfeffer, ed., "Special Issue: Trans Sexualities"; and Pfeffer, "Making Space."

17. See Butler, *Bodies That Matter*; and Davis, *Contesting Intersex*, for more discussion on doing sex, but here we focus on sexualities.

18. See, for example, Garcia, *Respect Yourself, Protect Yourself*; Katz, *The Invention of Sodomy*; Mathers, Sumerau, and Ueno, "'This Isn't Just Another'"; Mathers, Sumerau, and Cragun, "The Limits of Homonormativity"; Pascoe, *Dude*; Rich, "Compulsory Heterosexuality"; Schilt and Westbrook, "Doing Gender, Doing Heteronormativity"; and Seidman, "From Identity."

19. See, for example, Barringer, Sumerau, and Gay, "Examining Differences"; Chasin, "Making Sense"; Eisner, *Notes for a Bisexual Revolution*; Garber, *Bisexuality*; Gupta, "'And Now I'm Just Different'"; Mathers, "Sibling Relationships"; Moss, "Alternative Families, Alternative Lives"; Przybylo, "Crisis and Safety"; Scherrer and Pfeffer, "None of the Above"; Schippers, *Beyond Monogamy*; Vares, "My [Asexuality] Is Playing Hell."

20. Mathers, "Sibling Relationships"; Mathers, Sumerau, and Cragun, "The Limits of Homonormativity"; Sumerau, *Cigarettes & Wine*, *Homecoming Queens*, *That Year*, and *Essence*; Sumerau, "Embodying Nonexistence"; and Sumerau, Mathers, and Lampe, "Learning from the Experiences."

21. Costello, "Not a 'Medical Miracle'"; Costello, "Trans and Intersex Children"; Costello, "Nonconsensual Intersex Surgery"; Davis, *Contesting Intersex;* Davis, *Beyond Trans*; Karkazis, *Fixing Sex*; Kessler, *Lessons*.

22. Most LGBTQIA scholarship focuses instead on families, marriage and parenthood, identity construction and presentation, schools and colleges, public spaces, criminal justice systems, political movements, governmental regulations

and laws, subcultures, workplaces, demographics, media, language, sexual practices, economic conditions, and historical representations of the past. Religion and (scientific) education have been shown to significantly influence attitudes in all these areas of society.

23. See Adamczyk, *Cross-National*, for a review of LGBTQ attitudes studies; also see chapters 5 and 6 for discussion.

24. See Butler, *Gender Trouble*; Collins, *Black Feminist Thought*; Du Bois, *The Souls*; Foucault, *History of Sexuality*, vols. 1, 2, and 3; Marx, *Capital*; Warner, *The Trouble with Normal*; Weber, *The Protestant Ethic*.

25. Avishai, "'Doing Religion'"; Barton, *Pray the Gay Away*; Burke, *Christians under Covers*; Moon, *God, Sex, and Politics*.

Methodological Appendix

The seeds of this book were planted in a series of conversations we had beginning in the summer of 2013. At the time, J was preparing for their second year in a faculty position while Lain was preparing for zir second year in a master's program. Likewise, Lain was becoming more confident and open about zir sexual and gender fluidity, and J was becoming more open about her gender identities and journey in professional settings as part of her work with Lain and various transgender (and especially other transwomen) students in search of resources, support, and guidance. Together, we began having conversations about the difficulties of navigating academic spaces, finding academic resources in our disciplinary areas, and explaining our existence, even to fellow academics, as transgender people working in the social sciences.

As we both do now, J kept a list of transgender-inclusive resources, writings, and other materials that she regularly shared with students in search of more information at the time. As Lain became acquainted with the arts and scholarship on that list and our conversations continued, we began to discuss potential methods for bringing such information into the social sciences more broadly, the same way other transgender people working in various parts of the academy had been doing since at least the 1990s and as members of other marginalized communities had throughout the past few decades. To this end, we began to develop plans for individual and collaborative research projects utilizing our combined skill sets and standpoints to further integrate transgender experiences and scholarship into social scientific literatures and debates. In so doing, we began a series of projects examining cisgender, transgender, and otherwise gendered experiences in varied US settings and populations.[1]

Although these endeavors resulted in multiple projects of different sorts over the past five years, the present volume began as a hypothetical dream to do a large-scale qualitative study of transgender experience in the United States. We outlined this dream while Lain was working on zir master's thesis on cisnormative gendered harassment in public restrooms and J was traveling throughout the country on breaks from teaching, asking other transgender people what they would want to see in survey, interview, ethnographic, and other research protocols in the social sciences. This project became more than hypothetical sooner than expected, however, when Ryan T. Cragun, one of J's coworkers at the University of Tampa, added an option for identifying beyond cisgender categories in a survey he was doing with other researchers interested in gender within the Mormon Church. To his own surprise, Ryan found himself with a large collection of qualitative responses from transgender Mormons and ex-Mormons and sought out J and Lain to examine these materials.

Especially since religion was a common theme emerging in J's discussions with other transgender people about potential research needs and desires, we accepted the invitation and worked with Ryan to examine transgender experience in the Mormon Church. At the same time, J began working with Ryan on attitudinal surveys ascertaining opinions about transgender and other minority populations in the United States, while Lain completed their thesis and began preparing it for publication. In so doing, J asked about the possibility of utilizing the software and internet resources Ryan had used for the Mormon study to conduct a survey of transgender populations specifically. After a series of conversations about logistics and other matters, Ryan agreed to run the survey utilizing his server and software,[2] and both J and Lain began planning the form and shape of the survey instrument in a series of conversations with one another and other transgender people we reached through personal networks and J's ongoing travels.[3]

SURVEY DESIGN[4]

The survey itself was designed in an inductive manner. As transgender people required to take courses in social scientific statistical analysis to earn graduate degrees in our fields, we had both long been collecting notes about the limitations of such instruments in terms of sex/gender/sexualities. We were also aware of prior work demonstrating that often the best way to study non-cisgender populations on a broader level than any given case study relied upon designing new instruments capable of capturing the diversity of sex/ gender/sexual identities and experiences in ways not possible in most traditional (endosex- and cisgender-based) social scientific survey instruments to date. In fact, after we began this project, scholars in our own field would also begin publishing peer-reviewed articles outlining the importance of developing these types of surveys for studying transgender populations and revising traditional surveys for better capturing empirical sex/gender/sexual dimensions of social life. We thus approached our survey design more like ethnographers trying to understand a population from its own members rather than seeking to impose categories upon a population of interest based on established survey findings or precedent.[5]

To this end, J continued seeking out advice and guidance from transgender people while Lain organized themes in emerging interdisciplinary transgender studies and older work on transgender populations in the social sciences. In so doing, Lain developed a series of common questions social scientists ask varied populations and/or transgender people specifically for reference in our survey design. At the same time, J sought out the opinions and thoughts of people who occupied varied social locations (i.e., some were fellow academics and researchers, but many others were not; some were active in transgender rights work, but others were not; some were from similar social locations to J and Lain, but many others were not). In this way, we sought to build an integrated survey instrument that might speak to a wide variety of transgender standpoints, social locations, and perspectives at once.

Not surprisingly, this led to some complications as a result of the diversity of opinions and lived experiences within transgender populations. After the survey went live, for example, there were potential respondents who expressed issues with some of the gender identity options we provided and other types of questions that they found problematic in one way or another.[6] In each case, we empathized with their concerns; however, we also experienced instances where other potential respondents praised the same aspects of the survey. We point this out here to emphasize that there is no way any one type of survey or other research design will be likely to capture the entirety of perspectives within our populations, which reveals the importance of more systematic inclusion of transgender people into research endeavors throughout the social sciences. We further note this to again point out that our work here is by no means perfect, but rather an early case and call for more integrated empirical studies of sex/gender/sexual social life in the United States and, ultimately, beyond.

With these things in mind, we designed a survey where respondents answered open- and close-ended questions about sex assignment, gender identity, coming out, religious experience, medical experience, and experiences with both LGBTQIA communities and broader cisgender populations throughout US society.[7] We further captured quantitative responses concerning a host of demographic information such as racial identity, class identity, educational attainment, income, possession of medical insurance, religious and nonreligious identity, sexual identity, and attitudes concerning issues like abortion and same-sex marriage. Although the tables and statistics in this book each come from quantitative assessments, the bulk of the data here comes from qualitative responses to the questions displayed in table A.1.

Following earlier suggestions from transgender studies and mirroring current suggestions in other social sciences, we also departed from traditional survey methods in two ways. First, we allowed respondents the ability to write in answers that were not listed on every single demographic question. Rather than forcing respondents to pick the options we found in our lives and background studies, we left room for people to self-identify in the language that made the most sense to them.[8] Second, we did not require completion

Table A.1.   Open-Ended Questions in the Survey Utilized in This Analysis

Questions

(1) What was it like when you first came out to someone about your transgender identity?
(2) Why are you not open about your transgender identity?
(3) Would you please share any notable positive and negative experiences you have had with religious leaders?
(4) Would you please describe any notable positive and negative experiences you have had with Lesbian, Gay, Bisexual, Asexual, Pansexual, Transgender, Queer, Genderqueer, or Polyamorous (LGBTQIAP) groups?
(5) Would you please share any notable positive and negative experiences you have had with cisgender people?
(6) Would you please share any notable positive and negative experiences you have had with groups or organizations that are not explicitly religious or LGBTQIAP?
(7) Would you please share any notable positive and negative experiences you have had with healthcare?

of any survey question—qualitative or quantitative—throughout the instrument. Since we were not seeking to substantively generalize to all transgender people the demographic or statistical patterns that could emerge in the study and were well aware of work on the USTS and other instruments capturing broader statistical portraits, we instead allowed respondents freedom to provide answers including however much or little they wished to share. In this regard, we again treated the survey more like an ethnographic or interview-based instrument wherein respondents are granted the opportunity and autonomy to make their own decisions about what information to disclose throughout their participation in a study.[9]

RECRUITMENT AND SAMPLING

After completion of the survey design, the instrument was loaded onto Ryan's server and tested by each of us from different computers, access points, and operating systems. For recruitment and publicity purposes, we named the instrument the Transgender Religion Survey.[10] We chose this name for three interrelated reasons. First, the combination of the number of people we spoke with who brought up religion and Ryan's interest in religious studies led us to fashion an instrument that contained many questions about religion and nonreligion rarely captured on any survey that includes transgender respondents in any specific manner.[11] Second, in seeking funding to aid recruitment for the survey, we learned that the Association for the Sociology of Religion was potentially interested in transgender-inclusive projects for its annual funding options for research on gender, sexualities, and religion. Third, we were launching this survey at the same time that many other survey projects were being launched with the words *transgender* and *survey* in the title, and since we were planning to utilize social media in recruitment, we wanted a name that would both distinguish our survey in social media feeds and contain an aspect not often mentioned in other surveys or survey titles.

As a result of these decisions, we specifically focused our own marketing and publicity about the survey on explaining that the study *both* contained more questions related to religious and nonreligious experience than other surveys inclusive of transgender populations *and also* asked questions about other important areas and institutions in contemporary US transgender experience. To this end, we constructed social media posts, blog posts on the *Write Where It Hurts* academic blogs we run with Dr. Alexandra C. H.

Nowakowski, and informational documents we could share with potential respondents that noted both of these aspects of the study explicitly and clearly throughout the recruitment process. As noted in other works about survey design and dissemination, the goal was to offer a research opportunity that both spoke to a specific need in the community and captured broader responses beyond that specific topic from people occupying a wide variety of social and regional locations.[12]

At the same time, we applied for and received funding for recruitment from the Association for the Sociology of Religion.[13] As we sought to both conduct our study and give back to our populations in the process, we designed our grant proposal as an opportunity to provide financial resources to transgender organizations in the United States in exchange for their help informing members and online followers of their work to the existence of the survey. Specifically, we gave a total of $1,200 to four transgender organizations ($300 per organization) to simply share the survey with their members and online followers, who were then free to decide whether they wanted to participate in the study.[14] In so doing, we sought to use this project as an opportunity not only to study the experiences of transgender people but also to support others working on transgender issues and concerns more broadly throughout US society during the time period when we were distributing the survey. In addition to sharing the survey through these transgender organizations, we shared it in multiple transgender-focused social media groups, with permission from moderators when appropriate.[15]

For the purposes of recruitment, we primarily utilized social media and the contact with transgender organizations across the country for a specific reason. As Carla Pfeffer notes, researchers seeking to study marginalized populations (and especially those that have had negative experiences with science in the past) are often best served by sampling through the social networks within that population.[16] Put simply, social networks simultaneously serve as entrance points and gatekeepers that ascertain the efforts, standpoints, and any potential threat of researchers seeking to study a given population. J, for example, had previously both turned down many studies and warned others about them, and also participated in many studies that she then shared with other transwomen based on who was doing the study, how the study was constructed, and other factors about any given project over the course of her life. This is not uncommon in groups who are marginalized in society. In fact, it is incredibly common for populations like ours, which have experienced some of this marginalization at the hands of scientists themselves.

In fact, we experienced our own encounters with these dynamics throughout the recruitment process. There were occasions, for example, where J came out—privately and/or in other ways—for respondents understandably worried about any study that mentioned science, religion, and our population. There were similar occasions where J shared aspects of her experience with other transwomen who were—as J admits she would have been—suspicious of the research team's motives or relationships to transgender communities. There were other occasions where Lain had long conversations with leaders and members of transgender organizations about our own backgrounds, who the religious studies scientist working with us was, our plans for the data we collected, and questions about potential strings tied to the money we were providing to organizations during recruitment. There were many other cases we could share, but the point here is simple: Our own role as researchers and transgender people aided recruitment but also meant we had to navigate our own and others' complicated emotions about research in the process of collecting the data utilized throughout this book.

We want to stress three things here. First, these are understandable reactions from transgender people, as scientists have and continue to mistreat transgender people in many cases. Put simply, we know as well as anyone just how hard it is to exist and work openly as transgender people within scientific fields. Second, we expected these experiences and answered each question or comment we received as best we could. Even before we began designing this study, we talked at great length about how to navigate our own emotions and those of potential respondents as we sought to actively do transgender-inclusive empirical studies. Third, these factors demonstrate the importance of not just including transgender perspectives in science but also including transgender people in the design and implementation of scientific studies. We thus again join others calling for such efforts in the recruitment of students, faculty, and other researchers throughout the sciences within and beyond US society.

DATA ANALYSIS

As researchers who have published qualitative and quantitative research at various points in our respective careers to date, we approached our work here as a hybrid of these two traditions. Specifically, we utilized basic statistical techniques to establish the demographic contours of the sample and relevant points of interest for the broader analyses in comparison to the largest quantitative survey of transgender people in the United States to date, the USTS. At the same time, we pulled the qualitative responses to the questions in table A.1 for in-depth, focused, and comparative analyses. In so doing, however, we first examined the patterns in such data without the demographic markers tied to the respondent who shared a given statement (i.e., we looked at the responses without knowing the race, class, gender, sexuality, religion, or age of the respondent at first). We did this to capture the patterns in the data overall in the pursuit of a broad qualitative portrait of transgender experience throughout contemporary US society.

Especially because of the open-ended construction of the questions from which our data emerged, we approached such analyses in an inductive manner. We could not, for example, know ahead of time how much or how little people would say in response to each question. We also had no way of knowing the precise content of their responses to any of these questions.[17] As a result, we had no way of developing hypotheses or expectations ahead of time, and thus focused our work on outlining whatever patterns the responses revealed as important, commonly noted, and continuous throughout the data set. This also allowed us to stay very close to the data throughout our analysis (and while writing this book) because the inability to probe or ask follow-up questions with our respondents left us without a chance to effectively guess their motivations or other reasons for sharing what they chose to share in the survey.

As such, we went through the responses in their entirety, organizing them into recurring patterns and themes. We then went back and added the demographic labels that were applicable to each respondent throughout the organized data. In so doing, we pulled out some data subsets with specific populations that we are in the process of publishing as articles in academic journals. With the entirety of the data set, however, we went back through the responses and organized the patterns and themes in relation to varied social locations of the respondents who offered each example. In this way, we were able to search for patterns tied to specific demographic and other social locations that we share throughout this book. We continued this process in a back-and-forth manner, with each of us checking and rechecking the observations, notes, patterns, and interpretations of each set of quotes throughout the data.

As such, we organically induced the most common patterns and themes in the data set, which provide the content of the discussions throughout this book. Once we established and organized these themes throughout the data itself, we then turned to the existing literature—within and beyond the sciences—on transgender experience in US society. In so doing, we searched for similarities and differences in such work, and then extended such comparison to literatures focused on gender more broadly, scientific history and practice, religious history and practice, LGBTQIA communities and studies, and social scientific theoretical discussions and empirical examinations of sex/gender/sexualities more broadly. The combination of these endeavors created the discussions contained within this volume. Although it is only one snapshot from one set of transgender perspectives, this work provides an entry point for the ongoing emergence and expansion of transgender voices within the social sciences.

A NOTE ON THE LITERATURE

As we close this book, we find it prudent to discuss the literature we utilized throughout this book. Readers may have noticed that it is drawn from ongoing reading in the sciences (social, physical, and otherwise), arts, and media concerning transgender lives. As some prereaders noted while kindly looking over drafts of this work along the way, we have situated our work within a massive array of academic and other literature. In fact, academic colleagues who read over early drafts of this book universally commented on our use of significantly more literature than most other qualitative or quantitative books they have read on a given population. We are aware of this possible reaction from readers (academic or otherwise), and the decision to incorporate the amount and type of literature that we did was intentional on our parts, based in our experience as both researchers and transgender people in the United States today. We used this approach to compiling and incorporating relevant literatures for three very specific reasons.

First, as people who regularly seek to publish scholarship on transgender (and other marginalized) populations in the United States in scientific journals, we are all too familiar with assumptions that there is no—or at best, limited—literature on this topic, and that we, transgender people, are a "new" topic to many scholars who have not been exposed to transgender studies, histories, or discussions within and beyond the academy. We are further all too accustomed to editors and reviewers who (1) ask us to provide things in our work that are not required in other works in the same journals, (2) express concerns that integrating our perspectives into scientific fields may be too upsetting for other scholars in a given specialty area or discipline, and (3) define our work as niche (or marginal) in comparison to the subjects they believe are more important in their version of science. We thus offer this expansive bibliographical resource in hopes that scholars who, for whatever reason, are not familiar with transgender history, arts, and research will utilize these resources to educate themselves about our communities the same ways we are required by educational institutions to learn about cisgender beliefs, norms, and accomplishments throughout history.

Second, as transgender people who have had to search for the resources and literature to understand ourselves and have often provided this service to other transgender people, we offer this bibliographic collection to other transgender people seeking information about themselves, their history, their communities, and their accomplishments. Some of these readers may be fellow scholars seeking resources for navigating academic publishing, while others may be people making sense of their own gender identities who desperately wish—as we did—but are rarely afforded the opportunity to see themselves in dominant representations of the world. We cannot know who might need these resources the most or for what reasons, but we do know that each of us—and many others we have known and/or simply met along the way—would have cherished a collection like this, contained in one place, at different points throughout our lives.

Third and finally, as transgender people who now create our own artistic and scientific works, we are indebted more than words can say to the transgender artists, scientists, and other creators who came before us and gave us reasons to believe we could do this kind of work, find community and space where we might belong, and have a voice in the first place. We cannot overstate how much such works mean to us and so many other transgender people. We can tell you, however, that in many cases, access to literature, art, research, and film where one sees oneself can be the difference between life and death. We thus sought to use this volume to celebrate and elevate such endeavors by giving them space throughout the book. As such, we wish to take this moment to explicitly express our gratitude to every other transgender artist, scientist, or other content creator who came before us, and to every one of the ones who will be coming into these conversations in the future.

We also wish to note that despite the breadth and depth of the bibliographic examples throughout this work, this is not the whole picture. We understand that this may sound strange, especially to cisgender readers surprised by the number of sources we utilize here; however, even in a bibliography as large as the one in this book, we are not able to cite or note anywhere near the entirety of the works related to transgender people and experiences throughout the history of scientific, religious, and/or artistic thought. Rather, once again, we have offered a snapshot of the existing literature, knowledge, and history of transgender studies and lives, focused specifically on mostly US examples, and we would again urge readers to remember that there are even more of these works throughout the world.

As we've said throughout this book, we are not new and there are myriad perspectives, experiences, and other components to our lives, histories, and populations that we do not have the space to cover here. We thus provide a larger bibliography than most books like ours but also remind readers that there remains much to see, learn, read, and consider beyond even this selection of work by and/or about transgender experience. We hope, as you conclude this book, that you will continue to explore the various examples of the profound and multifaceted ways in which transgender people have influenced—and continue to influence—the world we all share together.

NOTES

1. Cragun and Sumerau, "The Last Bastion"; Cragun and Sumerau, "No One Expects a Transgender Jew"; Mathers, "Navigating Genderqueer Existence"; Mathers, "Bathrooms, Boundaries, and Emotional Burdens"; Mathers, "Expanding on the Experiences"; Mathers, Sumerau, and Cragun, "The Limits of Homonormativity"; Nowakowski, Sumerau, and Mathers, "None of the Above"; Sumerau, "Embodying Nonexistence"; Sumerau, Barbee, Mathers, and Eaton, "Exploring the Experiences"; Sumerau and Cragun, God Loves (Almost) Everyone; Sumerau, Cragun, and Mathers, "Cisgendering Reality"; Sumerau and Grollman, "Obscuring Oppression"; Sumerau, Grollman, and Cragun, "'Oh My God,'"; Sumerau, Mathers, and Cragun, "Incorporating Transgender Experience"; Sumerau, Mathers, and Lampe, "Learning from the Experiences"; Sumerau, Mathers, Nowakowski, and Cragun, "Helping Quantitative Sociology."

2. Ryan's only request was the inclusion of more religious questions/variables than we would have likely utilized on our own, which he and/or we may or may not utilize in individual or collaborative writing projects in the future.

3. Many of these people were and remain basically strangers J found attending meetings and functions hosted by and for transgender people in various cities as she traveled within Florida during semesters and elsewhere during summer and winter breaks. Others, however, were drawn from J's and Lain's respective individual and collective social networks.

4. For a more concise and traditionally academic discussion of the survey, see Sumerau, Barbee, Mathers, and Eaton, "Exploring the Experiences"; and Sumerau, Mathers, and Lampe, "Learning from the Experiences."

5. Berg and Lune, *Qualitative Research Methods*; Charmaz, *Grounded Theory*; Kleinman, *Feminist Fieldwork*.

6. These situations generally involved someone expressing concern about using a given term (i.e., *intersex* as a gender identity or the terms *transsexual* or *cross-dresser*) that one did not wish to be used (i.e., *intersex* is mostly used as a sex rather than gender label; *transsexual* and *cross-dresser* are older terms that many transgender people reject in the current climate for various reasons). In each case, however, the option was included because at least a few people (and in some cases, many people) J and/or Lain met when seeking guidance preferred these terms and this type of usage just as much as others do not want them used. In such cases, we tried to have the options for any and all respondents, but were also sensitive to and understanding about people who praised and/or had issues with certain inclusions in the instrument.

7. Copies of the survey instrument itself are available upon request.

8. These identifications were sorted into categories they fit with for the purposes of statistics in this book. In fact, most respondents who used write-in options simply wrote more detail about their identities rather than using specifically different language for how they identify.

9. Charmaz, *Grounded Theory*; Compton, Meadow, and Schilt, *Other, Please Specify*; Kleinman, *Feminist Fieldwork*.

10. See the posts "The Transgender Religion Survey" (https://writewhereithurts.net/2015/12/09/the-transgender-religion-survey/) and "Experiencing Gender Variation" (https://writewhereithurts.net/2015/12/16/178-2/) on www.writewhereithurts.net for more on this discussion.

11. We use this phrasing because it is entirely possible that transgender people are within any and all survey samples, but since explicit questions about sex/gender are rarely asked in the creation of most surveys, there is no way to identify whether or not this is the case.

12. Westbrook and Saperstein, "New Categories."

13. We received the Joseph H. Fichter Grant from the Association for the Sociology of Religion. See www.sociologyofreligion.com/lectures-papers/fichter-research -grant-competition/ for more information on our funding source.

14. The organizations we donated to in exchange for sharing the survey are Black Transwomen Inc., Black Transmen Inc., Black Trans Advocacy Group, and the Transgender American Veterans Association. In the process, we reached out to many other organizations that did not end up returning our contact, whether or not they may have utilized the survey in any way. In giving funds to these organizations, we made clear that provision of funds was not contingent on any specific number of members or social media followers completing the survey. These organizations received the funds regardless of whether any members or followers decided to take part in our research.

15. Some social media pages did not have moderators. As such, there were no moderators from whom to seek permission in these cases. Although we were prepared to remove the survey from any social media pages if members of the groups opposed us sharing it, no such situation occurred.

16. Pfeffer, "Queer Accounting."

17. For example, we each know people who could answer any of these questions in a wide variety of ways based on their own lives and relationships with others.

Bibliography

Acosta, Katie L. *Amigas y Amantes: Sexually Nonconforming Latinas Negotiate Family*. New Brunswick, NJ: Rutgers University Press, 2013.

Adamczyk, Amy. *Cross-National Public Opinion about Homosexuality: Examining Attitudes Across the Globe*. Berkeley: University of California Press, 2017.

Ahlm, Jody. "Respectable Promiscuity: Digital Cruising in an Era of Queer Liberalism." *Sexualities* 20, no. 3 (March 2017): 364–79.

Ahmed, Sara. *Queer Phenomenology: Orientations, Objects, Others*. Durham, NC: Duke University Press, 2006.

Alegría, C. Aramburu. "Relationship Challenges and Relationship Maintenance Activities Following Disclosure of Transsexualism." *Psychiatric and Mental Health Nursing* 17, no. 10 (December 2010): 909–16.

Almeling, Rene. *Sex Cells: The Medical Market for Eggs and Sperm*. Berkeley: University of California Press, 2011.

Ames, Jonathan, ed. *Sexual Metamorphosis: An Anthology of Transsexual Memoirs*. New York: Vintage Books, 2005.

Ammerman, Nancy Tatom. *Congregation and Community*. New Brunswick, NJ: Rutgers University Press, 1997.

Anzaldua, Gloria. *Borderlands/La Frontera: The New Mestiza*. San Francisco: Aunt Lute, 1987.

Armstrong, Elizabeth A. *Forging Gay Identities: Organizing Sexuality in San Francisco, 1950–1994.* Chicago: University of Chicago Press, 2002.

Aune, Kristin. "Feminist Spirituality as Lived Religion: How UK Feminists Forge Religio-spiritual Lives." *Gender & Society* 29, no. 1 (February 2015): 122–45.

Avishai, Orit. "'Doing Religion' in a Secular World: Women in Conservative Religions and the Question of Agency." *Gender & Society* 22, no. 4 (August 2008): 409–33.

Avishai, Orit, Afshan Jafar, and Rachel Rinaldo. "A Gender Lens on Religion." *Gender & Society* 29, no. 1 (February 2015): 5–25.

Badgett, M. V. Lee, Laura E. Durso, and Alyssa Schneebaum. *New Patterns of Poverty in the Lesbian, Gay, and Bisexual Community.* Los Angeles: Williams Institute, 2013.

Barrett-Fox, Rebecca. *God Hates: Westboro Baptist Church, American Nationalism, and the Religious Right.* Lawrence: University Press of Kansas, 2016.

Barringer, M. N., J. E. Sumerau, and David A. Gay. "Examining Differences in Identity Disclosure between Monosexuals and Bisexuals." *Sociological Spectrum* 37, no. 5 (2017): 319–33.

Barton, Bernadette. 2012. *Pray the Gay Away: The Extraordinary Lives of Bible Belt Gays.* New York: New York University Press, 2012.

Bauer, Robin. "Transgressive and Transformative Gendered and Sexual Practices and White Privileges: The Case of Dyke/Trans BDSM Communities." *Women's Studies Quarterly* 36, no. 3–4 (fall–winter 2008): 233–53.

Becker, Penny Edgell. *Congregations in Conflict: Cultural Models of Local Religious Life.* New York: Cambridge University Press, 1999.

Beemyn, Genny, and Susan Rankin. *The Lives of Transgender People.* New York: Columbia University Press, 2011.

Bellah, Robert N., Richard Madsen, William M. Sullivan, Ann Swidler, and Steven M. Tipton. *Habits of the Heart: Individualism and Commitment in American Life.* Berkeley: University of California Press, 1985.

Bellwether, Mira. *Fucking Trans Women.* Independently published, 2010.

Benjamin, Harry. *The Transsexual Phenomenon.* New York: Julian Press, 1966.

Bennett, Jeffrey. "'Born this Way': Queer Vernacular and the Politics of Origins." *Communication and Critical/Cultural Studies* 11, no. 3 (2014): 211–30.

Berg, Bruce L., and Howard Lune. *Qualitative Research Methods for the Social Sciences*, 8th ed. Essex, UK: Pearson Educated Limited, 2014.

Bernstein, Mary, and Verta Taylor, eds. *The Marrying Kind? Debating Same-Sex Marriage within the Lesbian and Gay Movement.* Minneapolis: University of Minnesota Press, 2013.

Bischof, Gary H., Bethany L. Warnaar, Mark S. Barajas, and Harkiran K. Dhaliwal. "Thematic Analysis of the Experiences of Wives Who Stay with Husbands who Transition Male-to-Female." *Michigan Family Review* 15, no. 1 (2011): 16–34.

Bishop, Katelynn. "Body Modifications and Trans Men: The Lived Realities of Gender Transition and Partner Intimacy." *Body & Society* 22, no. 1 (March 2016): 62–91.

Blank, Hanne, and Raven Kaldera. *Best Transgender Erotica.* Boston: Circlet, 2002.

Blumer, Herbert. *Symbolic Interaction: Perspective and Method.* Berkeley: University of California Press, 1969.

Blumer, Markie L. C., Y. Gavriel Ansara, and Courtney M. Watson. "Cisgenderism in Family Therapy: How Everyday Clinical Practices Can Delegitimize People's Gender Self-Designations." *Journal of Family Psychotherapy* 24, no. 4 (2013): 267–85.

Boenke, Mary, ed. *Trans Forming Families: Real Stories about Transgendered Loved Ones*, 2nd ed., expanded. Hardy, VA: Oak Knoll Press.

Bolin, Anne. *In Search of Eve: Transsexual Rites of Passage.* New York: Bergin and Garvey, 1988.

Bonilla-Silva, Eduardo. *Racism without Racists: Colorblind Racism and the Persistence of Racial Inequality in the United States.* Lanham, MD: Rowman & Littlefield, 2003.

Bornstein, Kate. *Gender Outlaw: On Men, Women, and the Rest of Us.* New York: Routledge, 2016.

Bourdieu, Pierre. *Cultural Reproduction and Social Reproduction.* London: Tavistock, 1973.

Boylan, Jennifer Finney. *She's Not There: A Life in Two Genders*. New York: Broadway Paperbacks, 2013.

Bridges, Tristan. "A Very 'Gay' Straight? Hybrid Masculinities, Sexual Aesthetics, and the Changing Relationship between Masculinity and Homophobia." *Gender & Society* 28, no. 1 (February 2014): 58–82.

Broad, K. L. "Coming Out for Parents, Families and Friends of Lesbians and Gays: From Support Group Grieving to Love Advocacy." *Sexualities* 14, no. 4 (August 2011): 399–415.

Brown, Nicola, R. "'I'm in Transition Too': Sexual Identity Renegotiation in Sexual-Minority Women's Relationships with Transsexual Men." *International Journal of Sexual Health* 21, no. 1 (2009): 61–77.

———. "The Sexual Relationships of Sexual-Minority Women Partnered with Trans Men: A Qualitative Study." *Archives of Sexual Behavior* 39, no. 2 (2010): 561–72.

———. "Stories from Outside the Frame: Intimate Partner Abuse in Sexual-Minority Women's Relationships with Transsexual Men." *Feminism & Psychology* 17, no. 3 (August 2007): 373–93.

Brown, Suzanne, Jo Kucharska, and Magdalena Marczak. "Mental Health Practitioners' Attitudes towards Transgender People: A Systematic Review of the Literature." *International Journal of Transgenderism* 19, no. 1 (2018): 4–24.

Brubaker, Rogers. *Trans: Gender and Race in an Age of Unsettled Identities*. Princeton, NJ: Princeton University Press, 2016.

Bryant, Karl. "In Defense of Gay Children? 'Progay' Homophobia and the Production of Homonormativity." *Sexualities* 11, no. 4 (August 2008): 455–75.

Buggs, Shantel Gabrieal. "Dating in the Time of #BlackLivesMatter: Exploring Mixed-Race Women's Discourses of Race and Racism." *Sociology of Race and Ethnicity* 3, no. 4 (October 2017): 538–51.

Burke, Kelsy. *Christians under Covers: Evangelicals and Sexual Pleasure on the Internet*. Oakland: University of California Press, 2016.

Burke, Mary C. "Resisting Pathology: GID and the Contested Terrain of Diagnosis in the Transgender Rights Movement." In *Sociology of Diagnosis*, edited by P. J. McGann and D. J. Hutson, 183–210. Advances in Medical Sociology 12. Bingley, UK: Emerald Group, 2011.

Butler, Judith. *Bodies That Matter: On the Discursive Limits of "Sex."* New York: Routledge, 1993.

———. *Gender Trouble: Feminism and the Subversion of Identity.* New York, Routledge, 1999.

———. *Undoing Gender.* New York: Routledge, 2004.

Calasanti, Toni M., and Kathleen F. Selvin. *Gender, Social Inequality, and Aging.* New York: Alta Mira, 2001.

Califia, Pat. *Sex Changes: Transgender Politics.* Jersey City, NJ: Cleis, 2012.

Carter, Shannon K., and Amanda Koontz Anthony. "Good, Bad, and Extraordinary Mothers: Infant Feeding and Mothering in African American Mothers' Breastfeeding Narratives." *Sociology of Race and Ethnicity* 1, no. 4 (2015): 517–31.

Castañeda, Claudia. "Developing Gender: The Medical Treatment of Transgender Young People." *Social Science & Medicine* 143 (October 2015): 262–70.

Chambre, Susan M. *Fighting for Our Lives: New York's AIDS Community and the Politics of Disease.* New Brunswick, NJ: Rutgers University Press, 2006.

Charmaz, Cathy. *Constructing Grounded Theory.* Thousand Oaks, CA: Sage, 2006.

Chasin, CJ DeLuzio. "Making Sense in and of the Asexual Community: Navigating Relationships and Identities in a Context of Resistance." *Journal of Community and Applied Social Psychology* 25 (2015): 167–80.

Chen, Mel Y. "Everywhere Archives: Transgendering Trans Asians, and the Internet." *Australian Feminist Studies* 25, no. 64 (2010): 199–208.

Cheng, Cliff. "Marginalized Masculinities and Hegemonic Masculinity: An Introduction." *Journal of Men's Studies* 7, no. 3 (June 1999): 295–315.

Chrisler, Joan C., and Paula Caplan. "The Strange Case of Dr. Jekyll and Ms. Hyde: How PMS Became a Cultural Phenomenon and a Psychiatric Disorder." *Annual Review of Sex Research* 13, no. 1 (2002): 274–306.

Cimino, Richard, and Christopher Smith. *Atheist Awakening: Secular Activism and Community in America.* New York: Oxford, 2014.

———. "Secular Humanism and Atheism beyond Progressive Secularism." *Sociology of Religion* 68, no. 4 (2007): 407–24.

Cohen, Cathy J. "Punks, Bulldaggers, and Welfare Queens: The Radical Potential of Queer Politics?" *GLQ: A Journal of Lesbian and Gay Studies* 3, no. 4 (1997): 437–65.

Coley, Jonathan S. *Gay on God's Campus: Mobilizing for LGBT Equality at Christian Colleges and Universities.* Chapel Hill: University of North Carolina Press, 2018.

Collins, Patricia Hill. *Black Feminist Thought: Knowledge, Consciousness, and the Politics of Empowerment,* 2nd ed. New York: Routledge, 2000.

———. *Black Sexual Politics: African Americans, Gender, and the New Racism.* New York: Routledge, 2004.

———. *Fighting Words: Black Women and the Search for Justice.* Minneapolis: University of Minnesota Press, 1998.

———. "Intersectionality's Definitional Dilemmas." *Annual Review of Sociology* 41 (August 2015): 1–20.

Collins, Sharon M. *Black Corporate Executives: The Making and Breaking of a Black Middle Class.* Philadelphia: Temple University Press, 1997.

Combahee River Collective. "A Black Feminist Statement." In *The Second Wave: A Reader in Feminist Theory.* New York, Routledge, 1997 [1977].

Compton, D'Lane, Tey Meadow, and Kristen Schilt, eds. *Other, Please Specify: Queer Methods in Sociology.* Oakland: University of California Press, 2018.

Connell, Catherine. "Doing, Undoing, or Redoing Gender? Learning from the Workplace Experiences of Transpeople." *Gender & Society* 24, no. 1 (February 2010): 31–55.

Connell, Raewyn. "Accountable Conduct: 'Doing Gender' in Transsexual and Political Retrospect." *Gender & Society* 23, no. 1 (2009): 104–11.

Connell, Raewyn, and James Messerschmidt. "Hegemonic Masculinity: Rethinking the Concept." *Gender & Society* 19, no. 6 (December 2005): 829–59.

Connell, R. W. *Gender and Power: Society, the Person, and Sexual Politics.* Stanford, CA: Stanford University Press, 1987.

Costello, Cary Gabriel. "Nonconsensual Intersex Surgery as Physical Conversion Therapy." The Intersex Roadshow (blog), August 20, 2018, https://intersex roadshow.blogspot.com/2018/08/nonconsensual-intersex-surgery-as.html.

———. "Not a 'Medical Miracle': Intersex Reproduction and the Medical Enforcement of Binary Sex and Gender." In *Maternity and Motherhood: Narrative and Theoretical Perspectives on Queer Conception, Birth, and Parenting*, edited by Margaret F. Gibson, 63–80. Bradford, ON: Demeter Press, 2014.

———. "Trans and Intersex Children: Forced Sex Changes, Chemical Castration, and Self-Determination." In *Women's Health: Readings on Social, Economic, and Political Issues*. Dubuque, IA: Kendall Hunt, 2016.

———. "Understanding Intersex Relationship Issues." In *Expanding the Rainbow: Exploring the Relationships of Bi+, Trans, Polyamorous, Asexual, Kinky, and Intersex People*, edited by Brandy L. Simula, J. E. Sumerau, and Andrea Miller. Boston: Brill Sense, forthcoming.

Cragun, Ryan T., and J. E. Sumerau. "The Last Bastion of Sexual and Gender Prejudice? Sexualities, Race, Gender, Religiosity, and Spirituality in the Examination of Prejudice toward Sexual and Gender Minorities." *Journal of Sex Research* 52, no. 7 (2015): 821–34.

———. "No One Expects a Transgender Jew: Religious, Sexual, and Gendered Intersections in the Evaluation of Religious and Nonreligious Others." *Secularism and Nonreligion* 6, no. 1 (2017): 1–16. DOI: 10.5334/snr.82

Cragun. Ryan T., Emily Williams, and J. E. Sumerau. "From Sodomy to Sympathy: LDS Elites' Discursive Construction of Homosexuality Over Time." *Journal for the Scientific Study of Religion* 54, no. 2 (May 2015): 291–310.

Creek, S. J. "'Not Getting Any Because of Jesus': The Centrality of Desire Management to the Identity Work of Gay, Celibate Christians." *Symbolic Interaction* 36, no. 2 (May 2013): 119–36.

Crenshaw, Kimberlé. "Mapping the Margins: Intersectionality, Identity Politics, and Violence against Women of Color." *Stanford Law Review* 46, no. 3 (July 1991): 1241–99.

Criminal Queers. Directed by Chris Vargas and Eric A. Stanley. Homotopia Films, 2016.

Cromwell, Jason. *Transmen and FTMs: Identities, Bodies, Genders and Sexualities*. Urbana: University of Illinois Press, 1999.

Cruel and Unusual. Directed by Janet Baus and Dan Hunt. CreateSpace, 2007.

Cruz, Taylor M. "Assessing Access to Care for Transgender and Gender Nonconforming people: A Consideration of Diversity in Combating Discrimination." *Social Science and Medicine* 110 (2014): 65–73.

Currah, Paisley. "Expecting Bodies: The Pregnant Man and Transgender Exclusion from the Employment Non-Discrimination Act." *Women's Studies Quarterly* 36, no. 3–4 (December 2008): 330–36.

Darwin, Helana. "Doing Gender beyond the Binary: A Virtual Ethnography." *Symbolic Interaction* 40, no. 3 (August 2017): 317–34.

Davidman, Lynn. *Tradition in a Rootless World: Women Turn to Orthodox Judaism.* Berkeley, University of California Press, 1991.

Davis, Georgiann. *Contesting Intersex: The Dubious Diagnosis.* New York: New York University Press, 2015.

Davis, Georgiann, Jodie M. Dewey, and Erin L. Murphy. "Giving Sex: Deconstructing Intersex and Trans Medicalization Practices." *Gender & Society* 30, no. 3 (June 2016): 490–514.

Davis, Heath Fogg. *Beyond Trans: Does Gender Matter?* New York: New York University Press, 2017.

DeCurtis, Anthony. *Lou Reed: A Life.* New York: Little, Brown, 2017.

Deer, Sarah. *The Beginning and End of Rape: Confronting Sexual Violence in Native America.* Minneapolis: University of Minnesota Press, 2015.

Demantas, Ilana, and Kristen Meyers. "'Step Up and Be a Man in a Different Manner': Unemployed Men Reframing Masculinity." *Sociological Quarterly* 56, no. 4 (fall 2015): 640–64.

Denny, D. "The Politics of Diagnosis and a Diagnosis Politics: The University-Affiliated Gender Clinics, and How They Failed to Meet the Needs of Transsexual People." *Chrysalis Quarterly* 1, no. 3 (1992): 9–20.

Devor, Holly. *FTM: Female-to-Male Transsexuals in Society.* Bloomington: Indiana University Press, 1997.

De Vries, Kylan Mattias de. "Intersectional Identities and Conceptions of the Self: The Experience of Transgender People." *Symbolic Interaction* 35, no. 1 (2012): 49–67.

Dewey, Jodie M. "Challenges of Implementing Collaborative Models of Decision Making with Trans-Identified Patients." *Health Expectations* 18, no. 5 (2015): 1508–18.

Dewey, Jodie M., and Melissa Gesbeck. "(Dys)Functional Diagnosing: Mental Health Diagnosis, Medicalization, and the Making of Transgender Patients." *Humanity and Society* 41, no. 1 (February 2017): 37–72.

Diamond, Lisa M. *Sexual Fluidity: Understanding Women's Love and Desire.* Cambridge, MA: Harvard University Press, 2008.

Dillon, Michele. *Postsecular Catholicism: Relevance and Renewal.* New York: Oxford, 2018.

Dingwall, Robert. "Notes toward an Intellectual History of Symbolic Interactionism." *Symbolic Interaction* 24, no. 2 (2001): 237–42.

Doan, Petra. "Coming Out of Darkness and into Activism." *Gender, Place, and Culture* 24, no. 5 (2017): 741–46.

———. "To Count or Not to Count: Queering Measurement and the Transgender Community." *Women's Studies Quarterly* 44, no. 3–4 (fall/winter 2016): 89–110.

Dozier, Raine. "Beards, Breasts, and Bodies: Doing Sex in a Gendered World." *Gender & Society* 19, no. 3 (June 2005): 297–316.

Drescher, Jack. "Queer Diagnoses: Parallels and Contrasts in the History of Homosexuality, Gender Variance, and the *Diagnostic and Statistical Manual.*" *Archives of Sexual Behavior* 39, no. 2 (April 2010): 427–60.

Driskill, Qwo-Li, Daniel Heath Justice, Deborah Miranda, and Lisa Tatonetti, eds. *Sovereign Erotics: A Collection of Two-Spirit Literature.* Tucson: University of Arizona Press, 2011.

Du Bois, W. E. B. *The Souls of Black Folk.* Chicago: McClurg, 1903.

Duggan, Lisa. *The Twilight of Equality? Neoliberalism, Cultural Politics and the Attack on Democracy.* Boston: Beacon Press, 2004.

Dzmura, Noach, ed. *Balancing on the Mechitza: Transgender in Jewish Community.* Berkeley, CA: North Atlantic Books, 2010.

Edgley, Charles, ed. *The Drama of Social Life: A Dramaturgical Handbook.* New York: Routledge, 2016.

Eisner, Shiri. *Bi: Notes for a Bisexual Revolution*. Berkeley, CA: Seal Press, 2013.

Ekins, Richard, and Dave King. "Towards a Sociology of Transgendered Bodies." *Sociological Review* 47, no. 3 (August 1999): 580–602.

El-Rouayheb, Khaled. *Before Homosexuality in the Arab-Islamic World, 1500–1800*. Chicago, University of Chicago Press, 2005.

Elledge, Jim, ed. *Gay, Lesbian, Bisexual, and Transgender Myths: From the Arapaho to Zuñi: An Anthology*. New York: Peter Lang, 2002.

Erickson-Schroth, Laura. *Trans Bodies, Trans Selves: A Resource for the Transgender Community*. New York: Oxford, 2014.

Erzen, Tanya. *Straight to Jesus: Sexual and Christian Conversions in the Ex-Gay Movement*. Berkeley: University of California Press, 2006.

Espiritu, Yen Le. "'We Don't Sleep Around Like White Girls Do': Family, Culture, and Gender in Filipina American Lives." *Signs: Journal of Women in Culture and Society* 26, no. 2 (winter 2001): 415–40.

Eyssel, Jana, Andreas Koehler, Arne Dekker, Susanne Sehner, and Timo O. Nieder. "Needs and Concerns of Transgender Individuals Regarding Interdisciplinary Transgender Healthcare: A Non-Clinical Online Survey." *PLoS ONE* 12, no. 8 (2017): e0183014.

Ezzell, Matthew B. "'Barbie Dolls' on the Pitch: Identity Work, Defensive Othering, and Inequality in Women's Rugby." *Social Problems* 56, no. 1 (February 2009): 111–31.

———. "Pornography, Lad Mags, Video Games, and Boys: Reviving the Canary in the Cultural Coal Mine." In *The Sexualization of Childhood*, edited by Sharna Olfman, 7–32. Westport, CT: Praeger, 2009.

Fausto-Sterling, Anne. *Sex/Gender: Biology in a Social World*. New York: Routledge, 2012.

———. *Sexing the Body: Gender Politics and the Construction of Sexuality*. New York: Basic Books, 2000.

Feinberg, Leslie. *Stone Butch Blues*. Old Chelsea Station, NY: Alyson Books, 1993.

———. *Transgender Warriors: Making History from Joan of Arc to Dennis Rodman*. Boston: Beacon Press, 1996.

———. *Trans Liberation: Beyond Pink and Blue*. Boston: Beacon Press, 1998.

Feliciano, Cynthia, and Rubén G. Rumbaut. "Gendered Paths: Educational and Occupational Expectations and Outcomes among Adult Children of Immigrants." *Ethnic and Racial Studies* 28(6) (2005): 1087–1118.

Fenstermaker, Sarah. "The Turn from 'What' to 'How': Garfinkel's Reach beyond Description." *Symbolic Interaction* 39, no. 2 (May 2016): 295–305.

Ferguson, Roderick A. "Race-ing Homonormativity: Citizenship, Sociology, and Gay Identity." In *Black Queer Studies: A Critical Anthology*, edited by E. Patrick Johnson and Mae G. Henderson, 52–67. Durham, NC: Duke University Press, 2005.

Fetner, Tina. *How the Religious Right Shaped Lesbian and Gay Activism*. Minneapolis: University of Minnesota Press, 2008.

Fetner, Tina. "Anti-LGBT Activism: Same as It Ever Was." Gender & Society (blog), April 27, 2016. https://gendersociety.wordpress.com/2016/04/27/anti -lgbt-activism-same-as-it-ever-was

Fetner, Tina, and Melanie Heath. "Studying the 'Right' Can Feel Wrong: Reflections on Researching Anti-LGBT Movements." In *Other, Please Specify: Queer Methods in Sociology*, edited by D'Lane Compton, Tey Meadow, and Kristen Schilt, 140– 53. Oakland: University of California Press, 2018.

Fetner, Tina, and Kristin Kush. "Gay-Straight Alliances in High Schools: Social Predictors of Early Adoption." *Youth & Society* 40, no. 1 (September 2008): 114–30.

Fields, Jessica. "Normal Queers: Straight Parents Respond to Their Children's 'Coming Out'." *Symbolic Interaction* 24, no. 2 (2001): 165–87.

———. *Risky Lessons: Sex Education and Social Inequality*. New Brunswick, NJ: Rutgers University Press, 2008.

Fine, Cordelia. "Explaining, or Sustaining, the Status Quo? The Potentially Self-Fulfilling Effects of 'Hardwired' Accounts of Sex Differences." *Neuroethics* 5, no. 3 (December 2012): 285–94.

Finley, Nancy J. "Skating Femininity: Gender Maneuvering in Women's Roller Derby." *Journal of Contemporary Ethnography* 39, no. 4 (August 2010): 359–87.

Foucault, Michel. *The Archaeology of Knowledge and Discourse on Language*. New York: Pantheon, 1972.

———. *Discipline and Punish: The Birth of the Prison.* New York: Vintage, 1995.

———. *The History of Sexuality.* Volume 1: *An Introduction.* New York: Vintage, 1978.

———. *The History of Sexuality.* Volume 2: *The Use of Pleasure.* New York: Vintage, 1985.

———. *The History of Sexuality.* Volume 3: *The Care of the Self.* New York: Vintage, 1988.

———. *The Order of Things: An Archaeology of the Human Sciences.* New York: Vintage, 1994.

France, David. *How to Survive a Plague: The Story of How Activists and Scientists Tamed AIDS.* New York: Vintage, 2016.

Fuhrmann, Arnika. *Ghostly Desires: Queer Sexuality and Vernacular Buddhism in Contemporary Thai Cinema.* Durham, NC: Duke University Press, 2016.

Gagné, Patricia, and Richard Tewksbury. "Conformity Pressures and Gender Resistance among Transgendered Individuals." *Social Problems* 45, no. 1 (1998): 81–101.

———. "Knowledge and Power, Body and Self: An Analysis of Knowledge Systems and the Transgendered Self." *Sociological Quarterly* 40, no. 1 (winter 1999): 59–83.

Gagné, Patricia, Richard Tewksbury, and Deanna McGaughey. "Coming Out and Crossing Over: Identity Formation and Proclamation in a Transgender Community." *Gender & Society* 11, no. 4 (August 1997): 478–508.

Gallardo, Gabriel. "The Transgender Muse that Helped Change the Music Scene of the 1970s." *Cultura Colectiva,* July 18, 2017. https://culturacolectiva.com/music/rachel-transgender-muse-lou-reed/

Garber, Marjorie. *Bisexuality and the Eroticism of Everyday Life.* New York: Routledge, 1995.

Garcia, Lorena. *Respect Yourself, Protect Yourself: Latina Girls and Sexual Identity.* New York: New York University Press, 2012.

Garfinkel, Harold. *Studies in Ethnomethodology.* Malden, MA: Blackwell, 1967.

Garrison, Spencer. "On the Limits of 'Trans Enough': Authenticating Trans Identity Narratives." *Gender & Society* 32, no. 5 (October 2018): 613–37.

Gay, Geneva. "Navigating Marginality en route to the Professoriate: Graduate Students of Color Learning and Living in Academia." *International Journal of Qualitative Studies in Education* 17, no. 2 (2004): 265–88.

Gehi, Pooja A., and Gabriel Arkles. "Unraveling Injustice: Race and Class Impact of Medicaid Exclusions of Transition-Related Health Care for Transgender People." *Sexuality Research and Social Policy* 4, no. 4 (December 2007): 7–35.

Gerber, Lynne. "Grit, Guts, and Vanilla Beans: Godly Masculinity in the Ex-Gay Movement." *Gender & Society* 29, no. 1 (February 2015): 26–50.

Giblon, Rachel, and Grata R. Bauer. "Health Care Availability, Quality, and Unmet Need: A Comparison of Transgender and Cisgender Residents of Ontario, Canada." *BMC Health Services Research* 17 (April 2017): 283.

Gibson, Andrea. *Hey Galaxy.* Tender Loving Empire Records 797822264399, 2018, vinyl.

———. *The Madness Vase.* Long Beach, CA: Write Bloody, 2011.

———. *Pansy.* Nashville: Write Bloody, 2015.

———. *Pole Dancing to Gospel Hymns.* Nashville: Write Bloody, 2008.

Gill, Michael. *Already Doing It: Intellectual Disability and Sexual Agency.* Minneapolis: University of Minnesota Press, 2015.

Goffman, Erving. "The Arrangement between the Sexes." *Theory and Society* 4, no. 3 (autumn 1977): 301–31.

———. *The Presentation of Self in Everyday Life.* New York: Anchor Books, 1959.

———. *Stigma: Notes on the Management of Spoiled Identity.* New York: Simon and Schuster, 1963.

Gorman, Bridget K., Justin T. Denney, Hillary Dowdy, and Rose Anne Medeiros. "A New Piece of the Puzzle: Sexual Orientation, Gender, and Physical Health Status." *Demography* 52, no. 4 (August 2015): 1357–82.

Gossett, Reina, Eric A. Stanley, and Johanna Burton, eds. *Trap Door: Trans Cultural Production and the Politics of Visibility.* Cambridge, MA: MIT Press, 2017.

Grace, Laura Jane, and Dan Ozzi. *Tranny: Confessions of Punk Rock's Most Infamous Anarchist Sellout.* New York: Hachette, 2016.

Grant, Jaime M., Lisa A. Mottet, Justin Tanis, Jack Harrison, Jody L. Herman, and Mara Keisling. *Injustice at Every Turn: A Report of the National Transgender Discrimination Survey.* Washington, DC: National Center for Transgender Equality and National Gay and Lesbian Task Force, 2011.

Green, Jamison. *Becoming a Visible Man.* Nashville: Vanderbilt University Press, 2004.

Grollman, Eric Anthony. "Multiple Disadvantaged Statuses and Health." *Journal of Health and Social Behavior* 55, no. 1 (March 2014): 3–19.

———. "Multiple Forms of Perceived Discrimination and Health among Adolescents and Young Adults." *Journal of Health and Social Behavior* 53, no. 2 (June 2012): 199–214.

Gupta, Kristina. "'And Now I'm Just Different, but There's Nothing Actually Wrong with Me': Asexual Marginalization and Resistance." *Journal of Homosexuality* 64, no. 8 (2017): 991–1013.

Gutiérrez, Jennicet, Steven Thrasher, Paulina Helm-Hernandez, Greggor Mattson, Salvador Vidal-Ortiz, Terry Roethlein, and Angela Jones. "Systemic Violence: Reflections on the Pulse Nightclub Massacre." In *The Unfinished Queer Agenda after Marriage Equality,* edited by Angela Jones, Joseph Nicholas DeFilippis, and Michael W. Yarbrough, 20–34. New York, Routledge, 2018.

Hagen, Whitney B., Stephanie M. Hoover, and Susan L. Morrow. "A Grounded Theory of Sexual Minority Women and Transgender Individuals' Social Justice Activism." *Journal of Homosexuality* 65, no. 7 (2018): 833–59.

Halberstam, J. *Female Masculinity.* Durhamn, NC: Duke University Press, 1998.

———. *In a Queer Time and Place: Transgender Bodies, Subcultural Lives.* New York: New York University Press, 2005.

Harding, Sandra, ed. *The Feminist Standpoint Theory Reader: Intellectual and Political Controversies.* New York: Routledge, 2004.

Hartke, Austen. *Transforming: The Bible and the Lives of Transgender Christians.* Louisville, KY: Westminster John Knox Press, 2018.

Hartless, Jaime. "Questionably Queer: Understanding Straight Presence in the Post-Gay Bar." *Journal of Homosexuality* (2018). DOI: 10.1080/00918369.2018.1491707

Heath, Melanie. *One Marriage under God: The Campaign to Promote Marriage in America.* New York: New York University Press, 2012.

Hines, Sally. *TransForming Gender: Transgender Practices of Identity, Intimacy and Care*. Bristol, UK: Policy Press, 2007.

———. "What's the Difference? Bringing Particularity to Queer Studies of Transgender." *Journal of Gender Studies* 15, no. 1 (2006): 49–66.

Hoffman-Fox, Dara. *You and Your Gender Identity: A Guide to Discovery*. New York: Skyhorse, 2017.

Hollander, Jocelyn. "'I Demand More of People': Accountability, Interaction, and Gender Change." *Gender & Society* 27, no. 1 (2013): 5–29.

hooks, bell. *Teaching to Transgress: Education as the Practice of Freedom*. New York: Routledge, 1994.

Hughes, Cayce C. "Not Out in the Field: Studying Privacy and Disclosure as an Invisible (Trans) Man." In *Other, Please Specify: Queer Methods in Sociology*, edited by D'Lane Compton, Tey Meadow, and Kristen Schilt, 111–25. Oakland: University of California Press, 2018.

Hughes, James. "Beyond the Medical Model of Gender Dysphoria to Morphological Self-Determination." *Lahey Clinic Medical Ethics Journal* 13, no. 1 (2006): 10.

Institute of Medicine. "The Health of Lesbian, Gay, Bisexual, and Transgender People: Building a Foundation for a Better Understanding." *Report Brief for the Institute of Medicine of the National Academies* (March 31, 2011).

Irving, John. *In One Person*. New York: Simon and Schuster, 2012.

Ivankovich, Megan B., Jami S. Leichliter, and John M. Douglas Jr. "Measurement of Sexual Health in the U.S.: An Inventory of Nationally Representative Surveys and Surveillance Systems." *Public Health Reports* 128, no. 1 (March/April 2013): 62–72.

Jacobs, Sue-Ellen, Wesley Thomas, and Sabine Lang, eds. *Two-Spirit People: Native American Gender Identity, Sexuality, and Spirituality*. Urbana-Champaign: University of Illinois Press, 1997.

James, S. E., C. Brown, and I. Wilson. *2015 U.S. Transgender Survey: Report on the Experiences of Black Respondents*. Washington, DC, and Dallas, TX: National Center for Transgender Equality, Black Trans Advocacy, and National Black Justice Coalition, 2017.

James, S. E., J. L. Herman, S. Rankin, M. Keisling, L. Mottet, and M. Anafi. *The Report of the 2015 U.S. Transgender Survey*. Washington, DC: National Center for Transgender Equality, 2016.

James, S. E., T. Jackson, and M. Jim. *2015 U.S. Transgender Survey: Report on the Experiences of American Indian and Alaska Native Respondents.* Washington, DC: National Center for Transgender Equality, 2017.

James, S. E., and G. Magpantay. *2015 U.S. Transgender Survey: Report on the Experiences of Asian, Native Hawaiian, and Pacific Islander Respondents.* Washington, DC, and New York: National Center for Transgender Equality and National Queer Asian Pacific Islander Alliance, 2017.

James, S. E., and B. Salcedo. *2015 U.S. Transgender Survey: Report on the Experiences of Latino/a Respondents.* Washington, DC, and Los Angeles, CA: National Center for Transgender Equality and TransLatin@ Coalition, 2017.

Jasinski, Jana L., Jennifer K. Weekly, James D. Wright, and Elizabeth E. Mustaine. *Hard Lives, Mean Streets: Violence in the Lives of Homeless Women.* Boston: Northeastern University Press, 2010.

Jauk, Daniela. "Gender Violence Revisited: Lessons from Violent Victimization of Transgender Identified Individuals." *Sexualities* 16, no. 7 (2013): 807–25.

Jenness, Valerie, and Sarah Fenstermaker. "Agnes Goes to Prison: Gender Authenticity, Transgender Inmates in Prisons for Men, and Pursuit of 'The Real Deal'." *Gender & Society* 28, no. 1 (February 2014): 5–31.

Johnson, Austin H. "Beyond Inclusion: Thinking toward a Transfeminist Methodology." In *At the Center: Feminism, Social Science, and Knowledge,* edited by Vasilikie Demos and Marcia Texler Segal, 21–42. Bingley, UK: Emerald, 2015.

———. "Normative Accountability: How the Medical Model Influences Transgender Identities and Experiences." *Sociology Compass* 9, no. 9 (2015): 803–13.

———. "Transgender People, Medical Authority, and the Lived Experience of Medicalization." Unpublished dissertation, Kent State University, 2017.

———. "Transnormativity: A New Concept and Its Validation through Documentary Film about Transgender Men." *Sociological Inquiry* 86, no. 4 (November 2016): 465–91.

———. "Rejecting, Reframing, and Reintroducing: Trans People's Strategic Engagement with the Medicalisation of Gender Dysphoria." *Sociology of Health and Illness.* DOI: 10.1111/1467-9566.12829

Jones, Angela. *African American Civil Rights: Early Activism and the Niagara Movement.* Santa Barbara, CA: Praeger, 2011.

Jones, Angela, ed. *A Critical Inquiry into Queer Utopias*. New York: Palgrave Macmillan, 2013.

Jordan, Mark D. *The Invention of Sodomy in Christian Theology*. Chicago: University of Chicago Press, 1997.

Jordan-Young, Rebecca, and Raffaella I. Rumiati. "Hardwired for Sexism? Approaches to Sex/Gender in Neuroscience." *Neuroethics* 5, no. 3 (December 2012): 305–15.

Karkazis, Katrina. *Fixing Sex: Intersex, Medical Authority, and Lived Experience*. Durham, NC: Duke University Press, 2008.

Katz, Jonathan Ned. *The Invention of Heterosexuality*. Chicago: University of Chicago Press, 1995.

Keller, Ursula, and Kathryn Harker Tillman. "Post-Secondary Educational Attainment of Immigrant and Native Youth." *Social Forces* 87, no. 1 (September 2008): 121–52.

Kennedy, Pagan. *The First Man-Made Man: The Story of Two Sex Changes, One Love Affair, and a Twentieth-Century Medical Revolution*. New York: Bloomsbury, 2007.

Kessler, Suzanne J. *Lessons from the Intersexed*. New Brunswick, NJ: Rutgers University Press, 1998.

Khalili, J., L. B. Leung, and A. L. Diamant. "Finding the Perfect Doctor: Identifying Lesbian, Gay, Bisexual, and Transgender-Competent Physicians." *American Journal of Public Health* 105, no. 6 (June 2015): 1114–19.

Khurshid, Ayesha. "Islamic Traditions of Modernity: Gender, Class, and Islam in a Transnational Women's Education Project." *Gender & Society* 29, no. 1 (February 2015): 98–121.

Kirkpatrick Johnson, Monica, and John R. Reynolds. "Educational Expectation Trajectories and Attainment in the Transition to Adulthood." *Social Science Research* 42, no. 3 (May 2013): 818–35.

Kleinman, Sherryl. *Equals before God: Seminarians as Humanistic Professionals*. Chicago: University of Chicago Press, 1984.

———. *Feminist Fieldwork Analysis*. Thousand Oaks, CA: Sage, 2007.

Kosenko, Kami A., Lance Rintamaki, Stephanie Raney, and Kathleen Maness. "Transgender Patient Perceptions of Stigma in Health Care Contexts." *Medical Care* 51, no. 9 (August 2013): 819–22.

Koyama, Emi. "Whose Feminism Is It Anyway? The Unspoken Racism of the Trans Inclusion Debate," In *The Transgender Studies Reader*, volume 1, edited by Susan Stryker and Stephen Whittle, 698–705. New York: Routledge, 2006.

Kraus, Cynthia. "Critical Studies of the Sexed Brain: A Critique of What and for Whom?" *Neuroethics* 5, no. 3 (December 2012): 247–59.

Krieger, Nick. *Nina Here nor There: My Journey beyond Gender*. Boston: Beacon Press, 2011.

Kruse, Kevin M. *One Nation under God: How Corporate America Invented Christian America*. New York: Basic Books, 2015.

Kuhn, Thomas S. *The Structure of Scientific Revolutions*. Chicago: University of Chicago Press, 1962.

Lamble, Sarah. "Retelling Racialized Violence, Remaking White Innocence: The Politics of Interlocking Oppressions in Transgender Day of Remembrance." *Sexuality Research and Social Policy* 5, no. 1 (March 2005), article 24.

Lampe, Nik, Lin Huff-Corzine, and Jay Corzine. "The Pulse Scrolls." In *Homicide on the Rise: The Resurgence of Homicide in Urban America?* edited by Wendy Regoeczi and John Jarvis, 156–60. Proceedings of the 2018 Annual Meeting of the Homicide Research Working Group, Clearwater Beach, FL.

LeBlanc, Fred Joseph. "Unqueering Transgender? A Queer Geography of Transnormativity in Two Online Communities." Unpublished master's thesis, Victoria University of Wellington, 2010.

Lee, Jooyoung. *Blowin' Up: Rap Dreams in South Central*. Chicago: University of Chicago Press, 2016.

LeDrew, Stephen. "Discovering Atheism: Heterogeneity in Trajectories to Atheist Identity and Activism." *Sociology of Religion* 74, no. 4 (2013): 431–53.

Lev, Arlene Istar. *Transgender Emergence: Therapeutic Guidelines for Working with Gender-Variant People and Their Families*. Binghamton, NY: Haworth Clinical Practice Press, 2004.

Lewins, Frank. *Transsexualism in Society: A Sociology of Male-to-Female Transsexuals*. South Melbourne, Australia: Macmillan, 1995.

Link, Bruce G., and Jo Phelan. "Social Conditions as Fundamental Causes of Disease." *Journal of Health and Social Behavior* 1995, Extra Issue: 80–94.

Loewen, James W. *Lies My Teacher Told Me: Everything Your American History Textbook Got Wrong*. New York: Touchstone, 2007.

Lombardi, Emilia. "Trans Issues in Sociology: A Trans-Centered Perspective," In *Other, Please Specify: Queer Methods in Sociology*, edited by D'Lane Compton, Tey Meadow, and Kristen Schilt, 67–79. Oakland, CA, University of California Press, 2018.

Loseke, Donileen R., and James C. Cavendish. "Producing Institutional Selves: Rhetorically Constructing the Dignity of Sexually Marginalized Catholics." *Social Psychology Quarterly* 64, no. 4 (December 2001): 347–62.

Lowell, Shalen. "Symbiotic Love: On Dating, Sex, and Interpersonal Relationships among Transgender People." In *Expanding the Rainbow: Exploring the Relationships of Bi+, Trans, Polyamorous, Asexual, Kinky, and Intersex People*, edited by Brandy L. Simula, J. E. Sumerau, and Andrea Miller. Boston: Brill Sense, forthcoming.

Lucal, Betsy. "What It Means to Be Gendered Me: Life on the Boundaries of a Dichotomous Gender System." *Gender & Society* 13, no. 6 (December 1999): 781–97.

Lynch, Michael J. "The Power of Oppression: Understanding the History of Criminology as a Science of Oppression." *Critical Criminology* 9, no. 1–2 (September 2000): 144–52.

MacDonald, Trevor, Joy Noel-Weiss, Diana West, Michelle Walks, Mary Lynne Biener, Alanna Kibbe, and Elizabeth Myler. "Transmasculine Individuals' Experiences with Lactation, Chestfeeding, and Gender Identity: A Qualitative Study." *BMC Pregnancy and Childbirth* 16, no. 106 (2016). DOI: 0.1186/s12884 -016-0907-y

Magliozzi, Devon, Aliya Saperstein, and Laurel Westbrook. "Scaling Up: Representing Gender Diversity in Survey Research." *Socius* 2 (2016): 1–11.

Mamo, Laura. *Queering Reproduction: Achieving Pregnancy in the Age of Technoscience*. Durham, NC: Duke University Press, 2007.

Manion, Jen. "Transbutch." *Transgender Studies Quarterly* 1, no. 1–2 (May 2014): 230–32.

Marine, Susan B., and Z. Nicolazzo. "Names That Matter: Exploring the Tensions of Campus LGBTQ Centers and Trans* Inclusion." *Journal of Diversity in Higher Education* 7, no. 4 (December 2014): 265–81.

Martin, Patricia Yancey. "Gender as a Social Institution." *Social Forces* 82, no. 4 (June 2004): 1249–73.

———. *Rape Work: Victims, Gender, and Emotions in Organization and Community Context.* New York: Routledge, 2005.

Martinez–San Miguel, Yolanda, and Sarah Tobias, eds. *Trans Studies: The Challenge to Hetero/Homo Normativities.* New Brunswick, NJ: Rutgers University Press, 2016.

Marx, Karl. *Capital,* volume 1. New York: Penguin Classics, 1990.

Mathers, Lain. "What Team? Some Thoughts on Navigating Monosexism." Write Where It Hurts (blog), July 16, 2015. http://writewhereithurts.net/2015/07/16/what-team-some-thoughts-on-navigating-monosexism/

Mathers, Lain A. B. "Bathrooms, Boundaries, and Emotional Burdens: Cisgendering Interactions through the Interpretation of Transgender Experience." *Symbolic Interaction* 40, no. 3 (August 2017): 295–316.

———. "Expanding on the Experiences of Transgender Nonreligious People: An Exploratory Analysis." *Secularism and Nonreligion* 6 (2017): 1–10. DOI: 10.5334/snr.84

———. "Navigating Genderqueer Existence within and beyond the Academy." In *Negotiating the Emotional Challenges of Conducting Deeply Personal Research in Health,* edited by Alexandra "Xan" C. H. Nowakowski and J. E. Sumerau, 125–34. New York, Routledge, 2017.

———. "Sibling Relationships and the Bi+ Coming Out Process," In *Expanding the Rainbow: Exploring the Relationships of Bi+, Trans, Polyamorous, Asexual, Kinky, and Intersex People,* edited by Brandy L. Simula, J. E. Sumerau, and Andrea Miller. Boston: Brill Sense, forthcoming.

Mathers, Lain A. B., J. E. Sumerau, and Ryan T. Cragun. "The Limits of Homonormativity: Constructions of Bisexual and Transgender People in the Post-Gay Era." *Sociological Perspectives* 61, no. 6 (2018) 934–52.

Mathers, Lain A. B., J. E. Sumerau, and Koji Ueno. "'This Isn't Just Another Gay Group': Privileging Heterosexuality in a Mixed-Sexuality LGBTQ Advocacy Group." *Journal of Contemporary Ethnography* 47, no. 6 (2018) 834–64.

McBee, Thomas Page. *Amateur: A True Story about What Makes a Man*. New York: Scribner, 2018.

McBride, Sarah, and Joe Biden. *Tomorrow Will Be Different: Love, Loss, and the Fight for Trans Equality*. New York: Crown Archetype, 2018.

McCabe, Katharine, and J. E. Sumerau. "Reproductive Vocabularies: Interrogating Intersections of Reproduction, Sexualities, and Religion among U.S. Cisgender College Women." *Sex Roles* 78, no. 5–6 (March 2018): 352–66.

McIntyre, Joanna. "'They're So Normal I Can't Stand It': *I Am Jazz, I Am Cait*, Transnormativity, and Trans Feminism." In *Orienting Feminism: Media, Activism, and Cultural Representation*, edited by Catherine Dale and Rosemary Overall, 9–24. New York: Springer, 2018.

McLean, Kirsten. "Hiding in the Closet? Bisexuals, Coming Out and the Disclosure Imperative." *Journal of Sociology* 43, no. 2 (June 2007): 151–66.

McQueeney, Krista. "'We Are God's Children, Y'all': Race, Gender, and Sexuality in Lesbian-and Gay-Affirming Congregations." *Social Problems* 56, no. 1 (February 2009): 151–73.

Mead, George Herbert. *Mind, Self, and Society*. Chicago, University of Chicago Press, 1934.

Meadow, Tey. *Trans Kids: Being Gendered in the Twenty-First Century*. Oakland: University of California Press, 2018.

Meyerowitz, Joanne. *How Sex Changed: A History of Transsexuality in the United States*. Cambridge, MA: Harvard University Press, 2002.

Miller, Lisa R., and Eric Anthony Grollman. "The Social Costs of Gender Nonconformity for Transgender Adults: Implications for Discrimination and Health." *Sociological Forum* 30, no. 3 (September 2015): 809–31.

Mize, Trenton D. "Sexual Orientation in the Labor Market." *American Sociological Review* 81, no. 6 (December 2016): 1132–60.

Mizock, Lauren, and Thomas K. Lewis. "Trauma in Transgender Populations: Risk, Resilience, and Clinical Care." *Journal of Emotional Abuse* 8, no. 3 (2008): 335–54.

Mock, Janet. *Redefining Realness: My Path to Womanhood, Identity, Love, & So Much More*. New York: Atria Paperback, 2014.

Monro, Surya, Sally Hines, and Antony Osborne. "Is Bisexuality Invisible? A Review of Sexualities Scholarship 1970–2015." *Sociological Review* 65, no. 4 (November 2017): 663–81.

Moon, Dawne. *God, Sex, and Politics: Homosexuality and Everyday Theologies.* Chicago: University of Chicago Press, 2004.

Moon, Dawne, and Theresa W. Tobin. "Sunsets and Solidarity: Overcoming Sacramental Shame in Conservative Christian Churches to Forge a Queer Vision of Love and Justice." *Hypatia* 33, no. 3 (summer 2018): 451–68.

Moore, Mignon R. "Articulating a Politics of (Multiple) Identities: LGBT Sexuality and Inclusion in Black Community Life." *Du Bois Review: Social Science Research on Race* 7, no. 2 (fall 2010): 315–34.

More, Sam Dylan. "The Pregnant Man: An Oxymoron?" *Journal of Gender Studies* 7, no. 3 (1998): 319–28.

Moss, Alison R. "Alternative Families, Alternative Lives: Married Women *Doing* Bisexuality." *Journal of GLBT Family Studies* 8, no. 5 (2012): 405–27.

Movement Advancement Project. "A Closer Look: Bisexual Transgender People." September 2017. http://www.lgbtmap.org/bisexual-transgender.

Najmabadi, Afsaneh. *Women with Mustaches and Men without Beards: Gender and Sexual Anxieties of Iranian Modernity.* Berkeley: University of California Press, 2005.

Nikoleyczik, Katrin. "Towards Diffractive Transdisciplinarity: Integrating Gender Knowledge into the Practice of Neuroscientific Research." *Neuroethics* 5, no. 3 (December 2012): 231–45.

Nowakowski, Alexandra C. H., and J. E. Sumerau. *Other People's Oysters.* Boston: Brill Sense, 2018.

———. "Out of the Shadow: Partners Managing Illness Together." *Sociology Compass* 11, no. 5 (May 2017): e12466.

Nowakowski, Alexandra C. H., J. E. Sumerau, and Lain A. B. Mathers. "None of the Above: Strategies for Inclusive Teaching with 'Representative' Data." *Teaching Sociology* 44, no. 2 (April 2016): 96–105.

Nutt, Amy Ellis. *Becoming Nicole: The Transformation of an American Family.* New York: Random House, 2015.

O'Brien, Jodi. "Seeing Agnes: Notes on a Transgender Biocultural Ethnomethodology." *Symbolic Interaction* 39, no. 2 (May 2016): 306–29.

———. "Wrestling the Angel of Contradiction: Queer Christian Identities." *Culture and Religion* 5, no. 2 (2004): 179–202.

Omi, Michael, and Howard Winant. *Racial Formation in the United States*, 3rd ed. New York: Routledge, 2015.

Padavic, Irene, and Barbara Reskin. *Women and Men at Work*. Thousand Oaks, CA: Pine Forge Press, 2002.

Pascoe, C. J. *Dude, You're a Fag: Masculinity and Sexuality in High School*. Berkeley: University of California Press, 2007.

Pattanaik, Devdutt. *The Man Who Was a Woman and Other Queer Tales from Hindu Lore*. Binghamton, NY: Harrington Park Press, 2012.

Pearce, Ruth. *Understanding Trans Health: Discourse, Power and Possibility*. Bristol, UK: Bristol University Press, 2018.

Peitzmeier, Sarah, Ivy Gardner, Jamie Weinand, Alexandra Corbet, and Kimberlynn Acevedo. "Health Impact of Chest Binding among Transgender Adults: A Community-Engaged, Cross-Sectional Study." *Culture, Health & Sexuality* 19, no. 1 (2017): 64–75.

Perkinson, James W. *White Theology: Outing Supremacy in Modernity*. New York: Palgrave, 2004.

Pfeffer, Carla A. "Bodies in Relation—Bodies in Transition: Lesbian Partners of Trans Men and Body Image." *Journal of Lesbian Studies* 12, no. 4 (2008): 325–45.

———. "'I Don't Like Passing as a Straight Woman': Queer Negotiations of Identity and Social Group Membership," *American Journal of Sociology* 120, no. 1 (July 2014): 1–44.

———. "Making Space for Trans Sexualities." *Journal of Homosexuality* 61, no. 5 (2014): 597–604.

———. "Normative Resistance and Inventive Pragmatism: Negotiating Structures and Agency in Transgender Families." *Gender & Society* 26, no. 4 (August 2012): 574–602.

———. "Queer Accounting: Methodological Investments and Divestments," In *Other: Please Specify*, edited by D'Lane Compton, Tey Meadow, and Kristen Schilt, 304–26. Oakland: University of California Press, 2018.

———. *Queering Families: The Postmodern Partnerships of Cisgender Women and Transgender Men*. New York: Oxford, 2017.

———. "'Women's Work'? Women Partners of Transgender Men Doing Housework and Emotion Work." *Journal of Marriage and Family* 72, no. 1 (February 2010): 165–83.

Pfeffer, Carla A., ed. "Special Issue: Trans Sexualities." *Journal of Homosexuality* 61, no. 5 (2014): 597–780.

Phelan, Jo C., and Bruce G. Link. "Is Racism a Fundamental Cause of Inequalities in Health?" *Annual Review of Sociology* 41 (August 2015): 311–30.

Pitt, Richard N. "'Killing the Messenger': Religious Black Gay Men's Neutralization of Anti-Gay Religious Messages." *Journal for the Scientific Study of Religion* 49, no. 1 (March 2010): 56–72.

———. "'Still Looking for My Jonathan': Gay Black Men's Management of Religious and Sexual Identity Conflicts." *Journal of Homosexuality* 57, no. 1 (2010): 39–53.

Plemons, Eric D. "Description of Sex Difference as Prescription for Sex Change: On the Origins of Facial Feminization Surgery." *Social Studies of Science* 44, no. 5 (October 2014): 657–79.

Plummer, Ken. *Telling Sexual Stories: Power, Change and Social Worlds*. London: Routledge, 1995.

Ponticelli, Christy M. "Crafting Stories of Sexual Identity Reconstruction." *Social Psychology Quarterly* 62, no. 2 (June 1999): 157–72.

Poteat, Tonia, Danielle German, and Deanna Kerrigan. "Managing Uncertainty: A Grounded Theory of Stigma in Transgender Health Care Encounters." *Social Science & Medicine* 84 (May 2013): 22–29.

Prickett, Pamela J. "Negotiating Gendered Religious Space: The Particularities of Patriarchy in an African American Mosque." *Gender & Society* 29, no. 1 (February 2015): 51–72.

Prosser, Jay. *Second Skins: The Body Narratives of Transsexuality*. New York: Columbia University Press, 1998.

Przybylo, Ela. "Crisis and Safety: The Asexual in Sexusociety." *Sexualities* 14 (2011): 444–61.

Psihopaidas, Demetrios. "Intimate Standards: Medical Knowledge and Self-Making in Digital Transgender Groups." *Sexualities* 20, no. 4 (June 2017): 412–27.

Quadagno, Jill. *The Color of Welfare: How Racism Undermined the War on Poverty.* New York: Oxford University Press, 1994.

———. *One Nation Uninsured: Why the U.S. Has No National Health Insurance.* New York: Oxford University Press, 2005.

Ramirez-Valles, Jesus. *Queer Aging: The Gayby Boomers and a New Frontier for Gerontology.* New York: Oxford University Press, 2016.

Raun, Tobias. *Out Online: Trans Self-Representation and Community Building on YouTube.* New York: Routledge, 2016.

Rebchook, G., J. Keatley, R. Contreras, J. Perloff, L.F. Molano, C. J. Reback, K. Ducheny, T. Nemoto, R. Lin, J. Birnbaum, T. Woods, J. Xavier, and the SPNS Transgender Women of Color Study Group. "The Transgender Woman of Color Initiative: Implementing and Evaluating Innovative Interventions to Enhance Engagement and Retention in HIV Care." *American Journal of Public Health* 107, no. 2 (2017): 224–29.

Redfern, Jan S., and Bill Sinclair. "Improving Health Care Encounters and Communication with Transgender Patients." *Journal of Communication in Healthcare* 7, no. 1 (2014): 25–40.

Reese, Teri Jo. "Gendered Identity Work: Motivations for Joining the Military." Unpublished master's thesis, Florida State University, 2012.

Reisner, Sari L., Judith Bradford, Ruben Hopwood, Alex Gonzales, Harvey Makadon, David Todisco, Timothy Cavanaugh, Rodney VanDerwarker, Chris Grasso, Shayne Zaslow, Stephen L. Boswell, and Kenneth Meyer. "Comprehensive Transgender Healthcare: The Gender Affirming Clinical and Public Health Model of Fenway Health." *Journal of Urban Health* 92, no. 3 (June 2015): 584–92.

Reisner, Sari L., Jaclyn M. White Hughto, Emilia E. Dunham, Katherine J. Heflin, Jesse Blue Glass Begenyi, Julia Coffey-Esquivel, and Sean Cahill. "Legal Protections in Public Accomodation Settings: A Critical Public Health Issue for Transgender and Gender-Nonconforming People." *Milbank Quarterly* 93, no. 3 (September 2015): 484–515.

Reynolds, John R., and Chardie L. Baird. "Is There a Downside to Shooting for the Stars? Unrealized Educational Expectations and Symptoms of Depression." *American Sociological Review* 75, no. 1 (February 2010): 151–172.

Reynolds, John, Michael Stewart, Ryan MacDonald, and Lacey Sischo. "Have Adolescents Become Too Ambitious? High School Seniors' Educational and Occupational Plans, 1976 to 2000." *Social Problems* 53, no. 2 (May 2006): 186–206.

Reynolds, John R., and Stephanie Woodham Burge. "Educational Expectations and the Rise in Women's Post-Secondary Attainments." *Social Science Research* 37, no. 2 (June 2008): 485–99.

Rich, Adrienne. "Compulsory Heterosexuality and Lesbian Existence." *Signs* 5, no. 4 (summer 1980): 631–60.

Ridgeway, Cecelia L. *Framed by Gender: How Gender Inequality Persists in the Modern World*. New York: Oxford, 2011.

Rinaldo, Rachel. *Mobilizing Piety: Islam and Feminism in Indonesia*. New York: Oxford, 2013.

Robinson, Brandon Andrew. "Conditional Families and Lesbian, Gay, Bisexual, Transgender, and Queer Youth Homelessness: Gender, Sexuality, Family Instability, and Rejection." *Journal of Marriage and Family* 80, no. 2 (2018) 383–96.

Robinson, Christine M., and Sue E. Spivey. "The Politics of Masculinity and the Ex-Gay Movement." *Gender & Society* 21, no. 5 (October 2007): 650–75.

Rodriguez, Eric M. "At the Intersection of Church and Gay: A Review of the Psychological Research on Gay and Lesbian Christians." *Journal of Homosexuality* 57, no. 1 (2010): 5–38.

Rodriguez, Eric M., and Lourdes D. Follins. "Did God Make Me this Way? Expanding Psychological Research on Queer Religiosity and Spirituality to Include Intersex and Transgender Individuals." *Psychology & Sexuality* 3, no. 3 (2012): 214–25.

Roen, Katrina. "Theory and Embodiment: The Risk of Racial Marginalization." In *The Transgender Studies Reader*, vol. 1, edited by Susan Stryker and Stephen Whittle, 656–65. New York: Routledge, 2006.

———. "Transgender Theory and Embodiment: The Risk of Racial Marginalisation." *Journal of Gender Studies* 10, no. 3 (2001): 253–63.

Romeo, Franklin H. "Beyond a Medical Model: Advocating for a New Conception of Gender Identity in the Law." *Columbia Human Rights Law Review* 36 (2004): 713–53.

Rosenberg, Rosalind. *Jane Crow: The Life of Pauli Murray*. New York: Oxford, 2017.

Rosenfeld, Dana. "Heteronormativity and Homonormativity as Practical and Moral Resources: The Case of Lesbian and Gay Elders." *Gender & Society* 23, no. 5 (October 2009): 617–38.

Rosh, Samuel. "Beyond Categorical Exclusions: Access to Transgender Healthcare in State Medicaid Programs." *Columbia Journal of Law and Social Problems* 51, no. 1 (2017): 1–37.

Rossi, Alice S. "The Formation of SWS: An Historical Account by a Founding Mother." *SWS Network News* (November 1985): 2–4.

Roy, Deboleena. "Neuroethics, Gender and the Response to Difference." *Neuroethics* 5, no. 3 (December 2012): 217–30.

Rubin, Henry. "The Logic of Treatment." In *Transgender Studies Reader*, vol. 1, edited by Susan Stryker and Stephen Whittle, 482–98. New York: Routledge, 2006.

———. *Self-Made Men: Identity and Embodiment among Transsexual Men*. Nashville: Vanderbilt University Press, 2003.

Ruin. "Discussing Transnormativities through Transfeminism." *Transgender Studies Quarterly* 3, no. 1–2 (May 2016): 202–11.

Samons, Sandra L. "Can This Marriage Be Saved? Addressing Male-to-Female Transgender Issues in Couples Therapy." *Sexual and Relationship Therapy* 24, no. 2 (2009): 152–62.

Samuels, Ellen. *Fantasies of Identification: Disability, Gender, Race*. New York: New York University Press, 2014.

San Francisco Human Rights Commission. "Bisexual Invisibility: Impacts and Recommendations." San Francisco, 2011. https://sf-hrc.org/sites/default/files/Documents/HRC_Publications/Articles/Bisexual_Invisiblity_Impacts_and_Recommendations_March_2011.pdf

Sanger, Tam. *Trans People's Partnerships: Towards an Ethics of Intimacy*. New York: Palgrave, 2010.

Scarce, Michael. *Smearing the Queer: Medical Bias in the Health Care of Gay Men.* Binghamton, NY: Harrington Park Press, 1999.

Scheim, A. I., G. Santos, S. Arreola, K. Makofane, T. D. Do, P. Herbert, M. Thomann, and G. Ayla. "Inequities in Access to HIV Prevention Services for Transgender Men: Results of a Global Survey of Men Who Have Sex with Men." *Journal of the International AIDS Society* 19, no. 2 (2016): 20779.

Scherrer, Kristin, and Carla A. Pfeffer. "None of the Above: Toward Identity and Community-Based Understandings of (A)sexualities." *Archives of Sexual Behavior* 46, no. 3 (2017): 643–46.

Schilt, Kristen. "'A Little Too Ironic': The Appropriation and Packaging of Riot Grrrl Politics by Mainstream Female Musicians." *Popular Music and Society* 26, no. 1 (2003): 5–16.

———. "The Importance of Being Agnes." *Symbolic Interaction* 39, no. 2 (May 2016): 287–94.

———. "Just One of the Guys? How Transmen Make Gender Visible at Work." *Gender & Society* 20, no. 4 (August 2006): 465–90.

———. *Just One of the Guys? Transgender Men and the Persistence of Gender Inequality.* Chicago: University of Chicago Press, 2010.

———. "The 'Not Sociology' Problem." In *Other, Please Specify: Queer Methods in Sociology,* edited by D'Lane Compton, Tey Meadow, and Kristen Schilt, 37–50. Oakland, CA: University of California Press, 2018.

Schilt, Kristen, and Danya Lagos. "The Development of Transgender Studies in Sociology." *Annual Review of Sociology* 43 (July 2017): 425–33.

Schilt, Kristen, and Laurel Westbrook. "Doing Gender, Doing Heteronormativity: 'Gender Normals,' Transgender People, and the Social Maintenance of Heterosexuality." *Gender & Society* 23, no. 4 (August 2009): 440–64.

Schippers, Mimi. *Beyond Monogamy: Polyamory and the Future of Polyqueer Sexualities.* New York: New York University Press, 2016.

———. "Recovering the Feminine Other: Masculinity, Femininity, and Gender Hegemony." *Theory and Society* 36, no. 1 (February 2007): 85–102.

Schleifer, David. "Make Me Feel Mighty Real: Gay Female-to-Male Transgenderists Negotiating Sex, Gender, and Sexuality." *Sexualities* 9, no. 1 (2006): 57–75.

Schneer, David, and Caryn Aviv, eds. *Queer Jews*. New York: Routledge, 2002.

Schrock, Douglas. "Transsexuals' Narrative Construction of the 'True Self.'" *Social Psychology Quarterly* 59, no. 3 (September 1996): 176–92.

Schrock, Douglas P., and Lori L. Reid. "Transsexuals' Sexual Stories." *Archives of Sexual Behavior* 35, no. 1 (February 2006): 75–86.

Schrock, Douglas, Lori Reid, and Emily M. Boyd. "Transsexuals' Embodiment of Womanhood." *Gender & Society* 19, no. 3 (June 2005): 317–35.

Schrock, Douglas, and Michael Schwalbe. "Men, Masculinity, and Manhood Acts." *Annual Review of Sociology* 35 (August 11, 2009): 277–95.

Schrock, Douglas, J. E. Sumerau, and Koji Ueno. "Sexualities." In *Handbook of the Social Psychology of Inequality*, edited by Jae McLeod, Edward Lawler, and Michael Schwalbe, 627–54. New York: Springer, 2014.

Schwalbe, Michael, Sandra Godwin, Daphne Holden, Douglas Schrock, Shealy Thompson, and Michele Wolkomir. "Generic Processes in the Reproduction of Inequality: An Interactionist Analysis." *Social Forces* 79, no. 2 (December 2000): 419–52.

Sedgwick, Eve Kosofsky. *Epistemology of the Closet*. Berkeley: University of California Press, 1990.

Seidman, Steven. "From Identity to Queer Politics: Shifts in Normative Heterosexuality and the Meaning of Citizenship." *Citizenship Studies* 5, no. 3 (2001): 321–28.

Serano, Julia. *Excluded: Making Feminism and Queer Movements More Inclusive*. Berkeley, CA: Seal Press, 2013.

———. *Whipping Girl: A Transsexual Woman on Sexism and the Scapegoating of Femininity*. Berkeley, CA: Seal Press, 2007.

Sevelius, J. M., E. Patouhas, J. G. Keatley, and M. O. Johnson. "Barriers and Facilitators to Engagement and Retention in Care among Transgender Women Living with Human Immunodeficiency Virus." *Annals of Behavioral Medicine* 47 (2013): 5–16.

Shearer, Annie, Joanna Herres, Tamar Kodish, Helen Squitieri, Kiera James, Jody Russon, Tita Atte, and Guy S. Diamond. "Differences in Mental Health Symptoms across Lesbian, Gay, Bisexual, and Questioning Youth in Primary Care Settings." *Journal of Adolescent Health* 59, no. 1 (2016): 38–43.

Shultz, Jackson Wright. *Trans/Portraits: Voices from Transgender Communities.* Lebanon, NH: Dartmouth College Press, 2015.

shuster, stef m. "Generational Gaps or Othering the Other." In *Expanding the Rainbow: Exploring the Relationships of Bi+, Trans, Polyamorous, Asexual, Kinky, and Intersex People,* edited by Brandy L. Simula, J. E. Sumerau, and Andrea Miller. Boston: Brill Sense, forthcoming.

———. "Passing as Experts in Transgender Medicine," In *The Unfinished Queer Agenda after Marriage Equality,* edited by Angela Jones, Joseph Nicholas DeFilippis, and Michael W. Yarbrough, 74–87. New York: Routledge, 2018.

———. "Punctuating Accountability: How Discursive Aggression Regulates Transgender People." *Gender & Society* 31, no. 4 (August 2017): 481–502.

———. "Uncertain Expertise and the Limitations of Clinical Guidelines in Transgender Healthcare." *Journal of Health and Social Behavior* 57, no. 3 (September 2016): 319–32.

Silva, Tony J. "'Helpin' a Buddy Out': Perceptions of Identity and Behavior among Rural Straight Men That Have Sex with Each Other." *Sexualities* 21, no. 1–2 (February 2018): 68–89.

Smith, Andrea. *Conquest: Sexual Violence and American Genocide.* Durham, NC: Duke University Press, 2015.

Smith, Dorothy, E. *The Everyday World as Problematic: A Feminist Sociology.* Boston: Northeastern University Press, 1987.

Snorton, C. Riley. *Black on Both Sides: A Racial History of Trans Identity.* Minneapolis: University of Minneapolis Press, 2017.

Somerville, Siobhan. "Scientific Racism and the Emergence of the Homosexual Body." *Journal of the History of Sexuality* 5, no. 2 (October 1994): 243–66.

Somerville, Siobhan B. *Queering the Color Line: Race and the Invention of Homosexuality in American Culture.* Durham, NC: Duke University Press, 2000.

Sontag, Susan. *Illness as Metaphor and AIDS and Its Metaphors.* 2nd ed. New York: Farrar, Straus and Giroux, 1988.

Spade, Dean. *Normal Life: Administrative Violence, Critical Trans Politics, and the Limits of the Law.* Durham, NC: Duke University Press, 2015.

Spicer, Shane S. "Healthcare Needs of the Transgender Homeless Population." *Journal of Gay & Lesbian Mental Health* 14, no. 4 (2010): 320–39.

Stanley, Eric A., Nat Smith, and Cece McDonald. *Captive Genders: Trans Embodiment and the Prison Industrial Complex, Expanded Second Edition.* Oakland, CA: AK Press, 2015.

Steele, Sarah M., Megan Collier, and J. E. Sumerau. "Lesbian, Gay, and Bisexual Contact with Police in Chicago: Disparities across Sexuality, Race, and Socioeconomic Status." *Social Currents* 5, no. 4 (August 2018): 328–49.

Stein, Arlene. *Unbound: Transgender Men and the Remaking of Identity.* New York: Pantheon, 2018.

Stewart, Quincy Thomas, Ryon J. Cobb, and Verna M. Keith. "The Color of Death: Race, Observed Skin Tone, and All-Cause Mortality in the United States." *Ethnicity & Health.* DOI: 10.1080/13557858.2018.1469735

Stone, Amy L. "Flexible Queers, Serious Bodies: Transgender Inclusion in Queer Spaces." *Journal of Homosexuality* 60, no. 12 (2013): 1647–65.

———. "Gender Panics about Transgender Children in Religious Right Discourse." *Journal of LGBT Youth* 15, no. 1 (2018): 1–15.

———. "The Geography of Research on LGBTQ Life: Why Sociologists Should Study the South, Rural Queers, and Ordinary Cities." *Sociology Compass* (2018). DOI: 10.1111/soc4.12638

———. "More than Adding a T: American Lesbian and Gay Activists' Attitudes towards Transgender Inclusion," *Sexualities* 12, no. 3 (June 2009): 334–54.

Stone, Sandy. "The Empire Strikes Back: A Posttranssexual Manifesto." In *Writing on the Body*, edited by Katie Conboy, Nadia Medina, and Sarah Stanbury, 337–59. New York: Columbia University Press, 1997.

Stroumsa, Daphna. "The State of Transgender Health Care: Policy, Law, and Medical Frameworks." *American Journal of Public Health* 104, no. 3 (March 2014): e31–38.

Stryker, Susan. "Transgender History, Homonormativity, and Disciplinarity." *Radical History Review* 2008, no. 100 (Winter 2008): 145–57.

———. *Transgender History: The Roots of Today's Revolution.* New York: Seal Press, 2017.

Stryker, Susan, and Aren Z. Aizura, eds. *The Transgender Studies Reader*, vol. 2. New York: Routledge, 2013.

Stryker, Susan, and Stephen Whittle, eds. *The Transgender Studies Reader*, vol. 1. New York: Routledge, 2006.

Suen, Yiu Tung. "Older Single Gay Men's Body Talk: Resisting and Rigidifying the Aging Discourse in the Gay Community." *Journal of Homosexuality* 64, no. 3 (2017): 397–414.

Sumerau, J. E. *Cigarettes & Wine*. Boston: Sense, 2017.

———. "Embodying Nonexistence: Experiencing Cis and Mono Normativities in Everyday Life." In *Body Battlegrounds: Transgressions, Tensions, and Transformations*, edited by Samantha Kwan and Christina Bobel. Nashville: Vanderbilt University Press, forthcoming.

———. *Essence*. Independently published, 2017.

———. "Experiencing Gender Variation." Write Where It Hurts (blog), December 16, 2015. www.writewhereithurts.net/2015/12/16/178-2/

———. *Homecoming Queens*. Boston: Sense, 2017.

———. "I See Monsters: The Role of Rape in My Personal, Professional, and Political Life." In *Negotiating the Emotional Challenges of Conducting Deeply Personal Research*, edited by Alexandra C. H. Nowakowski and J. E. Sumerau, 147–58. New York: Routledge, 2018.

———. "Mobilizing Race, Class, and Gender Discourses in a Metropolitan Community Church." *Race, Gender, and Class* 19, no. 3–4 (2012): 93–112.

———. "'Somewhere between Evangelical and Queer': Sexual-Religious Identity Work in a LGBT Christian Church." In *Selves, Symbols, and Sexualities: An Interactionist Anthology*, edited by Thomas S. Weinberg and Staci Newmahr, 123–34. Thousand Oaks, CA: Sage, 2013.

———. "'That's What a Man Is Supposed to Do': Compensatory Manhood Acts in an LGBT Christian Church." *Gender & Society* 26, no. 3 (June 2012): 461–87.

———. *That Year*. Independently published, 2017.

———. "'They Just Don't Stand for Nothing': LGBT Christians' Definitions of Non-Religious Others." *Secularism and Nonreligion* 5, no. 8 (2016): 1–12.

———. "The Transgender Religion Survey." Write Where It Hurts (blog), December 9, 2015. http://writewhereithurts.net/2015/12/09/the-transgender-religion-survey/

Sumerau, J. E., Harry Barbee, Lain A. B. Mathers, and Victoria Eaton. "Exploring the Experiences of Heterosexual and Asexual Transgender People." *Social Sciences* (2018): DOI: 10.3390/socsci709016

Sumerau, J. E., and Ryan T. Cragun. *Christianity and the Limits of Minority Acceptance in America: God Loves (Almost) Everyone.* Lanham, MD: Lexington Books, 2018.

———. "The Hallmarks of Righteous Women: Gendered Background Expectations in the Church of Jesus Christ of Latter-Day Saints." *Sociology of Religion* 76, no. 1 (January 2015): 49–71.

———. "'I Think Some People Need Religion': The Social Construction of Nonreligious Moral Identities." *Sociology of Religion* 77, no. 4 (December 2016): 386–407.

———. "'Why Would Our Heavenly Father Do That to Anyone': Oppressive Othering through Sexual Classification Schemes in the Church of Jesus Christ of Latter-Day Saints." *Symbolic Interaction* 37, no. 3 (August 2014): 331–52.

Sumerau, J. E., Ryan T. Cragun, and Harry Barbee. "'This Incredible Monster Was Always in the Way': The Moral Career of a Sexual Sinner in the Church of Jesus Christ of Latter-Day Saints." *Qualitative Report* 23, no. 3 (2018): 662–76.

Sumerau, J. E., Ryan T. Cragun, and Lain A. B. Mathers. "Contemporary Religion and the Cisgendering of Reality." *Social Currents* 3, no. 3 (September 2016): 293–311.

———. "'I Found God in the Glory Hole': The Moral Career of a Gay Christian." *Sociological Inquiry* 86, no. 4 (November 2016): 618–40.

Sumerau, J. E., and Eric Anthony Grollman. "Obscuring Oppression: Racism, Cissexism, and the Persistence of Social Inequality." *Sociology of Race and Ethnicity* 4, no. 3 (July 2018): 322–37.

Sumerau, J. E., Eric Anthony Grollman, and Ryan T. Cragun. "'Oh My God, I Sound Like a Horrible Person': Generic Processes in the Conditional Acceptance of Sexual and Gender Diversity." *Symbolic Interaction* 41, no. 1 (February 2018): 62–82.

Sumerau, J. E., Lain A. B. Mathers, Ryan T. Cragun. "'Can't Put My Finger on It': A Research Report on the Non-Existence and Meaninglessness of Sin." *Qualitative Report* 21, no. 6 (June 2016): 1132–44.

———. "Incorporating Transgender Experience toward a More Inclusive Gender Lens in the Sociology of Religion." *Sociology of Religion* 79 no. 4 (2018): 425–48.

Sumerau, J. E., Lain A. B. Mathers, and Nik Lampe. "Learning from the Experiences of Bi+ Trans People," *Symbolic Interaction* (2018). DOI: 10.1002/symb.387

Sumerau, J. E., Lain A. B. Mathers, Alexandra C. H. Nowakowski, and Ryan T. Cragun. "Helping Quantitative Sociology Out of the Closet." *Sexualities* 20, no. 5–6 (September 2017): 644–56.

Sumerau, J. E., Douglas P. Schrock, and Teri Jo Reese. "Transsexuals' Gender Presentations," In *Life as Performance: A Dramaturgical Handbook*, edited by Charles Edgley, 245–60. Burlington, VT: Ashgate, 2013.

Sweet, Paige L., and Claire Laurier Decoteau. "Contesting Normal: The DSM-5 and Psychiatric Subjectivation." *BioSocieties* 13, no. 1 (March 2018): 103–22.

Thomas, Jeremy N., and Daniel V. A. Olson. "Beyond the Culture War: Managing Sexual Relationships inside a Congregation of Gay Evangelicals." *Review of Religious Research* 54, no. 3 (September 2012): 349–70.

Thomas, W. I., and Dorothy Swaine Thomas. *The Child in America: Behavior Problems and Programs*. New York: Alfred A. Knopf, 1928.

Thumma, Scott. "Negotiating a Religious Identity: The Case of the Gay Evangelical." *Sociology of Religion* 52, no. 4 (December 1991): 333–47.

Tolbert, TC, and Tim Trace Peterson, eds. *Troubling the Line: Trans and Genderqueer Poetry and Poetics*. Callicoon, NY: Nightboat Books, 2013.

Torres, Carlos G., Megan Renfrew, Karey Kenst, Aswita Tan-McGory, Joseph R. Bentancourt, and Lenny López. "Improving Transgender Health by Building Safe Clinical Environments that Promote Existing Resilience: Results from a Qualitative Analysis of Providers." *BMC Pediatrics* 15 (November 2015): 187.

Towle, Evan B., and Lynn Marie Morgan. "Romancing the Transgender Native: Rethinking the Use of the 'Third Gender' Concept." *GLQ: A Journal of Lesbian and Gay Studies* 8, no. 4 (2002): 469–97.

Travers, Ann. *The Trans Generation: How Trans Kids (and Their Parents) Are Creating a Gender Revolution*. New York: New York University Press, 2018.

Trotsenberg, M. "Gynecological Aspects of Transgender Healthcare." *International Journal of Transgenderism* 11, no. 4 (2009): 238–46.

Unger, Cecile A. "Care of the Transgender Patient: A Survey of Gynecologists' Current Knowledge and Practice." *Journal of Women's Health* 24, no. 2 (December 2014): 114–18.

Vaccaro, Christian Alexander. "Male Bodies in Manhood Acts: The Role of Body-Talk and Embodied Practice in Signifying Culturally Dominant Notions of Manhood." *Sociology Compass* 5, no. 1 (January 2011): 65–76.

Valentine, David. *Imagining Transgender: An Ethnography of a Category*. Durham, NC: Duke University Press, 2007.

Vares, Tiina. "'My [Asexuality] Is Playing Hell with My Dating Life': Romantic Identified Asexuals Negotiate the Dating Game." *Sexualities* 21, no. 4 (June 2018): 520–36.

Vidal, Catherine. "The Sexed Brain: Between Science and Ideology." *Neuroethics* 5, no. 3 (December 2012): 295–303.

Vidal-Ortiz, Salvador. "The Figure of the Transwoman of Color through the Lens of 'Doing Gender.'" *Gender & Society* 23, no. 1 (February 2009): 99–103.

———. "Queering Sexuality and Doing Gender: Transgender Men's Identification with Gender and Sexuality." In *Gendered Sexualities*, Advances in Gender Research, vol. 6, edited by Patricia Gagné and Richard Tewksbury, 181–233. New York: Elsevier Science Press, 2002.

———. "Transgender and Transsexual Studies: Sociology's Influence and Future Steps." *Sociology Compass,* 2, no. 2 (March 2008): 433–50.

Vidal-Ortiz, Salvador, Brandon Andrew Robinson, and Cristina Khan, eds. *Race and Sexuality*. Medford, MA: Polity Press, 2018.

Vincent, Ben. *Transgender Health: A Practitioner's Guide to Binary and Non-Binary Trans Patient Care*. Philadelphia: Jessica Kingsley, 2018.

Walters, Mikel L., Jieru Chen, and Matthew Breiding. *The National Intimate Partner and Sexual Violence Survey (NISVS): 2010 Findings on Victimization by Sexual Orientation.* Atlanta: National Center for Injury Prevention and Control, Centers for Disease Control and Prevention, 2013. https://www.cdc.gov/violenceprevention/pdf/nisvs_sofindings.pdf.

Walters, Suzanna Danuta. *The Tolerance Trap: How God, Genes and Good Intentions Are Sabotaging Gay Equality*. New York: New York University Press, 2014.

Ward, Jane. *Not Gay: Sex between Straight White Men*. New York: New York University Press, 2015.

———. *Respectably Queer: Diversity Culture in LGBT Activist Organizations*. Nashville: Vanderbilt University Press, 2008.

Warner, Michael. *The Trouble with Normal: Sex, Politics, and the Ethics of Queer Life*. Cambridge, MA: Harvard University Press, 1999.

Washington, Harriet A. *Medical Apartheid: The Dark History of Medical Experimentation on Black Americans from Colonial Times to Present*. New York: Harlem Moon, 2006.

Weber, Max. *The Protestant Ethic and the Spirit of Capitalism*. New York: Scribner, 1958.

West, Candace, and Sarah Fenstermaker. "Doing Difference." *Gender & Society* 9, no. 1 (February 1995): 8–37.

West, Candace, and Don H. Zimmerman. "Doing Gender." *Gender & Society* 1, no. 2 (June 1987): 125–51.

Westbrook, Laurel, and Aliya Saperstein. "New Categories Are Not Enough: Rethinking the Measurement of Sex and Gender in Social Surveys." *Gender & Society* 29, no. 4 (August 2015): 534–60.

Westbrook, Laurel, and Kristen Schilt. "Doing Gender, Determining Gender: Transgender People, Gender Panics, and the Maintenance of the Sex/Gender/ Sexuality System." *Gender & Society* 28, no. 1 (February 2014): 32–57.

Wilcox, Melissa M. *Coming Out in Christianity: Religion, Identity, and Community*. Bloomington: Indiana University Press, 2003

———. "Of Markets and Missions: The Early History of the Universal Fellowship of Metropolitan Community Churches." *Religion and American Culture: A Journal of Interpretation* 11, no. 1 (winter 2001): 83–108.

———. *Queer Nuns: Religion, Activism, and Serious Parody*. New York: New York University Press, 2018.

———. *Queer Women and Religious Individualism*. Bloomington: Indiana University Press, 2009.

———. "When Sheila's a Lesbian: Religious Individualism among Lesbian, Gay, Bisexual, and Transgender Christians." *Sociology of Religion* 63, no. 4 (winter 2002): 497–513.

Wolkomir, Michelle. *Be Not Deceived: The Sacred and Sexual Struggles of Gay and Ex-Gay Christian Men.* New Brunswick, NJ: Rutgers University Press, 2006.

———. "Making Heteronormative Reconciliations: The Story of Romantic Love, Sexuality, and Gender in Mixed-Orientation Marriages." *Gender & Society* 23, no. 4 (August 2009): 494–519.

Worthen, Meredith G. F. "An Argument for Separate Analyses of Attitudes toward Lesbian, Gay, Bisexual Men, Bisexual Women, MtF, and FtM Transgender Individuals." *Sex Roles* 68 (2013): 703–23.

Xavier, Jessica, Judith Bradford, Michael Hendricks, Lauretta Stafford, Ryan McKee, Elaine Martin, and Julie A. Honnold. "Transgender Health Care Access in Virginia: A Qualitative Study." *International Journal of Transgenderism* 14, no. 1 (2013): 3–17.

Yavorsky, Jill E. "Cisgendered Organizations: Trans Women and Inequality in the Workplace." *Sociological Forum* 31, no. 4 (December 2016): 948–69.

Young, Iris Marion. "Throwing Like a Girl: A Phenomenology of Feminine Body Comportment Motility and Spatiality." *Human Studies* 3, no. 2 (April 1980): 137–56.

Zamantakis, Alithia. "'I Try Not to Push It Too Far': Trans/Nonbinary Individuals Negotiating Race and Gender in Intimate Relationships." In *Expanding the Rainbow: Exploring the Relationships of Bi+, Trans, Polyamorous, Asexual, Kinky, and Intersex People*, edited by Brandy L. Simula, J. E. Sumerau, and Andrea Miller. Boston: Brill Sense, forthcoming.

Zion-Waldoks, Tanya. "Politics of Devoted Resistance: Agency, Feminism, and Religion among Orthodox Agunah Activists in Israel." *Gender & Society* 29, no. 1 (February 2015): 73–97.

Index

Avishai, Orit, 93

Barton, Bernadette, 102

cisgender: aggression from cisgender
people, 84–87; awareness of
transgender people, 21n41, 75, 78–
81, 88n4; definition of, 4–5, 19n25
cisgendering reality: in everyday life,
4–6, 12–13; foundation of cisgender
realities, 87–88; in LGBTQIA
community, 60–63; in medicine,
114–19; in religion, 92–94, 96–100
cisnormativity, 7, 75–79
Collins, Patricia Hill, 9, 14, 67, 75, 134
coming out: invisibility, 35–37; negative
experiences, 37–38; not coming out,
41–44; to partners, 40–41, 49–50n34;
positive experiences, 38–39
complementarity, 22n48, 92–93, 95–97,
114, 117
conditional acceptance, 55, 127–28

Davis, Georgiann, 117
discursive aggression, 82–84
doing cisgender, 135–37
doing difference, 19n28, 93
doing endosex, 139–40
doing gender, 5–6, 73, 135–39
doing sexualities, 137–39

existential urgency, 90n32

Fetner, Tina, 94, 96

Grollman, Eric Anthony, 55

health disparities among transgender
people, 119–20
Heath, Melanie, 95
heteronormativity, 138
homo/hetero flexibility, 70–71n23
homonormativity, 54, 95

intersex, 70n18, 117, 139–40

Johnson, Austin, 114, 131n21

knowledge production: alternative,
    9–12; cisnormative, 7–8, 49n29,
    89nn10–11; metrocentric, 108–
    109n11; sciences of oppression,
    115–16

Lee, Jooyoung, 90n32
LGBTQIA: definition of, 19n26; intra
    community conflicts, 59–60

medical science: ignorance about
    transgender populations, 122–24;
    medical gatekeeping, 117–19,
    131n22; potential for change,
    126–27; refusal of medical care,
    120–22; surviving cisgender medical
    providers, 124–26
mononormativity, 138
monosexism, 58, 63, 70–71n23
monosexualizing reality, 63–64, 127
Moon, Dawne, 92

othering, 42, 64–67
outsider within, 14, 67, 74, 78

Pfeffer, Carla, 40

religion: comparison to medical science,
    128; in LGBTQIA community, 57,
    70n20; LG-Christian organizations,
    94; positive religious experiences,
    102–6; in relation to sex, gender,
    sexualities, 92–94; Religious Right,
    94; religious-spiritual journeys, 98–
    100; transgender people's experience
    with Christianity, 100–102

sexual normativity, 138
shuster, stef, 42, 64, 66–67, 82
Smith, Dorothy, 3, 14, 134–35
the study: methodological appendix,
    147–59; sample demographics, 30–34,
    47n18, 98; outline of, 12–13, 47–48n20
Stryker, Susan, 10, 15–16n1, 21n41

Tobin, Theresa, 92
toxic masculinity, 60–61
transgender: definition of, 5, 16n1;
    historical variation of the term, 23n57
transnormativity, 72n37

U. S. Transgender Survey (USTS), 29–
    30, 35, 48n26, 77, 85, 97–98

Wilcox, Melissa M., 98–99

CPSIA information can be obtained
at www.ICGtesting.com
Printed in the USA
LVHW091453151219
640589LV00001B/35/P